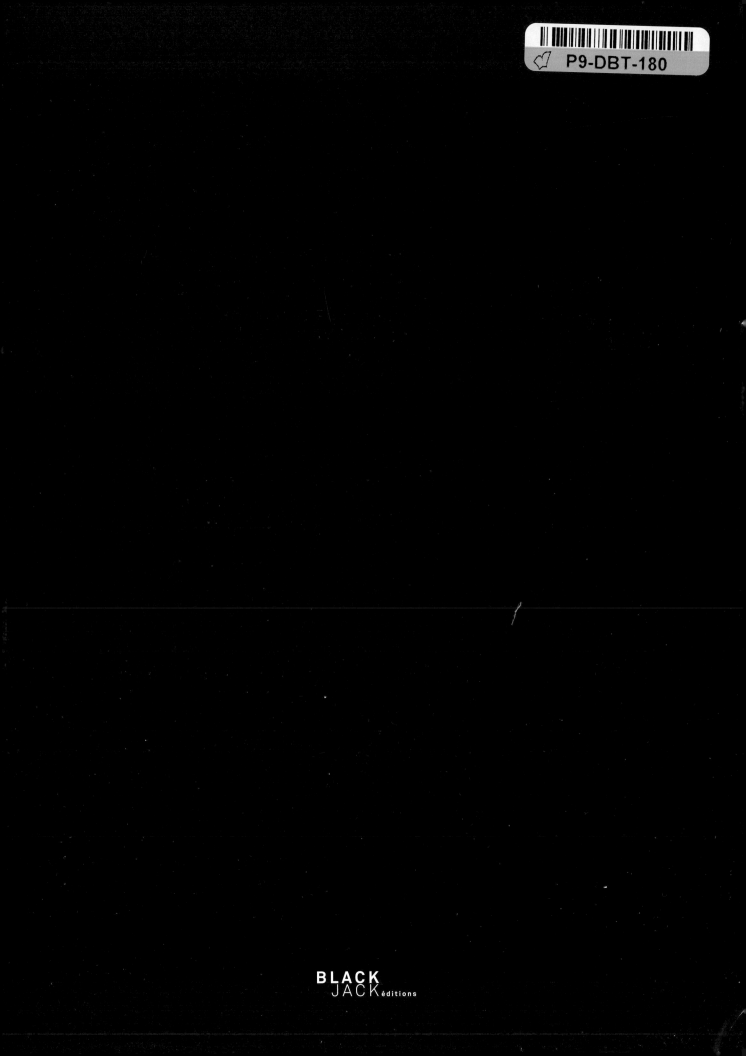

BLACK
JACK éditions

RepaiRepaiRepaiRepaiRepaiRepaiRepaiRepaiRepa

epaiRepaiRepaiRepaiRepaiRepaiRepaiRepaiR

"Life is just one small piece of light
between two eternal darknesses."
(Vladimir Nabokov)

FOREWORD

This book is undoubtedly a monograph in the traditional sense of the word, considering it contains reproductions of the majority of Kader Attia's body of work since his early career. Within it, you'll discover the multiple facets of his work. And yet, for every installation he also produces films, photographs, collages, drawings, and objects, if you ask him to define himself in one word (which he does only grudgingly) he would say that, above all, he's a sculptor. Throughout this multiplicity of media, it's actually the plasticity of realities, histories and identities that he explores as material.

We decided to structure this publication not along chronological lines but with an emphasis on the organic, pre-existing relationships between projects. The book contains 9 sections, entrances into his body of work that converge as both reflexive lines of thought and critical standpoints. Kader Attia wanted to "use" his work to initiate (or continue) conversations with people who, in some cases, are quite distant from the art world. He hoped to reveal the process by which his plastic research is elaborated, which draws a great deal on exchange, association and displacement. Each section contains archive pages where visual and textual documents gravitate as satellites to his work. These archives have no didactic intent, nor are they exhaustive, rather they contribute to exploding the narrative, or more precisely the attempt at narrative. And even here, it's a sculptural act: from this flow of documents, Kader Attia extracts certain ingredients to shape a unique history of his artistic process and commitment.

The work in this context is a source for investigation that attests directly to the function and power of art today, also operating within the fields of architecture, medicine, psychoanalysis, natural science, political science and the methods along which their respective histories are built.

In a way, this publication acts as an invitation from the artist for you to enter his mental studio. It not only speaks to scholars of the art world or of his body of work, but to all those who consider themselves wardens of the present. So the term "monograph", though not exactly false, does not entirely articulate the intention of this book: the voices expressed here within are multiple, the angles are open, the approaches complex.

Perhaps, in the spirit of introductions, I should start at the beginning, with the title: *RepaiR*. And, to shed light on this word, it seems fitting to share an anecdote, an origin story or perhaps the triggering event. More than 20 years ago, while Kader Attia was finishing his service in the Congo (in France at the time, people who refused their military service were called "conscientious objectors"), a friend gave him an old loincloth that once belonged to his great aunt and had been patched together with bits of Vichy fabric (gingham) (1). Kader Attia held on to this object without really looking at it, until one day he realized that the repair done to the cloth was in fact a powerful and assertive act of cultural reappropriation. His friend's great aunt made an exogenous item her own, an item belonging to a culture that, by way of colonization, had repressed hers, and yet she managed to mark this object with her own individuality. Double wounds: insects had eaten the cloth, colonizers had devoured her country, and by using Vichy fabric (gingham) to repair the cloth, the old woman had engaged in a double reparation, that of the object and of her own identity. On a symbolic and concrete level, she in turn devoured the other. I'm using the word "devour" here intentionally, to echo the *Manifesto Antropófago* written by Oswald de Andrade in 1928 (2). The poem is an assertion of Brazilian singularity in the face of Europe, a case in favor of the anthropophagy practiced by the Tupi Indians (original inhabitants of the Brazilian coast), who devoured their enemy to access their power, literally incorporating and becoming the other. Thus the great aunt of Kader Attia's friend succeeded, through a traditional method of cloth repair, in incorporating an otherness, assimilating and, in a sense, digesting it.

Continuing his investigation, Kader Attia understood the fundamental difference between the idea of reparation in the modern West and reparation in the non-Occident. Western modernism (introduced by the Quattrocento) advocates reparation as an ideal and ideological return to the same: it strives, then, to retain the integrity of the original object. On the other hand, most non-Occidental cultures value the act of repairing in and of itself and make these repairs visible rather than hide them. These cultures have no pretensions about returning the object to a pseudo-original, perfect state. Was Western expansionism (through conquest and colonies), led by concepts of progress and humanism, not legitimized by an ideology of reparation? Is reparation not at the very heart of so many exchanges between the West and other countries, be it in regard to restitution, compensation or recognition? While we live in a word where Western-centrism no longer applies and a new definition of humanism in a post-colonial context is required, the polysemic dimensions of reparation take ethical, political and, yes, aesthetic turns. In one of the texts you will find quoted in the archive pages, Achille Mbembe writes: "Restitution and reparation therefore lie at the very heart of a possible construction of a shared consciousness of the world, that is to say the accomplishment of universal justice. The concepts of both restitution and reparation are founded on the idea that there is an intrinsic part of humanity under the protection of every human being. This irreducible part lies in every one of us. It enables us to be objectively different, yet the same" (3). Indeed, because reparation, be it material or immaterial, challenges the most individual and the most universal simultaneously, it is a choice approach for an artist such as Kader Attia.

Another significant specificity in reparation is its unique relationship to time. Any repair involves a link between the past, history (individual and/or collective) and the present. Any repair is a contemporary reading/writing of history. In this sense, a repair is the past reincarnated and offers a chance to rebuild foundational narratives. Repair is therefore the here-and-now of a storytelling gesture that recounts history. Arthur Danto wrote that one of the characteristics – and perhaps opportunities – of contemporary artists is their access to the past, which they can grasp as they please since the course of things no longer obliges them to follow the dictates of novelty, progress or manifestos, as was the case for the modernists (4). Kader Attia takes full hold of this opportunity in this book, just as he does in his work in general.

RepaiR addresses the different aspects of reparation/reappropriation that operate in Kader Attia's artistic research, but it is also an act of repair in itself. It manifests the plasticity of the world and speaks to our present, to our place, to the responsibility we can create foundations for and even vindicate, especially now, through a historical conscience and the need for transdisciplinarity and dialogue. This publication is two years in the making, and stands now as a direct invitation for discussion and reflection, a call addressed personally to you.

Léa Gauthier
Translated from French by Maya Dalinsky

Léa Gauthier is a philosopher, she teaches Art Theory at The Royal Academy of Fine Arts in Brussels. She is also an art critic and a publisher.

(1) See photo p.73.
(2) Oswald de Andrade, "Manifesto Antropófago" in *Revista de Antropofagia*, 1928.
(3) Achille Mbembe, *Critique de la Raison Nègre*, éditions La Découverte, 2013. Cf. p.82 of this book.
(4) Arthur Danto, *After the End of Art. Contemporary Art and the Pale of History*, Princeton University Press, 1997.

REAPPROPRIATIONS

KASBAH, 2008.
SITE SPECIFIC INSTALLATION, VARIABLE DIMENSIONS, WOOD, LEFTOVERS OF CORRUGATED IRON, METAL, AND
WOOD BOARDS, TV ANTENNAS, TRUCK TIRES, WIRES, BRICKS, FOUND MATERIALS, INSTALLATION VIEW AT
CENTRO DE ARTE CONTEMPORANEO HUARTE - HUARTE, 2008.

KASBAH, 2008.
INSTALLATION VIEW AT CCC DE TOURS - TOURS, 2009.

KASBAH, 2008.
INSTALLATION VIEW AT BEIRUT ART CENTER - BEIRUT, 2014.

KASBAH, 2008.
INSTALLATION VIEW AT SALA DE ARTE PÚBLICO SIQUEIROS - MEXICO DF, 2009.

KASBAH, 2008.
INSTALLATION VIEW AT THE 17TH BIENNALE OF SYDNEY - SYDNEY, 2010.

KOBENA MERCER: Art and architecture have become ever more closely connected but, in contrast to artists whose sculpture explores the purely formal properties of space, or architects who have constructed gallery spaces for the exhibition of art, your work has a strong historical or even archeological dimension with regards to our understanding of architecture in colonial or post-colonial contexts. How did your research interests in colonial architecture come about, and how would you characterize the conceptual issues that you set out to explore in works such as *Kasbah* (2007)?

KADER ATTIA: In my opinion, the history of art and architecture shows us ways to create images that have both an aesthetic and ethical interest. You can see this from the Egyptian pyramids to medieval European cathedrals and modern skyscrapers. But, whereas sculpture's reason for being has always been to raise questions about space, architecture aims at both containing space and, at the same time, occupying it. Like sculpture, architecture deals with volume located in space, but it also contains an inner space with a purpose: it could be a private space in which you spend a part of your life, or offices in which you work, a jail, or perhaps a public space. One architect whose work is, for me, very much related to this issue is Roland Simounet. Though born in Algeria in 1927 at Guyotville, Simounet was a student of Le Corbusier. As an architect, Simounet has an interesting background. Indeed, before he became a student of Le Corbusier, Simounet had graduated from the Paris School of Fine Arts. The influence of Le Corbusier on all his students was incredibly strong, especially with the Modulor. The Modulor is a theoretical project that deals with the balance between private space and the way a human being occupies it.

In the early 1950s, Simounet built his first social housing projects in Morocco and Algeria. He discovered that, at the end of each day, the workers — who generally came from the countryside to the city to get jobs — would take some materials left in the garbage at the building site, such as big sticks of wood, corrugated iron, or pieces of broken bricks.

At this time, following the idea of the Modulor, Simounet was looking for the best way to use the private space of his social housing project. So, at the end of one workday, out of curiosity, he followed some of his workers as they went back home, in order to see how they used these materials. Not far from the building site, he discovered an area where the workers had built a shantytown. Simounet asked his assistant to take all the dimensions of the inner spaces of the workers' shantytown or bidonville — to measure the space between two different houses and to take note of the difference between the public and the private space, the features of these private spaces, and so forth. Then, he compared these dimensions to the Modulor and what Roland Simounet found was that the shantytown's dimensions were almost exactly the same as those of the Modulor. Why? Because the poverty of these workers had led them to reduce the features of the private spaces in this shantytown to the essential. After he had taken the measurements of how the inner spaces were shared in these houses, Simounet discovered that everything was brought to its essential necessity: no superficiality, no unneeded details. The simplicity of the private space was almost the same as the ideal one described by the Modulor.

After that, most of the private spaces of Simounet's housing projects were based on theories that had been inspired through both the Modulor and the observation of the shantytown built by his workers.

He also found out that this group of vernacular constructions was organized in a way very similar to the Casbah in Algiers or to other old medinas. Like Le Corbusier, who discovered the Casbah in Algiers at the end of the 1920s, Simounet shared his master's fascination with Mediterranean architecture. You could say that, of Le Corbusier's students, Roland Simounet was one of the most aware of what he had seen in the city of Ghardaïa, when he spent five weeks there in 1931, amazed when he saw Maghreb vernacular architecture for the first time (1).

Le Corbusier used to say to his students: "We will always come back to the eternal architecture of the Mediterranean Sea." For him, Mediterranean architecture had something to do with spirituality and functionality: spirituality, for the relation with the elements — light, wind, etc. — and functionality, for its roofs and terraces, on which people were living, spending time, walking… For instance, he noticed that you can cross Algiers' Casbah walking from one roof to the other.

Hence *Kasbah* is an installation based on these historical issues, both aesthetic and ethical, about the real roots of aesthetic modernity in European architecture. As an artwork made by an Algerian artist born in France, this work is one sign of reappropriation among endless possibilities. A syncretism between tradition and modernity that projects itself into another time: contemporaneity. The time I have spent, since I was born, between France and Algeria has always been psychologically tough. Through a work like *Kasbah* I'm trying to rebuild something that seemed to be missing — a historical lapse.

In North Africa, shantytowns have grown with Modernity, but they have always been seen as its garbage. But that's not what they are. They are a Modernity, the one belonging to the people who built them without being architects. At that point, *Kasbah* speaks as a tribute to this aesthetics and to this freedom that people take to build their home with whatever they find.

K. M.: I'm curious about this aspect of rebuilding something that has gone missing. Although there is a tendency to interpret post-colonial issues in identity-based terms, so that what is missing is a psychological lack or deficit, I understand what you are saying as a critique of the standard narrative of modernism — what is missing is the cross-cultural dynamic of borrowing and appropriation.

In *Kasbah* the body of the building has gone missing and only the roofs remain — which underlines your point about the zinc material, like the satellite dish, as one of the "signs of reappropriation" which are an important concept of yours to which I hope we can return. But first, in light of what you say about Simounet, what are your thoughts on why Le Corbusier was so attracted to the Mediterranean in general and to the ancient Mzab architecture of Ghardaïa in particular? Was it "otherness" or some element of sameness between his utopian vision and the formal simplicity found in these non-Western dwellings?

K. A.: Yes, indeed, in *Kasbah* the body of the building is missing, but its absence makes us think of its presence. I often represent something by its absence, as sometimes the evocation of something is stronger than its presence. Anything that is not represented may be strongly present because its absence works as its trace. It is what I try to show with works like *Untitled (Plastic Bags)*, *Ghost* or *Sleeping from Memory*. So what is missing in colonial architecture and the history of art has actually always been very present as soon as we think through what Michel Foucault used to call "the archive" of something. The archive of modernist architecture is embodied by both official history and its hidden side. Everything takes part in an endless structure that sometimes has failures. And in these rare failures, art can exist... Like the piece *Kasbah,* for instance.

Maybe Le Corbusier was more able than anybody else at that time to see through a failure of this cultural continuity in architecture, because of his "intuition". When Le Corbusier was claiming that architecture will come back to the Mediterranean area, he actually was referring to Western architectural influences that exist everywhere in classical architecture – from the Louvre to Washington and Moscow, you can see Greek columns, pediments, pilasters, friezes, and so on – so the influence of this Mediterranean architecture is worldwide. Therefore, he was not initially referring to the vernacular desert architecture of the Mzab, because, at that time, he had not seen it yet. But of course, after he discovered it in 1931, he continued to speak about the "necessity to go back to the eternal architecture of the Mediterranean Sea", now also referring to Mzab.

Regarding its otherness or some element of sameness between his utopian vision and the formal simplicity found in these "non-Western dwellings", as far as I'm concerned, I think he found both, and that's why Le Corbusier was so interested in this vernacular architecture. But he also went beyond this, inventing a way to look at it: a specific way to integrate these elements of another culture into his Western aesthetics. This way of looking is an appropriation of this thought, this culture, this aesthetics, because neither he nor history has ever recognized its importance as an inspiration for Le Corbusier's work until now.

K. M.: Did Le Corbusier adopt an ethnographic attitude, or did his admiration stem from a different relationship to the civilization of the desert?

K. A.: It looks as if one of the first contacts Le Corbusier had with the Mzab valley was through the book of a sociologist named Marcel Mercier (2). I think that this ethnographic insight on Mzab civilization came into Le Corbusier's life at a time when he was looking for something new in architecture, which would have existed in the Mediterranean area.

Accordingly, Le Corbusier started his Algerian trip with an observation based on an ethnographic text. But the real issue of this story is, I think, that Le Corbusier invented a new way of looking, as Picasso did with both Iberian sculpture and African masks. The way they both felt, interpreted, represented what they were looking at, the insight they had into it, is very close to the one that non-Western civilizations have nowadays about the Occident's manufactured goods: a mythological reading of something that comes from the outside, not so far from a kind of exoticism that first seems exciting, then kitsch, and in the end gets recycled into something that belongs to the perceiver.

K. M.: The issue of recycling is important, and especially so in your concept of "signs of reappropriation" that exist in the historical dialectic between various modernist utopianisms in their encounter with different vernaculars. I wonder whether you could say how these "signs of reappropriation" affected the mass housing projects that were built in Algeria and Morocco during the era of decolonization?

K. A.: First of all, my concept of reappropriation is not only related to the idea of physical recycling. It is also a more natural notion, whereas, for me, recycling is typically cultural. The abstract aspect is natural because it is based on the simple principle that there is reappropriation as soon as there is a dispossession of a geographical, religious, or cultural territory.

So the signs of reappropriation affected the mass housing projects that were built in Algeria and Morocco during the era of decolonization in a very unexpected way, especially in the early years of independence.

These first visible signs of reappropriation immediately changed the aesthetic of the façade. People started to hang personal items and food, red chilis, pieces of fatty lamb and sheep meat, and of course their clothes in order to dry them.

While the functionality of modern social architecture used to work as a uniform aesthetic order, it was not the space for any expression of identity. This dogma or apology for the notion that "identical is respect for equality" rather than "equality is respect for identities" meant that living in these buildings entailed becoming the object of the control that was built into their design, whereas, when people were living in their home villages and houses they were taking part in their environments and were their subjects.

So while the balconies had a similarity based on the same pattern and design – no colours, simple forms – this was one of the most relevant visual aspects of architectural modernism because, rather than being the object of this modern functionality, people are always re-appropriating their spaces naturally, as subjects in their own right.

K. M.: *The Cité Pouillon* apartment complex, for example, seems to implicate architecture as a tool of social control of the rural populations moving into the cities. Does this mean that the architecture of colonial modernism expressed the continuing power of the West during the very moment of decolonization? What would be your interpretation in the case of the *Cité Verticale* in Casablanca, which was a focus for the interdisciplinary analysis that Marion Von Osten put together for the 2008 exhibition and conference *In the Desert of Modernity,* held in Berlin.

K. A.: It is worth noting that all the social housing built by Fernand Pouillon during the 1950s in Algeria was commissioned by the French colonial power. Why? After World War II, the soldiers from the colonies (Senegal, Mali, Morocco and Algeria, for instance) who were sent to the battlefields came back to their colonized home countries and started to claim the same rights as settlers. But they were denied those rights. So demonstrations, riots and the creation of independence organizations – from Algeria to Indochina, or from the Middle East to India – began to develop, essentially in poor countrysides where the revolutionary wind blew the hardest. The colonial order responded to these developments with immediate violence – for example, in Messali Hadj's trial and in the 1945 riots in Setif in Algeria. But why there? Why did colonial resistance start mostly in the poor rural areas? Because, as Jean-Paul Sartre described in his preface to Frantz Fanon's book *The Wretched of the Earth,* everywhere in the world, people from the countryside have always been those who suffer more than people from the city, even the working classes. Because the peasantry has always had to fight both the oppression of "colonial inequalities" and the tough and unpredictable climate, they have always been the ones most likely to get involved in revolution.

In this social context, then, the colonial administration scheduled a whole series of architectural projects aiming, officially, to provide housing for all. But in reality, the aim was to identify, register, and control contesting individuals from the countryside, who were growing in number and gaining more and more political influence over the urban populations. By making these farmers and peasants move from the houses they'd built themselves to planned housing on a mass scale, the colonial administration transformed them from subjects to objects of the place where they lived. In the end, this was a strategy where modernism played a part in the political goals of seeking better control of the colonized – having a monthly rent, electricity, water and other bills to pay meant that colonial subjects became the consuming objects of their apartments.

Regarding Cité Verticale, first of all, I would highly recommend Marion Von Osten's essay "Architecture Without Architects – Another Anarchist Approach", whose title alludes to the famous title of Bernard Rudofsky's 1964 exhibition at MoMA.

For me, Cité Verticale is important because it reminds us of the way modernist architecture is implicated in stealing original patterns from non-Western cultures, while pretending that it is inventing a fair and functional environment for the people.

Rolland Simounet's observations of shantytowns who ultimately found them to be almost similar to Le Corbusier's Modulor, certainly changed the idea of social architectures in many ways. And so, in this sense, Simounet's observations indeed represented a beginning of thinking in postmodern architecture that arose in the colonial context. The concept of Cité Verticale was also based on the analysis of local architectural behaviours and necessities. But, in my opinion, this conceptual approach, among many others, had already been sketched by Le Corbusier, who used to compare the Cité Radieuse – a project building in Marseille (1945 - 1952) – to the oldest city of Ghardaïa, named Beni Isguen. Le Corbusier was fascinated by the very simple and easy way that the streets of Beni Isguen were connected to each other and to the surrounding habitations. He claimed that his Cité Radieuse was "a vertical application of Beni Isguen". That's why I think that the idea of the verticality of the urban space was both invented and applied before the Cité Verticale of Georges Candilis and Shadrach Woods.

The transfer of vernacular African-Arab-Berber urbanism and its promiscuity between private and public space had begun with the Cité Radieuse. In this building, Le Corbusier created corridors so wide and long that he called them "les rues" (streets). Through these streets, kids could go directly to school by bicycle, moving through their home streets to elevators that would bring them to the ground floor where the street of the school was located. So the conception of verticality of the cité was already a modernist project, also inspired in the colonial space, like the Cité Horizontale.

What the architects of the Cité Verticale did, like Simounet in his research, is in continuity with this appropriation, with a certain amnesia, even if they were claiming the contrary. The irony of both this amnesia and these fantasies Is the way they spread their theories.

The Team X group created the biggest rupture with Le Corbusier's and Walter Gropius' legacy. One of their core ideas was to create an architecture aimed at taking its subject (the inhabitant's culture, social habits, economic situation and so on) as the complementary issue of the home space. For instance, in the Cité Verticale, balconies are inspired by patios that originally are the spaces which bind the home space to the outside. In Morocco, this works amazingly, but unfortunately, it doesn't work worldwide. That's why I think it is an irony. An experimentation in the colonial space, especially in Africa, can be relevant, but only in its own context. This is exactly what happened with Jean Prouvé's Maison Tropicale built in Brazzaville. Two years ago, I saw this Maison Tropicale installed in Paris, in front of the Seine river. It was sad. I think we should pay attention to projects that have been created in tropical areas by their inhabitants, whose style – "tropicalism" – is the beginning of an interesting reappropriation of modernity, like Lina Bo Bardi in Brazil.

Last year, when I was in Sheffield in the UK, I had another example of this application of experiments in the colonial space taken out of their original context and applied in a Western country without being adapted to this new environment. I visited a series of buildings made by the same architects that created Cité Verticale – Georges Candilis and Shadrach Woods. I found it very interesting how these five or six buildings were bound together with bridges that worked as both outside corridors and streets for the milk delivery man. The fact that the public and the private spaces were that close, without interfering with each other, made me think about the Cité Verticale. But this delocalization of observations that had begun in North African shantytowns and their application in other situations raise some questions about whether this approach could work in a Western context.

The core issue of the Sheffield housing projects is the emphasis on circulation through the outside corridors, which are, in effect, streets that connect all the buildings of this city. They are wide enough to allow a small car to deliver milk to each door, as well to function as playgrounds for kids, just as in the Cité Radieuse. So this application of a spatial order that is both functional and promiscuous, and which was derived from the Mediterranean medina, was interesting to me because it was totally unexpected. But is this unexpectedness relevant?

The fact that Sheffield buildings were empty and undergoing reconstruction gained my attention most of all. The people who used to live here were "socially excluded". The buildings' location was outside the city's center. So the more I examined these buildings, the more my feelings about the project grew bitter. Did Candilis and Woods truly believe in their theories about considering the humanity of the inhabitants rather than the formal design of the architecture in these buildings? If that was their concept, then they failed, not only because the buildings were placed outside of the city center, but also because the appropriation of the "self-centrist" urbanist structure of the African vernacular city had nothing really to do with North Occidental urban behaviour. In all the old African medinas – from the Kasbah of Algiers to Ghardaïa, Timimoun, Fez, Djenné and Mopti, for instance – vernacular architectures are alive without the need for state planning. The life that goes into the city is the last architectural element of the quality of urban space, but it is what binds spaces together and makes a city truly alive.

K. M.: Perhaps the last aspect of the relationship between modernism and colonialism, as seen through the lens of architecture, is evoked by the video piece of yours, *Normal City*, included in the *In the Desert of Modernity* exhibition. This concerns the modernist high-rise apartment block that, in suburbs of Paris and other French cities, has become the social setting for the political protests articulated by post-migrant generations. Is it fair to say that such mass housing projects have a necessary correlation with the politics of post-colonialism?

K. A.: I think that, at the beginning, when these housing projects were built, there was indeed a correlation with the politics of post-colonialism, as most of the inhabitants were, and are still now, from the ex-colonies. I grew up in Garges-lès-Gonesse, a *cité* in the north of Paris, in the 1990s, where more than 60 different languages and dialects were registered in the same living space, all coming from the former French and British colonial empires.

Besides this, all these housing projects were built in the outskirts of the big cities, in their peripheries, so they were isolated and outside the economic centers. The plan was to colonize the people who live there. There is a clear continuity with how colonized people were always on the periphery of the political, economic and cultural power. So while ex-colonial migrants are tolerated as a productive workforce, there is no way they mix with the rest of the population. They are here to be economically exploited, not to be a part of the society. One significant example of this post-colonial politics is that, as of right now, such migrant workers do not have the right to vote. Moreover, their standard of living is much lower than that of the rest of society. These poor populations are then gathered in what we can call social ghettos.

For me, this urban organization embodies, in the most perverse way, the concept of "man exploiting man". And the most absurd aspect of this exploitation is the fact that these people, coming from the former colonies, who live in these buildings, are exactly the same people who actually built them in the 1960s.

As during colonial times, these people from the former colonies have not been integrated into the larger society. This is an original failure that has been passed on to the following generations. Successive governments have let this situation deteriorate, maintaining these neighbourhoods in the status of areas of "exclusion". This is directly in line with post-colonial politics, but it pushes the residents of these housing projects to another level of exclusion by creating such ghettos in which ethnic, social and economic minorities are gathered in grey monotone and uniform buildings that more or less just annihilate their identity. So in this situation, colonization is then reproduced by such housing as colonization of the mind, even if, nowadays, we are not officially in the colonial era anymore. I think that what is now at stake when the term "post-colonial" is used is the prolongation of the desire for domination by one society over its minorities.

The social housing built between the 1960s and the 1980s that I show in the three video films called *Normal City* is, indeed, an examination of the following on of the relation between colonialism and social housing in massive buildings that have been erected outside the former colonial empires' capitals and main cities, particularly in France. The videos show facades of social housing buildings that

are shot in the same neighbourhood. On each facade, all the apartments look the same, except one of them. In this apparently normal and ordered grid, one balcony is different. We don't know why, but we feel that something is not really working as it should...

But I should add that *Normal City* aims at speaking beyond colonialism as a historical and a geographical issue. It goes beyond this issue, as I think it also has to do with human beings' natural desire for power over the other, which always exists in two ways: domination and contempt. This is why areas outside the major cities – the so-called peripheries and banlieues – always embody the place of excluded people for the European psyche. These phobias actually come from the Middle Ages, when such areas used to be zones of containment of leprosy. Even after the disappearance of leprosy as a disease, which was the worst imaginable fear of the Middle Ages, these "excluded" spaces outside cities have remained, for centuries, the embodiment of fear (3).

Creating such poor, grey, monotonous and impersonal buildings, outside economic, political and cultural centers, in which any subject is alienated as just a small part of a huge grid of identical rectangular windows, is maybe the way to control his otherness. This "other", as a subject that power actually fears as its death, is maybe the answer to the question we will have to solve for future generations.

Kobena Mercer writes and teaches at Yale University on the visual arts of the black diaspora, examining African American, Caribbean, and Black British artists in modern and contemporary art. His courses and research address cross-cultural aesthetics in transnational contexts where issues of race, sexuality and identity converge.

Notes

1. Alex Gerber, "L'Algérie de Le Corbusier, Les Voyages de 1931" Thesis No 1077 (1992), presented at the Department of Architecture at l'École Polytechnique Fédérale in Lausanne, Switzerland.

2. Marcel Mercier, *La Civilisation urbaine au Mzab, Étude de sociologie africaine*, 1922.

3. Michel Foucault, *Madness and Civilization: A History of Insanity in the Age of Reason*, New York: Vintage, 1988.

KADER ATTIA: This conversation could begin on an American road, between Los Angeles and San Antonio. You know, the endless roads scattered with old cheap motels, like the ghosts of the modern dream designed with 50s aesthetics and acting as a link to a so-called era of great progress. Back when the West was a symbol of conquest, and capitalism was an ideal...

I thought about you when I was in San Antonio. I visited several 17th century Spanish Christian missions, or rather what was left of them. Most of these beautiful architectures can easily be compared to any Mediterranean Christian architecture. If you remember that Spain was colonized by Muslims for five centuries, you can see and understand better how Spanish colonial style took root in America thanks to characteristic Arabian-Muslim vernacular architecture. This brings up my first question to you, instigator of the amazing project *Colonial Modern*: is colonialism responsible for the evolution of architecture through and towards a Modern agenda?

MARION VON OSTEN: Historically speaking, the purpose of any colonial plan was to create new settlements and to bring new housing solutions for a distinct non-indigenous population arriving from some other part of the world. When I say "distinct", I mean separated; these constructions were created for colonists, colonial settlers, and separated them from other already-existing habitations and social communities. The colonial settlement is thus a biopolitical entity, a satellite community in a partially unfamiliar area and that does not want to mingle. But as it has been proved, this will to segregate itself from the local environment always fails. In relation to your comment about Spanish missions, I just visited the historical Franciscan missions in California where I learned that the church and cloister in Santa Barbara, for example, were built by local Comanche tribes. This is important, for the Franciscan monks would not have survived without the Comanche, as the latter fed them when they arrived in the 18th century. Also, the Indians handled the construction of the cloister, church and houses while teaching the monks how to craft textiles and pottery. After the mission was established, the natives were given free food and Christian education as a reward for their labor. Here it becomes interesting because even though their survival was completely dependent on the Comanche's local knowledge and food, the monks assumed Indians to be naive people who needed education and to be taken care of. This is what makes any colonial civilizing mission so paradoxical, as it depends on local people's knowledge, yet it does not acknowledge them as *de jure* subjects. This is also expressed in architecture. You can find some transcultural translations in these specific places. The church design is based on drawings from Vitruv's famous architecture book. However, the monks only followed Virtruv's model of a roman temple because they had no other example. Plus, in this strange church-temple you can also find small transpositions of Comanche ornaments on the ceiling and Mexican figurative elements beside paintings with belated baroque aesthetics. This eclecticism, or conscious or unconscious translation – praised as California's multicultural heritage – conceals how Christian and Roman aesthetic traditions remained hegemonic while other transcultural elements remained marginal. This hierarchy in the use of aesthetics is mostly expressed in the settlement designed by monks for First Nations converts. The Comanche housing facility next

to the cloister showed very modern lines; it was designed like a camp, built in a grid-like structure. This small-scale housing grid, specifically created for the natives, echoes Jacques Rancière's words about distributing the sensible, and therefore, about domination. Even when we need to constantly highlight transfers and exchanges created through specific cross-continental encounters, like between the Comanche and the Franciscans, as they later became a particular Christian group following early communist ideals, architecture still reveals this hierarchy and dominance that denied the Comanche's rights to be represented as gifted fishers, sailors and farmers or as spiritual collaborators, political allies or even fighters. When the economic and military interests of Spain, Russia, the Mexican Empire and later the United States caused never-ending conflicts on this territory, the first to suffer abuses and die were the Comanche. And there again, what is striking is the specific rationality in the Comanche settlement from Santa Barbara mission, for it consequently used this same grid pattern. The grid, as a planning principle, can be found in the organization of most colonial process. It already existed during the Roman Empire, so in the end, Spain was not the first one to use it. This grid structure is an artificial and rational pattern, free from any context and that can be expanded anytime. It is about expansion, identifying and conquering new territories in any part of the world. It is about housing a great number of people, about future population growth, since the grid can easily spread into any direction. It is also the same pattern as the famous Philadelphia grid developed during the 18th century, and yet when you come to studying colonial cities, you realize it had already been adopted for years in each and every of them. A village or town based on this structure is the very basis for creating any new artificial site or, just like in Caracas, for example, a colonial town similar to many other places you might add to your own research. New urban planning and the grid structure, which are nowadays perceived as high modernist aesthetic items, were brought into modern discourse on building practices through colonial expansion.

K. A.: Your answer reminds me of how Spanish Emperor Charles V, ordered Mexico's city planning, following a parallel and perpendicular street pattern. And do you know why? To have control over the population. When Technotican was taken over by the Spanish, they decided to slowly develop their new city on top of the former Aztec capital. These days, some architectures from this colonial settlement project, such as the *catedral del Zócalo*, are slowly falling down because of the old Aztec temples underneath. These "conscious and unconscious forms of cultural translations" seem to be another kind of "repairing", because they act as endless cultural translations from one cultural space and time to another. To come back to this colonial settlement planning, and to why it reminds me of the first urban plans in Mexico during the early 16th century that aimed at controlling people, do you sometimes think that architecture consists of filling a given space, while actually it is the contrary, thus making urban plans more important than the buildings themselves in the end? Do you think that projects led by you and I, among others, like Michel Écochard in Casablanca, aimed at controlling people through some vertical panopticon, or on the contrary, providing intimate spaces for the inhabitants? And what eventually drew them to totally close their own balconies?

Yes, I think you are right, colonial settlement is mainly about organization and urban landscaping but not so much about establishing an individual house for one particular settler. Biopolitical implications are quite obvious when we think of them as closed entities. What most people ignore, as your question pointed out, is that this vision of colonial planning has considerably influenced modern building concepts like, for instance, Ebenezer Howard's famous *Garden City*. A book entitled *The Art of Colonization*, written by Howard Edward Gibbon Wakefield, which also served as propaganda to convince the British government to build a settler colony in New Zealand, mainly influenced Howard's concept. But Howard's goal with the *Garden City*, which actually started his career in the United States before being published in the UK, went even further than its colonial blueprint. The idea was to sustain, through a satellite city concept, "a healthy, natural, and economic combination of town and country life" thanks to balanced work and relaxation times. This concept aimed at getting away from the contentious relations between industrialization and countryside. Just like in future replicas of the *Garden City* – such as the *Satellite City* or the *Cité Nouvelle* – life, production and education were strongly connected. Moreover, spatial organization of confined islands, segregated from the heart of the city and from other social groups, must have been based around new ideas about labor conditions and accumulating wealth as well. In Howard's original vision of a confined settlement, discipline and control were obviously part of the strategy. It is also strongly related to hygienic and epidemic argumentations. Only later was consumption added to the *Garden City* movement and following new town planning systems created in the 20th century. From then on, the *New Town* emerged not as a sign of total enclosure but as a place that was organized from A to Z. The principle of neighborhood units also appeared there and then developed in the United States with Clarence Stein.

When living in Casablanca under the French Protectorate, Louis Lyautey, Marshal of France, followed ideas close to North American industrial development plans and Howard's *Garden City* concept in his vision of the European colonial town of Casablanca. This concept, first introduced in European cities, was later used as a strategy to shut the local community out of the center when building what they called *Habous* neighborhoods, or the new Medina. Later on, in the 1940s, Verlieer, a French town-planner and socialist, appropriated the *Garden City* model again in his new planning for the huge Ain Chok settlement, a fantasy of a Moroccan village using the grid plan; local workers then lived far away from the heart of Casablanca. A few years later, Michel Écochard established a housing grid for his constructions – applying the "Housing for the Greatest Number" principle – because of the increasing number of colonized factories or even service workers. This housing grid, as the main instrument for new urban neighborhoods, was also meant to replace the numerous slums from the late 1940s to the mid 1950s that where mostly inhabited by rural migrants. In fact, the large-scale housing programs were French Protectorate's attempts to build modern settlements for the colonized just when anti-colonial uprising emerged, as Morocco obtained independence in 1956. In those times of resistance, the French urban planning services strategies varied from re-ordering the slums (*restructuration*) to temporary re-housing (*relogement*) while also creating new housing estates with controlled rents (*habitations à loyer modéré*) – all according to Écochard's grid. His master plan applied notions of "culturally specific" housing, making – according to his vision – local construction practices the starting point for developing a variety of housing typologies adapted to each category of inhabitants. These categories were still confined to already existing definitions of cultural and racial differences. However, it was only under colonial rules that categorization reinforced and turned into a means of exercising governmental power. Écochard's plan divided the city into different residential zones for European, Moroccan, and Jewish residents, as well as industrial and trading areas. "Muslim" housing estates were built far from the "European" colonial city, by creating a so-called *zone sanitaire* (sanitary zone), whose boundaries were actually the newly built motorway. This spatial separation was also inherited from the colonial apartheid regime, during which Moroccans were forbidden to enter the protectorate city unless employed as domestic servants in European households, and likewise constituted a strategic measure, facilitating military operations against any possible resistance.

K. A.: Do you remember, Marion, how we first met many years ago? I think it was for a video work called *Normal City* (which depicted the façades of social housing units from my teenage years in the suburbs of Paris). Could you find a link between European Western or Eastern aesthetics in social architecture, and what has been functionally experimented as a modern housing ideal for the native people and "adapted" in former colonial areas (during pre-independence times)? Again, I'm thinking about Écochard in Morocco, or Pouillon in Algeria, who apparently tried to adapt their designs to local indoor and outdoor living traditions. I always have the feeling that it is only possible to live in (not to say survive) such a neighborhood, just like in millions of other social housing blocks built for immigrants in the West, because the inhabitants re-created a social structure that is identical to the village most of them came from. Everyone knows each other, and says "hello", and if something wrong is about to happen, someone can see it from their window, and (for instance) advise you to remove the bag you forgot in your car, or park it in another place so that you can have an eye on it. So again, here is my question: how do you deal with this dialectic between social housing aesthetics and ethics, this complementarity of minimal functionality and aesthetics? Does it make sense to you? Does this aesthetics fit its own time, in which it was considered "nice", or is it, on the contrary, hostile? And last but not least, could this aesthetics have been part of a project of control that happened through standardization of the subjects (the inhabitants) as the objects of the modern social order?

M. V. O.: I think you are right in both cases, since the modernist project was and is about ambivalences – on the one hand to grant people with a better life, but on the other, to control and educate them. The Écochard grid was dimensioned according to a typology of houses with court-yards, believed to be appropriate for future inhabitants, who used to live in slums. His so-called culturally specific "Housing Grid for Muslims" measured eight by eight meters and consisted of two rooms and a wide outdoor space, related to Arabic patios. Part of the ensuing 64 square meters was organized as a so-called neighborhood unit, resulting in an intricate ground-level structure of patio-houses, alleys, and public squares. A single house in this grid consisted of two or three rooms and a patio accessed through the entrance. Using a variety of combinations, it was designed to be flexible enough to eventually adapt to creations seen in other housing types (individual or collective), states the architectural historian Catherine Blain. The patio house in Ecochard's vision allowed "growth" through usage. As Monique Eleb stated in the *Colonial Modern* conference, which you attended in 2008, the patio reference was not a copy of a traditional courtyard house but a European (mis-) interpretation. On the other hand, the patio house structure developed in French colonies should be understood as a modernist synthesis, a eurocentric translation that also carried pedagogical intentions to teach people modern industrial production and consumerism.

Though housing programs in French colonies from the 1950s and 1960s did take certain specific local, regional, or cultural conditions into account when they were conceived, with decolonization, these conditions turned out to be much more complex than originally thought. The single-floor mass-built modernist patio houses, intended to facilitate control upon Moroccan workers, is now so altered that one can no longer distinguish the original base structure. The builders simply used on the original design and foundations to construct three or four floor apartments. The many ways of appropriating space and architecture by people can also lead one to assume that neither colonialism nor post-colonial governments ever managed to establish complete control over the population.

K. A.: I agree, and it sounds very interesting, as an investigation process, to reveal how and why reappropriation emerges. As far as I'm concerned, it took me years of thinking to be able to observe early "signs of reappropriation". From architecture to any item, even human behaviors... Jacques Rancière offered an interesting analysis in *The Emancipated Spectator,* which is a reference to another article called *Le Tocsin des travailleurs*, published in the 19th century in an old French union newspaper... To sum it up, the article describes a worker cleaning the wooden floor in a bourgeois house, removing the old surface with a large blade (a tough job). After long hours of effort, he decides to stand up and look out the window. He slowly ends up appreciating the view, as well as the perspective leading to the horizon of French "classic" gardens... The pleasure he takes there makes him dream of how to set up all furniture in the room just like he would at home, following his own tastes to decide the kind of furniture he would buy as well as where and why he would put a given item in a given place, etc.

Rancière explains how, from bending on the floor and working hard to standing up in order to stretch a bit and look out the window, the worker switched from one state to another: from "the manual state" to the "visual state". At this very moment, he stopped being only hands executing orders so as to "reappropriate" his own self by watching and coming up with his own conclusions. From the hands to the eyes, his individuality reappropriates its freedom by reappropriating the perspective his social position has shut him out of, and from which his eyes had been taken off. Pierre Joseph Proudhon was the first to highlight "reappropriation". Remember his "Property is theft"... It also

meant social struggle is a reappropriation of what has been dispossessed by the bourgeois and bureaucratic system... Another personality you made me discover in one of your essays, "Architecture Without Architects – Another Anarchist Approach" published in the e-flux journal, issue #6, in 2009, is the British anarchist and architect Mark Crinson (perhaps you did it on purpose). The questions raised by such an interesting political figure and personality, within the understanding of contemporary social architecture, are in the continuity of Proudhon's thought. I would definitely compare him to Paul Robeson: a multi-talented personality. This African American former athlete, who was physically impressive due to his height and voice, was an actor, singer, and active communist. In a movie, I saw him sing the Chinese national anthem on a stage right in the middle of the street! The notion of cliché might not exist in human nature. It is probably a product of the modern mind, as a consequence of rationalism based on two obsessions: measuring the world using classification (through categories) and the fantasy of progress as a pure sign of evolution.

Edward Said beautifully summarized the relation between anarchism and architecture through the Western cliché of the Orient, with this quote: "The Orient has been orientalized by the Occident." It sounds like a legacy of the Western desire to control otherness, first culturally, then politically...

The way windows and balconies were arranged in so many social housing buildings designed by European minds in non-Western colonized contexts, from Asia to North Africa (in Casablanca for instance), raises two questions. If these transformations of balconies into kitchens or closed rooms turned towards the inside are "reappropriations", then what about freedom? In the *Cité Verticale*, why have all the large and comfortable balconies, which aimed at opening each apartment to the outside so as to take advantage of both public and private spaces at the same time, just like a private courtyard, been covered and closed by the inhabitants? Was it for self-protection, for moral issues, which is linked to Islam and privacy, in response to a design generated by another culture from another time, the culture of colonial domination imposing its utopian vision on another culture?

Could we say that adding confinement to these constructions is a "reappropriation"? When in Arabian Berber Muslim culture, home privacy takes women away from outside eyes so there is no way to see their faces and bodies in their private apartment, could we say that the modern European architecture gender issue failed here? Or as Edward Said investigated it in his essay *Orientalism*, is it a purely Western fantasy to think it is easy to reach Muslim Arabian women?

I'm sure you have seen examples of these thousands of old colonial postcards representing such "Western fantasies", like half-naked women in their apartment...

M. V. O.: I vaguely remember an article about veiling in North Africa stating the first forms of veiling noticed by natives were English ladies covering themselves from the sun and sand. And the author then highlighted the invention of sunglasses, with which you can look around even though no one can know what you are looking at since your eyes cannot be seen. So, I have no answer to your last questions but perhaps some more comments on your first one that might lead to a whole set of future investigations on what we like to call production and what is called appropriation. There is a concern about the use of the word appropriation and its concept: in it sleeps the very notion of property as you pointed out when you quoted Rancière. The concept of appropriation thus suggests that something used to belong to something/somebody, and was later developed by somebody or/and used in another geographical context or fashion. This concept suggests no original articulation in itself. Notions like copy, imitation and appropriation deny any immediate emergence, yet in the meantime, this emergence is claimed by Western modernists like the architects we were talking about. In the last decades of cultural anthropology and post-colonial thinking, appropriation was used to mark tactics and strategies in a De Certauian sense, I believe, to show that programs and concepts from above can be altered and subverted from below. But somehow, it also suggests that there would be no "first" voicing but always a belated reaction, only existing because there already was a first voicing by somebody else. The problem I started to feel about this concept is that it is mainly used in describing social class relations or in non-European articulations. When you talk about reappropriation, it aims at making this all a bit more complicated, since it is not clear to whom a concept and idea originally belonged. And, as I discuss it in my own research, this is also true about Modernism, as it can only be understood as a constant translation or synthesis of vernacular practices into a more rationalizing and universalizing concept that was later called modern. Still, it was a concept that appropriated the Arabian Kasbah, the Indian bungalow, the courtyard house, arts and crafting from the colonies, etc. According to this, it escaped the classical and renaissance past, but in the same way the classical era claimed to have higher taste and value, to be more civilized and universal in the end. What I try to highlight is that it is a product of worldly relations and many forms of transculturations, mainly triggered by colonialism. But when we think about the uses and adaptations the inhabitants made, which can be so easily spotted in Casablanca, it becomes incredible; actually the modifications are not mere changes or adaptations, some houses have been completely overworked. Then it brings us back to different issues about biopolitics and government matters specific to each society.

One could say people who lived in Écochard's grid, in Casablanca, adapted a non-functional house and rebuilt it. Écochard surely thought his system was functional and so people would get used to it. But what actually happened is that they built a new house upon an old structure that did not offer many possibilities because it was too small, as it aimed at creating nuclear family households. Therefore, one could agree on the fact that inhabitants have altered, adapted, and appropriated existing structures to their needs, thus subverting European programs. But when you sort of ignore the original structure, is this still appropriation, is this not production? Nowadays, scholars tend to link appropriation to the concept of freedom. Yet, it can only be done in such a case as the one I'm talking about – this is what I'm criticizing here – European ground structure is considered the ultimate model from which all other activities emerged. If you do not follow this eurocentric idea, you need to accept that the inhabitants have built new structures on top, if that was possible. Until now, this local "growing house" building practice or culture was associated with the already existing construction methods in North Afri-

can Medina. Many studies ended there so far. But when you read documents that show more concern about the history of the Medina as a transcultural encounter site than about French colonial cultural politics aiming at orientalizing and museumizing the Medina as a site of pre-modern forms of productions, it gets even more complicated to distinguish whose building practices and cultures we are talking about. And this is what lies at the heart of the problem, that architecture was and is still read as the expression of one cultural identity and not of a different way of living, trading and articulating that had been exchanging with other cultures long before the beginning of colonial modern projects and in which the northern hemisphere was not always the ruling colonizing power, since other local imperial forces had their own way of governing people and handled war, trade and exchanges in their own fashion. These transcultural traces are seldom found in current discourses as they are mainly based on binaries of the modern and premodern, on political identity, and do not focus on transfers, translations and exchanges.

K. A.: Achille Mbembe speaks of boundaries in an interview about the Berlin Conference. Before that, the nature of boundaries was different. There were areas between ethnic groups whose purpose was to both separate and bind them. In fact, these were places for traditional trade, war, language exchanges, etc. They were exchange areas of a different kind; they would revitalize both cultures...
I would like to come back to the complex reappropriation concept, and whether any situation or item that embodies it is born from nothing, or, on the contrary, is linked to some already existing thing or not...
Let's take the example of Écochard's *Cité Verticale* and the balconies that have been "re-covered" by all the inhabitants.
Indeed, the use of "re" (for reappropriation or repair), as an intellectual Western speculation and deduction, occurs through the prism of Western modern intellectual values and references. From Kant's critique on Hume's analysis, we know that the way we read the world is based on the relation between cause and effect: "causality". It is true that we are unable to think things from within themselves. If you watch a house or a flower, you can be sure than neither of them will be able to think of what they are. And so there is no human mind able to think this house or this flower by and within themselves. It always has to think them through the "relation" that exists between this thing and the mind. The relation between themselves consists of both the experience of the object and all the references linked to this relation. This relation is called "correlation"...
So when we have a close look at a house and a building that has been "rebuilt" by its inhabitants, then we are just part of this "correlation"...
Thus, if social architectures that developed through a modern political agenda in North Africa tried to provide the natives with a Western vision of modern housing, but have been quickly "re"-adapted by them, then it is just an endless process of human knowledge based on "correlation". Indeed you can make a very simple analogy to link such a behavior by native people to modern Western "new" architecture: this is how traditional homes and cities were built. There is not a single house isolated from another in a Medina. Each one is built against another so as to provide a strong load-bearing wall to the new house and a connection

to another area from the terrace. Even when the first one is in construction, the second one is being built at the same time. In vernacular urbanism, the notion of "city" is the accumulation of houses built "one against another", which I have been able to observe in North and South Sahara... What Louis Jeanneret, also known as Le Corbusier, found fascinating in a city like Ghardaïa, for instance, is the fact that every street of this Medina puts town facilities (market, madrassa, mosque, grocery stores...) within walking distance. When he created his first *Cité Radieuse* in Marseille, he claimed it was a "vertical Ghardaïa," and each corridor in this modern social housing was called a "street", as they linked all flats to social facilities you can find in the building, such as a swimming pool, a kindergarten, a school, a church, etc. Just as people from North Africa constantly adapted to their natural environment for centuries, they similarly adapted to their new artificial environment... And to push the "re-adaptation" process further, I would add Le Corbusier's "re-enactment" on a so-called personal creation, which sounds just like a repair of his modern building project, yet with traditional functionalism.

When you pointed out that the first veil story we heard about was a British woman protecting herself from sand, you also meant that in the Sahara, men are veiled too. Therefore, indeed, what you see is never the reality. Especially from a Western perspective.

I recently came upon an interesting story about a vernacular iconic architecture made of clay, in the Sahara – a story I had already heard but that was never established as true. Did you know that Djenne's mosque, in Mali, is a fake? Actually, what looks like an authentic 12th century mosque is not... This beautiful architecture has been "re"-built by the French at the beginning of the 20th century (in 1907).

As far as I'm concerned, this is extremely interesting, as we always point out that there is "reappropriation because of dispossession." But what if the reconstruction of a mosque, which has been destroyed several times by local people and foreigners, is ordered by a colonial power, in this case, by William Ponty, the French governor?

People in Mali do not complain, but in all former colonies, especially French ones, relations with colonial architecture are highly problematic. In Morocco, associations such as Casamémoire are doing a great job at protecting the architectural legacy, but in Algeria, protecting constructions led under the former colonial administration is still considered nonsense. Except for religious buildings. As a matter of fact, almost all churches were saved due to the fact they became mosques; this is another process of reappropriation, just like so many Ottoman mosques were turned into churches during colonization... It is an endless process, and reappropriation is a loop, too.

M. V. O.: Cultural articulations always have these incredibly rich multiple trajectories, but traces and transfers are likewise valued differently than the people producing culture: The architect earns cultural and symbolic wealth, the carpenter does not. On colonial grounds, this perception, or creation, of value starts with the ideological construction of traditional behaviors and acts against modern behaviors. In this binary pattern, there is competition between two value systems. This pattern is mostly due to European scholars. French orientalists' analysis and texts about local economies, crafts and building traditions either stated Moroccan local production were non-original

copies of an Arabian style, or called Berber crafting authentic indigenous art, as long as it had no disturbing contact with Arabian aesthetics. These euro-centric and anti-Arabian classifications caused great problems to the post-independence generation, and it also does not help to understand what a non capitalist local economy is, even nowadays.

Still, crafts production – the way French powers categorized it – was the local Moroccan economy's way of playing a part in trade relations and style exchanges over centuries. In opposition to what French people believed, not only was it more than a mere stable canon reproducing itself and simply influenced by the Ottoman Empire, but like in the Medina district, local production was also an expression and meeting point for different aesthetic trajectories and translocal trade relations with Africa and Europe. Moreover, guilds were in charge of controlling the local market, rewards, trades and production standards in Morocco over centuries, too.

When the French Protectorate took over the government, one of the first interventions concerned guilds, that is to say local economy and local production. New goods were introduced from other markets, shoes produced in Asia for instance, partially destroying local shoe production. That, had an impact on European markets because Moroccan leather products were imported to Europe as well, however trade relations changed with the introduction of Asian products. Therefore, it also modified the classification of local production, trade relations and local and traditional crafts, since the intervention into Moroccan guilds by French officials caused these manufactured goods to be seen as traditional and outdated. On the one hand, the local economy was now considered traditional/pre-modern, and on the other, the French argued that these forms of 'cultural production' would need to be protected and supported by French officials in the future, when Morocco would be completely modernized. This double faced destruction, devaluing and finally protecting the local economy, made it possible to declare it a mere extra, a boutique element decorating the real thing, which would be consumer goods made from industrialization.

For all of these reasons, the Medina district was protected by the Marshal of France, Louis Hubert Gonzalves Lyautey, as a kind of living museum about ancient living habits, surrounded by the *Cité Nouvelle* built for French colonists. To help Moroccan local trade, Lyautey had an oriental-modern *Habous* neighborhood constructed; by the way, it still exists as a central market area isolated from the former European city center. I'm talking about this because it is linked to your last comment, the fact is we missed this very point in our first project in Berlin at the *Haus der Kulturen der Welt*, in 2008, as we did not focus on who were actually the construction workers involved in building the new modern city of Casablanca. We were focusing on governance ideologies and anti-colonial resistance, but not so much on how working relations dramatically changed after French intervention. So how were these workers recruited? Obviously, most of them were Moroccans, while the planners, architects and technicians were Europeans. I only understood it after reading about it, but the Moroccan workforce was there because of the same intervention upon local economy and because of the catastrophic decrease in handicraft skills that occurred after Protectorate intervention in Morocco. So, first you have to destroy local production and value systems, then you have a highly skilled workforce build the new city for Europeans as well as some houses for the Moroccan workforce.

But these free floating skills were not just used in the name of colonial powers, they also served a lot of other purposes. As you know, the Medina house has always been an adapted and growing house. It was always accommodated according to a family's need, then it could be made bigger when it became too small. This actually was the local building practice, and you can find it in the whole Mediterranean area. Italian villages and smaller cities were built the same way, thanks to an adapted construction practice through which buildings could grow. This practice has not been erased by the colonial power, alongside many others, this skill survived industrialized means of production and can still be found nowadays. But as a result of colonial rule, local production, being marginal to industrial chains of production, has been turned into folklore and transformed into a souvenir culture. But still, this is an economy with its own logics next to other globalized forms of production, and it also makes it possible for people to let houses grow and adapt to the population's needs.

Marion Von Osten is an artist and cultural researcher. She works with curatorial, artistic, and theoretical approaches that converge through the medium of exhibitions, installations, video, and text productions. Her main research interests concern cultural production in postcolonial societies, technologies of the self, and the governance of mobility.

FROM THE SERIES **FOLLOWING THE MODERN GENEALOGY, 2012.**
SERIES OF COLLAGES, 100 X 75 CM, CARDBOARD, VINTAGE DOCUMENTS, PHOTOGRAPHS.

DÉ-CONSTRUIRE RÉ-INVENTER, 2012.
LIGHTBOX, 100 X 120 X 19 CM.

SATELLITE DISHES, 2009.
LIGHTBOX, 146 X 181 X 17 CM.

FROM THE SERIES **THE ARCH OF TAZOULT, 2012.**
SERIES OF LIGHTBOXES, 100 X 120 X 19 CM.

NARCISSE, 2012.
INSTALLATION, MIRROR, CONCRETE BLOCK, WIRE, VIEW AT GALLERIA
CONTINUA - SAN GIMIGNANO, 2012.

HALAM TAWAAF, 2008.
INSTALLATION, BEER CANS, VIEW AT THESSALONIKI BIENNALE - THESSALONIKI, 2009.

UNTITLED (CONCRETE BLOCKS), 2008.
FLOOR SCULPTURE, 5 M IN DIAMETER, CONCRETE BRICKS, VIEW AT CENTRO
ATLÁNTICO DE ARTE MODERNO - LAS PALMAS DE GRAN CANARIA, 2008.

UNTITLED (CONCRETE PILLARS), 2007.
SCULPTURE, CONCRETE, STEEL STICKS, VIEW AT FRIEZE ART FAIR, SCULPTURE PARK - LONDON,
PROJECT OF GALERIE CHRISTIAN NAGEL - 2007

UNTITLED (CONCRETE BLOCKS), 2008.
FLOOR SCULPTURE, CONCRETE BRICKS.

HALLAL, 2004.
INSTALLATION, EPHEMERAL STORE OF THE CLOTHING BRAND "HALLAL",
CLOTHES, MANNEQUINS, FURNITURES, PHOTOGRAPHS, BANDEROLE,
PRESS ARTICLES, VIEW AT GALERIE KAMEL MENNOUR - PARIS, 2004.

HALLAL, 2004.
INSTALLATION VIEW AT VILLA ARSON - NICE, 2004.

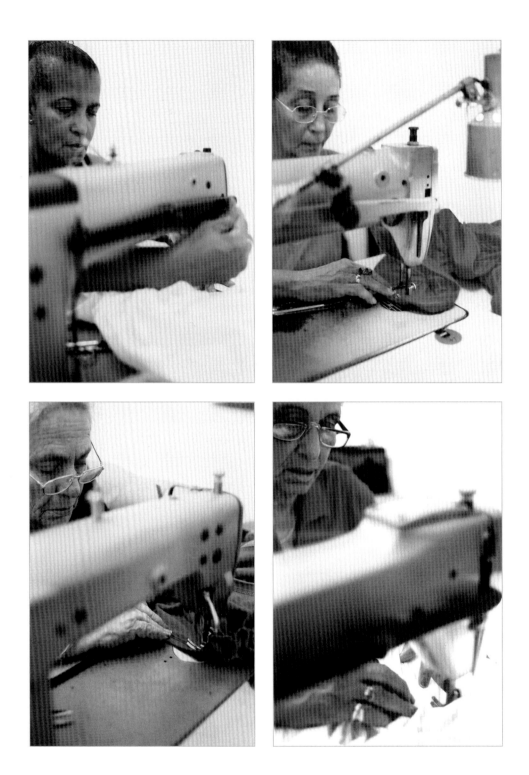

THE SWEATSHOP, 2004.
INSTALLATION, EPHEMERAL SWEATSHOP, DRESSMAKERS, SEWING MACHINES, CLOTHES, FURNITURES, VIEW
AT ART BASEL - MIAMI, 2004.

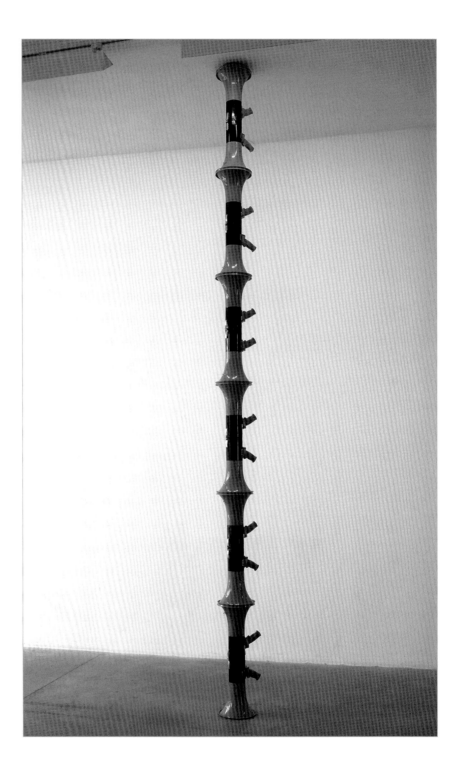

COLONNE SANS FIN, 2008.
SCULPTURE, VARIABLE DIMENSIONS, MEGAPHONES.

RECOVERY AS RESISTANCE, 2011.
INSTALLATION, CHEQUERED SKELETON OF A CAR, SEATS FROM DIFFERENT CARS,
VIEW AT GALLERIA CONTINUA – LES MOULINS, 2011.

CORRESPONDANCE, 2003.
VIDEO AND PHOTO INSTALLATION, VIDEO, 26 MIN, VIDEO STILLS.

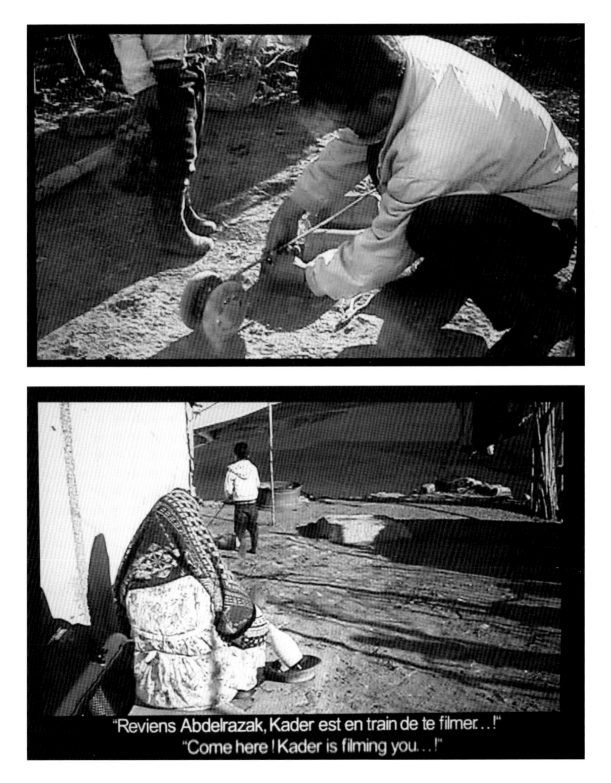

"Reviens Abdelrazak, Kader est en train de te filmer…!"
"Come here! Kader is filming you…!"

19th century etching, view of Kharthoum, Sudan.

In our attempt to undercut the cult
of genius, in our explanations, we
searched for the events that decidedly
affected Le Corbusier as a child,
as a young boy and as an adult, and
led him to become what he was in the
end: the most effective spokesman
for modernism – what it is, what it
might be and what it ought to be. The
summary of our search is simple and
reads as follows: because early in his
childhood he became intimate with the
elements of geometry in a playful way
(through Froebel), soon after that
he became enthralled with dwelling
above water as the earliest kind of
life in history, and through his own
acquaintance with Rousseau he realized
that this original constellation was
not entirely lost but could be found
again. He therefore knew for certain
that the architecture of modernism
had to be geometrically pure and
elevated above ground on stilts.

Adolf Max Vogt, *Le Corbusier, The Noble Savage:
Toward an Archaeology of Modernism*, 2000.

Top: Villa Savoye planned by Le Corbusier and Pierre
Jeanneret, Poissy, France, 1928 (photo. Paul Koslowsky).
19th century etchings showing stilt constructions, Congo.

Portrait of Fernand Pouillon, Algiers.

Climat de France housing complex planned by Fernand Pouillon in 1957, Algiers. The estate is now nicknamed "Climat de Souffrance" (literally "suffering climate") by its inhabitants

Algeria has been spoiled by the foolishness and the neglect of governments from, let's say, 1917 to 1958, to limit the duration of its responsibilities. If, from the most humble European to the great landowner, everyone became O.A.S, it was not the doing of a spontaneous generation. Succesive governments wanted that. Today, I can say that I have not known many clear - thinking Europeans. They were quite unintelligent, profoundly selfish and their minds had been prepared for segregation. The brutal repression which took place in Setif (1) was equal to Budapest's in its violence and cruelty. This is the spirit of this repression which animated all the Europeans of Algeria for so long. At that time, it was too late to embark on the right path. Chevallier (2) knew, he was one of the few who understood this. Today all this is finished, and it is the poor who suffer and will suffer the consequences again; such as the little Pieds-Noirs of Bab-El-Oued or of the Redoute. The ringleaders cannot suffer the consequences of the Algerian succession. They don't care at all. Some try to forget by worrying about new investment problems. Others, those in power, think with reason that they are responsible for the disaster and its sequelae. Chevallier continued to think and suffer in his flesh. This great patriot probably became stateless or opted for Algeria. But at that time, he was mostly concerned with urgent problems: how to find housing for the shantytown population, how to organize and sanitize Algiers in an exemplary fashion.

Fernand Pouillon, *Memoirs of an Architect*, 1968, translated from French by Joël Mallet.

(1) The massacres of Setif: bloody repressions of nationalist riots which occurred in May 1945 in the region of Constantine.
(2) Jacques Chevallier (1911-1971) was an industrialist and Franco-Algerian politician. He was elected to the general council of Algiers from 1945 to 1956 and was mayor of Algiers from 1953 to 1956.

Church in Diar es Saada, planned by Fernand Pouillon, later turned into a mosque

19th century etching depicting the interior of Algiers mosque, turned into a bishop's

FELIX THORIGNY

Middle East mud brick vernacular construction. Yemen

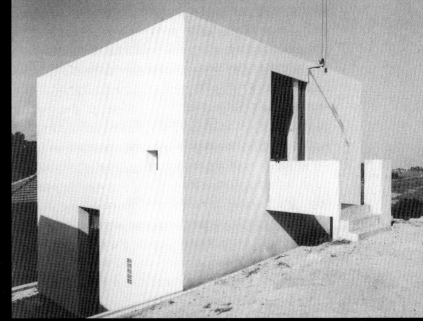

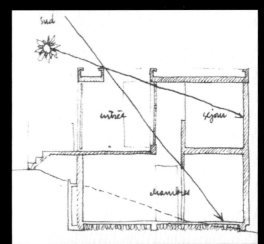

Top: A cargo cult nkisi, object representing a radio, West Africa.
Middle: Motorcycle designed by West African children during the 1970s.

Ntchakokot Kuba. Congo. Loincloth patched with bits of Vichy fabric (gingham).

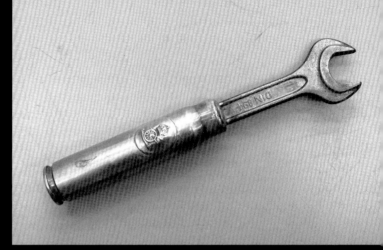

During World War I, soldiers in trenches used cartridges and shells to make tools, decorative objects, toys or even religious items. Likewise, in colonized countries, metropolitan coins were often turned into jewellery and worship objects (here Berber necklaces and pins).

Top: Construction of mud brick buildings at the border between Cameroon and Chad.
Bottom: Building maintenance in Yemen.

View of Marseilles colonial exhibition, 1922. Replica of Dogon African architecture in the foreground and replica of Cambodian architecture in the background.

Top: View of Marseilles colonial exhibition, 1931. Replica of a mosque in Sudan (currently Mal:
Bottom: View of Marseilles colonial exhibition, 1931. Replica of an Oceanic house.

European staging of natives playing the piano and listening to the music.

dern staging of private and professional life inside Buckminster Fuller's Dymaxion house

ACHILLE MBEMBE

THERE ONLY IS ONE WORLD

The birth of the race subject - and therefore of the Negro - is bound to the history of capitalism. Capitalism's primitive motivation is the double urge for unlimited violation of all kinds of interdiction, on the one hand, and for complete abolition of distinction between the means and the end, on the other. In his gloomy splendor, the Negro slave - being the very first race subject - is the product of both those urges, he becomes the emblematic figure of the possibility of unleashed violence and dangerous instability. As a power born from capture, control and polarization, capitalism always needed racial subsidies to exploit global resources. What was true yesterday still is today, even when capitalism is re-colonizing its own heart, and now that the perspectives for the Negro-future of the world have never been so obvious. The logic of distributing violence on a planetary scale spares no area of the world any more, nor does the current huge operation aiming at depreciating productive forces. Though there will be no secession regarding humanity, there will be no holding back on restitution, reparation, nor justice. Restitution, reparation and justice are the conditions for a common rise in humanity. The thought of what is to come will necessarily be a thought of life, of preserving life, of what must escape sacrifice. Necessarily, it will also be a circulating thought, a thought of crossing, and a world-thought. The issue of the world - what it is, relations between different areas, the extent of its resources and who they belong to, how to live in it, what makes it evolve or threatens it, where it is heading, its borderlines and boundaries, its probable end - will have existed through us from the moment that man made of flesh, bones and mind appeared under the sign of the Negro, meaning man-merchandise, man-metal and man-money. Fundamentally, that issue will have been ours, and it will remain so as long as to speak the world will equal to speak humanity and vice versa. For indeed, there is only one world. The latter is a Whole made of thousands of pieces. It is made of the entire world. It is made of the worlds. This living entity with multiple aspects was given a name by Édouard Glissant: the World-Whole, as if to highlight the ecumenical dimensions and the epiphany lying in the very concept of mankind… a concept without which the world in itself, in its essence as a thing, has no meaning at all. Thus it is entire mankind that gives the world its name. By doing so, human beings are delegating in the world and receive from it a confirmation of their own singular yet fragile, vulnerable and incomplete position, at least from the perspective of other forces in the universe - animals and plants, objects, molecules, divinities, skills, materials, the ground shaking, volcanoes blazing, winds and storms, waters flooding, the sun bursting and burning and so on. Therefore,

there is only a world due to naming, delegation, mutual action
and reciprocity. Nevertheless, if entire mankind delegates
itself in the world and receives from the latter a confirmation
of its own being and its fragility as well, then the difference
between the human world and the non-human world is not based
on external order anymore. When standing against the non-
human world, humanity is standing against itself. Because,
in the end, it is through the relation we develop with every
part of the living that the truth of what we actually are
is being revealed in the last moment. In ancient Africa, the
manifest sign of epiphany mankind embodied was the seed that
is buried in the ground, dies, comes to life again and gives
the tree, the fruit and life at the same time. It is mostly
to celebrate the union of the seed and life that ancient
Africans invented words and language, objects and skills,
ceremonies and rituals, works of art, perhaps even social and
political institutions. The seed was meant to create life in
a fragile and hostile environment, inside which mankind would
work and rest, while also protecting it. This environment
had to be repaired every time. Most vernacular knowledge had
no use but to be the link with this endless repair work. It
was assumed that nature was a force in itself. It could not
be shaped, transformed nor controlled without its agreement.
For all that, such a double transformation and regeneration
task took part in some cosmological assembly aiming at always
consolidating relations between human beings and other living
beings inside the world they shared. Sharing the world with
other living beings, such was the ultimate debt. Above all,
such was the key to durability for both humans and non-humans.
In this system made of trade, reciprocity and mutuality, humans
and non-humans were each other's silt. Silt, Édouard Glissant
did not mention it as mere material waste - seemingly dead
substance or elements, something that seemed to be of no use,
bits and pieces taken from their source and carried away by
water. He also saw it as a residue dropped on river shores,
in the middle of archipelagos, in the deepest of oceans, along
valleys or at the foot of cliffs - it can be found everywhere,
and especially in those dry desert lands where, if you move a
bit of manure, you will find unexpected and previously unseen
life, work and language forms. Our world's durability, he
stated, was to be thought through the back side of history,
from the slave and the cannibal structure of our modernity,
the one that took shape during the slave trade and fed from
it for centuries. The world emerging from this cannibal
structure is made of uncountable human bones buried under
the ocean, slowly turning to skeleton and flesh. It is made
of tons of bits and limbs and scattered pieces of words, soon
brought together and from which, miraculously, language is

reconstructed at the meeting point of the human being and its own animal. The durability of the world depends on our ability to reanimate beings and things that appear lifeless – the dead man, dried out and turned to dust by an economy that, for lack of enough people, traffics in bodies and life. Thus, the world will only last if mankind gets to constituting what has to be honestly called Life preservation. If our will to not perish makes us beings of history and allows the world to then our will to last can only be achieved if our craving for life becomes the cornerstone of a new way of thinking politics and culture. For the ancient Dogon, this never-ending repair labor had a name – the dialectics of meat and seed. The purpose of social institutions was to battle against human death and to prevent corruption of the body, meaning decay and rotting. The mask perfectly symbolized this will of the living to fight against death. It was a mock dead body and a substitute for the ephemeral shell, and its function did not only consist of commemorating the dead. It also served as proof of the body's transfiguration (as an ephemeral shell) and of the world's apotheosis and rot-resistant aspect. Therefore, this repair is an invitation to come back to the idea of life as an imperishable and rot-resistant form. In such conditions, you can try hard to erect borders, build walls and fences, divide, classify, rank and segregate from humanity the men and women who have been belittled, despised or who just do not look the same, or with whom you think you will never get along. There is only one world and we are all its beneficiaries. This world also belongs to everyone, and we are all co-heirs, even when we inhabit it differently – and this is exactly why you can find a real plurality of cultures and ways of living. Saying it does not mean forgetting the brutality and cynicism that still characterize the encounter of peoples and nations at all. It is simply a reminder of immediate and inexorable data surely finding its origins in the early years of modern Times – that is to say the irreversible process intermingling and intertwining cultures, peoples and nations. So, there is only one world, at least for the time being, and it is everything that exists. Consequently, we share a common sentiment or desire, each and every one of us, to be human beings in our own right. This desire for fulfillment in humanity is something we all share. In addition to that, what is more and more common to us now is the proximity of distance. It is the fact of sharing, willingly or not, the world as both everything that exists and everything we have. In order to build this common world of ours, men and women who, in a certain point in history, had to undergo any abstraction process and were considered as objects, will have to be restituted the part of humanity that was stolen from them. In this perspective, the concept of reparation, in addition to being an economic category, echoes the act of mending amputated pieces, repairing broken links, reviving the reciprocity game without which humanity cannot rise. Restitution and reparation therefore lie at the very heart of a possible construction of a shared consciousness of the world, that is to say the accomplishment of universal justice. The concepts of both restitution and reparation are founded on the idea that there is an intrinsic part of humanity under the protection of every human being. This irreducible part lies in every one of us. It enables us to be objectively different, yet the same. As a result, the ethics of restitution and reparation implies acknowledging what could be called other people's share, which is not mine, even though I am its guardian, regardless of whether I want it or not. Taking hold of the others' share would impact the very idea of self, justice, rights, and perhaps even just mankind, or even the universal project, should that be the final destination in and of itself. Reparation is also necessary because history has left scars and injuries. The historical process was, for most of our humanity, one of habituation to other people's death — slow death, suffocating death, sudden death or delegated death. This habituation to the death of a man or a woman you feel shares nothing with you, those multiple living sources of life being dried up in the name of race or difference, all of that left very deep scars in our imagination, in our culture and in our socio-economic relations. Those scars and injuries prevent us from forming a community. Indeed, constructing the common cannot be separated from reinventing community. By definition, the question of a universal community must be asked in terms of inhabiting the Open, of taking care of the Open — which is entirely different than an approach that first encloses and then remains locked into our so-called immediate relations. This non-relational form is the exact opposite of difference. In most cases, difference results from building up a desire. It is also born from working on abstraction, classification, division and exclusion — working on power which is later internalized and reproduced in everyday gestures and even by those who are excluded. The desire for difference often stems precisely from some intense experience of exclusion. In such conditions, proclaiming difference is the inverted language of the desire to be acknowledged and included. However, if as a matter of fact difference takes shape in desire (perhaps envy), the latter does not necessarily mean lust for power. It can also be a desire to be protected, to be spared, or kept from danger. On the other hand, the wish for difference is not necessarily the opposite of the project to determine what is *in-common*. Actually, for those who suffered colonial domination or those whose humanity was partially stolen at a given point in history, recollecting this part of humanity often goes through claiming their difference. Still, as it can be seen sometimes in modern Negro critique, claiming difference is but a moment in some wider plan – the plan for a world to come, one that is ahead of our time, with a universal destination, a world unburdened by race, by the desire or sense of vengeance that can stem from any racist situation.

Achille Mbembe, *Critique de la raison nègre*, La découverte, 2013. Translated from French by Joël Mallet.

FULLNESS AND EMPTINESS

GHOST, 2007.
INSTALLATION OF SCULPTURES, ALUMINUM FOIL,
VIEW AT STIFTUNG FEDERKIEL - HALLE 14 - LEIPZIG, 2007.

GHOST, 2007.
INSTALLATION VIEW AT GALERIE CHRISTIAN NAGEL - BERLIN, 2007.

GHOST, 2007.
INSTALLATION VIEW AT TRI POSTAL - LILLE, 2010.

ON VOID AND WHAT IT CONTAINS

Any plastic material conveys socio-political meanings, even when its forms are clean, simple, seemingly anodyne and neutral, as though completely transparent. Donald Judd, amongst others, never ceased to assert this, thereby showing the error of excessively formalist readings of his work. In addition to the fact that a majority of receivers feigns time and again to separate content and form, content and appearance, or meaning and representation, such an attitude pushes us into the trap we wish to avoid, since such a dichotomy would be due in large part to socio-political prejudice. Seeing only form at the expense of content is not the result of the "intention of the piece", much less of its author who always produces form to some degree, but of a prior decision on behalf of the receiver who does not question himself as to the possible or impossible aesthetic legitimacy of the break, nor on the implicit criteria which, conversely, might drive him to highlight the moral, ethical and socio-cultural stakes of the object in ignoring shape. Strictly remaining on the practical-sensorial or on the practical-moral level leads to two fatal errors: aestheticizing the object for various purposes which de-semanticize it, and being unable to judge of its success or failure as a piece of art. Kader Attia's pieces bind together the autonomy of the work and the social fact not only because we produce all sorts of things which are full of various meanings – at this level the work of art cannot distinguish itself from these things other than by a certain qualitative measure – but especially because the artist works in a field where politics, economics and religion intersect, and he therefore cannot ignore the ideologies and visions of reality which arise from it under the pretext that we are in the supposedly magnifying world of art. Beyond the issues of Muslim culture's more or less conflictual relationships with secularism, finance, money, democracy, civil liberties, women's rights, among many other contentious issues, Kader Attia's work touches on deeper structures of our imagination, our values and our practices. Structurally or anthropologically speaking, we find similar problems at the point where we thought they had disappeared, all the more so in that they move around, modify themselves and emerge elsewhere in forms which, literally and figuratively, ultimately express the nature of these very same problems.

Thus, in the *Halal* series with its products and its voluntarily derived by-products, we saw the conditioned reaction to the commodification of everything and anything, since clothing could become a brand under the powerful pressure of supply and demand. Whether they were food or clothing items, or objects originally intended for a use defined by religious rules, it appeared that not only did being labeled "halal" endow them with an aura that the trading system couldn't give them, but that furthermore, this whole merchandising operation was fully accepted, recognized, justified, and sanctified. Religions, monotheistic or not, give a symbolic and market value to hundreds of objects, usually junk, supposedly in order to strengthen faith while at the same time filling coffers. A number of dominant religions impose their earthly power simply because they have money, either clean or dirty, involved in the vast system of neoliberalism. This was evident, for example, during a period of the severe financial crisis (2010-2012), when civil society, institutions, industries and banks had to tighten their belts, submit to restrictions and economic austerity, but it was in no way possible to touch the material assets of the Greek Orthodox Church, nor those of the Vatican. This makes sense, since "his kingdom is not of this world." The money from the other world must not, therefore, be given to the needy who ultimately must take responsibility for the financial mistakes of their earthly world.

All religions are also businesses that make a profit because symbolic power is one of the communicating vessels of commodity fetishism that is greatly abstracted into the highly symbolic value of capital. It is neither an inevitable reversal nor an error, but a perfect match between the material spectacle of goods and the symbolic spectacle of belief. In order for the miracle of the transfiguration of the material into the symbolic, and in particular, as fundamental dramaturgy would have it, for the transfiguration of the symbolic into the material to take place, the spectacle must occur. Common man is neither an ascetic, a hermit, a martyr nor a penitent. Contrary to what is often argued, faith requires tangible, palpable, and concrete proof which can attest to the unverifiable, the hereafter, and the transcendent. The unseen is proved by the visible. The intangible by the material value. Or, as Samuel Beckett wrote in *The Unnamable*: "It is easier to build a temple than to make the deity appear in it". Thus, we increase the number of temples we build in inverse proportion to the absence of their object: the presentification of the void.

But is it so strange to think that religion and the capitalist system are both based on symbolic and abstract values which exist because we believe in them? In the eyes of someone who believes in heaven, the presentification of the void is the essence of his faith and it could not be otherwise. For the atheist, this void and its presentification are confined to superstition coupled with market fetishization, which extends to the socio-political field. As can be seen on a daily basis, it is absolutely wrong to say that the spiritual is separated from the material, that being is not contaminated by having. It is no secret that Islamic religious practices in the middle classes and the upper classes are very often a front and that what is done in private is exactly the opposite of what these practices prescribe. Depending on whether one is rich, comfortable, modest or poor, precepts have neither the same weight nor, indeed, the same value. This situation is echoed in other religions and societies. Instead of being emancipatory, religions continue to be the main engine of social hierarchy (think of the caste system in India), of maintaining order, of permanent constraints, senseless rules, heavy and obsolete prohibitions, of a kind of contemporary feudal system in which the spiritual promises supposedly made to one and all create a huge system of market equivalence. Ultimately the owners of capital always benefit and accumulate material wealth which is not redistributed to the general public. In general, the public feeds on spirituality, as is the case, for example, in the majority of the population of Latin America, which, in fact, has no other option.

If, as many economists believe, the violence of human passions has been diverted to benefit the search to satisfy one's own interests and the maximizing of one's own material well-being, it is clear that self-interest dominates the quest for disinterestedness, for gratuity, altruism and mutual aid. Moreover, these ideas may only be found in a text that prescribes the true path. Islam still forbids usury and interest, but it has not been difficult to circumvent religious law, and therefore morality and ethics, to increase property and investments in order to speculate without remorse and develop capital by making significant gains. The accumulation of capital is thus consistent with Islamic law. By means of an often twisted interpretation along the lines of the dominance of material values, these naturally lead to various hedonisms to which the capitalist system is supposed to give us access, so that none can be surprised that Kader Attia's neon sign, where the word "mosque" alternates with the word "nightclub" (*Mosque/Night Club*), represents two sides of the same coin. Through ironic, sarcastic, and especially lucid pieces, one of the characteristics of Attia's work is to expose the double bind in which the contemporary generation is caught. It isn't so much that this generation has a hard time choosing between so-called modernity – the wonderful neoliberal world – and such and such traditional society, but because it chooses the capitalist society as if there were no other solution. As leaders on all sides and all religions continually repeat, echoing Margaret Thatcher's sinister formula: "There is no alternative".

Capital and religion have in common, at the very least, the fact that they are based on an absence, an abstraction, an imaginary construct or an emptiness, what Marx called "the supersensible sensitive" drawing an analogy between both terms. For Marx, fetishism and even the mystique of the goods are imaginary and abstract representations in which the relationships between men are substituted with the value ratios between things. The more importance is given to the supersensible things, the greater their persuasiveness.

Hence the analogy between religious fetishism and commodity fetishism: "The religious world is but a reflection of the real world. A society in which the product of work usually takes the form of goods and in which, therefore, the most frequent relationship between producers is to compare the values of their products and under this envelope, to compare their private work with each other as equal human labor, such a society may find in Christianity with its cult of abstract man, and especially in its bourgeois types such as Protestantism, deism, etc., the most suitable form of religion (1)". In today's terms, when Kader Attia literally shapes the supersensible out of the sensible – i.e., the work he creates – he deals with that which is the central concern of people torn between being and having, spirituality and materialism, namely with an empty signifier. This signifier is a product of the human imagination understood as a temporary and material substitute for a supersensible world, also entirely invented, which thus creates a double fetishization of goods and the invisible. Nonetheless, it is a meaning that almost everyone wants to achieve in order to possess it and especially to use it in order to improve their existence, although it is empty by nature, will remain empty and will deliver only emptiness.
But which emptiness are we talking about? Kader Attia's work is situated in the Chinese philosophy of Liezi's *True Classic of Perfect Emptiness*, of Lacan's empty signifier, or also in the criticism of the great void of the speculation that enables Capital to function at full power. Having understood the double discourse of other notions of the mortified voids, since they are made up of pure appearance and illusion, and as if he were adopting an attitude of non-action in relation to them, Kader Attia opposes them with work which is just as equally empty, but which is not filled, so to speak, with a similar void.

With an efficiency worthy of a Taoist aphorism, Kader Attia plays subtly and quite literally – hence the dialectic of action and non-action – with real-life situations. These situations are depicted, for instance, in *The Void*, a photograph showing arches through which we see a mosque, and in its counterpart, *The Complete*, where huge slabs of concrete block a street in the neighbourhood of a Palestinian territory, specifically in Ramallah. We might obviously think of, with almost obligatory reference, Yves Klein's exhibition *Void* which was immediately followed by the exhibition *Complete* by his friend Arman who filled that same gallery with rubbish. Additionally, the socio-political importance of Klein's material, spiritual and mystical *Void* both opposes and complements Arman's material and disgusting *Complete*; these are, in short, two antagonistic visions of society.
For it is indeed a representation of the social, its practice and its uses, which we tend to quickly move away from in favour of post- and neo-eclectic movements derived from Pop, assemblage, and Dadaism, movements which are themselves already embalmed and museified even though they expressed and still express socio-political positions. To paraphrase Marx, our relationship to human history is not mainly about the true or truth but about practicality. And the void is an integral part of practicality, as has already been said a long time ago in the *Tao Te Ching*:

Thirty spokes share the wheel's hub,
But it is the center hole
That renders the care useful

We shape clay to make vases,
But it is on the hollow space within
That their use depends

We build a house by cutting out
Doors and windows,
But again it is on the void which
Its use depends

Thus "what is" constitutes
The possibility of every thing,
"what is not"
constitutes its function

Philosophical meditation like artistic creation is therefore, above all, practical. We have to invent, imagine, and think, but especially to be doing, to be in action, embodiment, and effectuation. In order for this to happen, there is no need for huge aesthetic machinery or grand objects, simple grocery bags are enough, placed just as they are in a venue, or given shape through drawing. The bags presented and designed by Kader Attia are empty, dangling, soft, and perfect. Their total banality and platitude cannot even qualify as a postmodern conceit. Because they are empty, they can be used for all kinds of uses and functions, and therefore it is indeed on the "internal void that its use depends," which any follower of the Way would certainly recognize. This void creates uses ranging from the most detrimental to the most convenient, so it is quite clear that their utility depends, in the literal and figurative sense, on what is placed inside it. Their outer form will be based on the things they contain. When they contain nothing, they take on, paradoxically, the shape of this thing. And because there is nothing in these bags, all kinds of imaginary projections, more or less fair and legitimate, are allowed. They are then filled with these things imagined by the audience, which, hopefully, are not nothing, of nothing or nothing. The belief that these bags are uninteresting is immediately contradicted by the vast socio-economic and socio-political processes through which environmental, commercial, advertising, and ethical issues are synthesized by this strange profession we call "packaging". We can sell you anything and everything if the packaging is attractive. It is more important and valuable than its content. Packing void reaps millions on a daily basis. These millions are themselves quite real.

In the installation *Ghost*, the empty aluminum envelopes which remain after the bodies of the models are removed also pertain to what the receiver places there. The emptying may be viewed as both that which takes part in the external material form and in a symbolic form literally built around this void and its envelope. We do not know if in fact they were men or women, although we inevitably think of women's clothing, such as those molded on women in prayer. Usually, only the women wear several scarves – like leaves here – that hide and cover their hair, whether in Islamic practices or in some Christian practices such as during Holy Week in Spain. If we refer to the title, *Ghost*, then we might have figures of prostrating – or at least kneeling – ghosts. Why women ghosts, and why so many? Why those sheets of aluminium, a ductile and lightweight material, often used for protection? Kader Attia has achieved one of his most striking and plastically successful pieces with almost nothing, with a void to be filled with meaning. Or emptied of meaning. The strength of this work lies precisely in the absence of the body of which only the ghostly shell remains, a final avatar of the concrete presence of missing beings, broken, faded and dead. Upon initial viewing of the piece we might actually think of of dead women. Specters of women. Absence is part of presence.

In order for the artist to fill the empty space with void – as he claims to have done – it was necessary to appropriate and occupy the venue in order to make present the void which, paradoxically, could not have appeared and become visible if these carnal husks had not been placed there. If you see these hundreds of bodies or figures of bodies in prayer from the back, their mass and luminosity fill the place powerfully. As seen from the front, so to speak, since they do not have faces, the same elements reverse immediately into their opposites since these contours, these envelopes and these clothes do not contain anything. It was necessary for the nothing or the internal void to take on an external shape – as in the vase, or in architecture – for that which is not there, not seen and yet which addresses us like a human figure signaling itself as absent, to become sensible. Each envelope seems to say: I'm here in my absence and by my absence. I am my absence.

We can not elide readings of *Ghost* which might view it as a denunciation of some of the servitudes of woman – including religion and morality – because in fact we are dealing with a large group of women in close ranks who seem to be either submitting to an authority, or, conversely, ready to rebel. We can only reject these possible interpretations if we are wary of the fatal separation previously discussed in which we only see the content at the expense of form. The notion of "content" is apt here since it refers to an empty content for each object and a content filled with voids with regards to the locus of representation. The language is also misleading: they are not women nor even metaphors for women, they are above all fictional objects. For everything that we see plays on this ambivalence in which we perceive both an excessively present object and an absent being. These things are not literal, precisely because they are things, nothing but aluminium foil to be filled with what we want, like common plastic bags. The object is present but the being is defective. The Being is literally hollow – a person was a living model for an envelope which thus refers to it – without delivering a figure, a face, that which grants human beings their humanity. No face, no being. But these women whose faces are hidden, or who willfully conceal them, are not things. Kader Attia absolutely knows this, artistically and as a citizen, and it would be a reductive assessment of this work to view in it only a denunciation of the status of Arab women. One could quite understand this deletion of the face from a Jewish perspective, specifically that of the philosopher Emmanuel Levinas, whose thinking attaches fundamental importance to the face of others. This is an unexpected connection but no more so than those established by Levinas between the Jewish tradition and the contemplation on phenomenology from which he philosophically originates and through which the idea has developed – from Husserl to Merleau-Ponty and Sartre – that I am constituted by the gaze of the Other. I exist in large part through the gaze focused on me, through a vis-à-vis, a concrete flesh-and-blood face-to-face. Once we get past our surprise at the objects in *Ghost*, which are ultimately only rolled up and stacked up materials which have taken on a human shape, our confusion, embarrassment, perhaps our discomfort arises from the fact that I am not viewed by others as might be expected, and in return, I can not watch a full representation of another. The void constitutes me, or more exactly, the gaze of the void or of this empty thing constitutes me. The great plastic and aesthetic intensity of *Ghost* stems from the fact that I am perceived by all these assembled voids, and the question is literally to know by which void I am in turn constituted.

No faces or bodies, no interiors or consistency. Yet this group, which one hesitates to refer to as people or beings, has an overwhelming presence. In fact, these hollow sculptures are true impressions of someone, their form is that of a living being, the trace or residue of this contact and a temporary recovery. The material is extremely fragile, ephemeral, very malleable, very resistant; it can be reduced to almost nothing, a few balls or heaps, as we know through use. We are ultimately neither stronger nor more permanent than these aluminum sheets, these sculptures of void in which we can see the final image of our emptiness.

These bright, luminous, frankly spectacular sculptures, which capture the reflections of the surrounding lights, are reminiscent of a certain tradition of baroque silver statues on which the scarcity of material vies with the vanitas. One cannot also help but think of the Western iconography that represents Death, usually a skeleton, completely covered from head to toe in a long cloth. However much fun we poke at these seemingly distant aesthetic games, from a bygone era, it does not change anything in our condition; we will all die. We're here, walking in the room and looking at these ghostly things and we can disappear forever in the blink of an eye.

What affects us physically in the empty, presentified void of *Ghost* is a possible shape, although palpable and present, of our finitude. It is not the skulls, flowers and hourglasses that give us the image of the passage of time, the fragility of our existence, but precisely that which seems to wrap up existence, contain it, hold it inside until the container fades away. The presence is part of the absence. The aesthetic and artistic experience of the sculptures is diverse, and must primarily be an aesthetic and artistic experience, a most material and sensory experience that does not point to the supersensible, since it is, on the contrary, a live interaction between our own bodies and these envelopes of absent bodies. The number of sculptures also affects the games of "presence-absence" and makes us feel even more sharply that we don't amount to much against this army of ghosts. We all know that life is fleeting but we still do not see it. We prefer denial. Ambition, wealth and power do not protect us from death, and all these themes that are considered trite cannot change our status, our destiny and our purpose.

We have learned nothing from multisecular formulas, such as the the Latin adage which asserts: "certain Death, uncertain hour" (*Mors certa, hora incerta*). *Ghost*'s great achievement is to make sensitive, to shape esthesiologically, so to speak, the confrontation with our finitude and our futility. In this sense, the envelopes may certainly be understood as that which surrounds and contains the void - and the void is that by which they took shape - but also the incorporation of the void. The envelope does not truly have an inside or an outside, but is rather the thin, weak and fragile joint between being and non-being, visible and invisible, presence and absence and, quite naturally, between full and empty. These experiments are supported by sheets that are 0.02 mm thick.

They are clearly feminine forms, and only feminine (no men or children), so that the risk of a literal understanding can reappear again and drag a gendered interpretation of the work. The first of these literal interpretations is that women are physically separated from men during prayer and that we might have a representation of such a moment here. This is a possible reading and in fact a legitimate one, which should be approached from a critical angle: religious inequalities may take the form of these envelopes making manifest the objectification of women. That clothes which are more or less closed are recognized by some activists or intellectuals (such as Tahar Ben Jelloun who has spoken on this issue several times) as indeed being a reification of women's bodies and, more broadly speaking, a denial of their civil liberties, immediately involves an attack on the shapes of the body through that which covers it. We have a plastic body, a shape, a physical structure, a configuration - what Merleau-Ponty sums up perfectly by saying that we are also a *Gestalt* - and controlling this external shape inevitably leads to a grasp on what it contains, both on the moral and on the physical levels. The forms are not only here in the pieces and as though detached from the concrete *Gestalt* of the models; rather, they are their image and their imprint.

Both perfectly singular and repetitive, these forms apply to each individual body and to all the bodies into the bodies of human beings in general. If, as Roland Barthes remarked that clothes are "a self-image that is worn on our selves", it is quite different if the image, that is this form, is imposed on me by another that is not always benevolent, friendly and my equal. I am then truly attacked in my image and in my representation. It is then no longer the

forms I have chosen that are delivered to the gaze and the touch of others, but a social image that has been adopted for me without my consent. This imaginary form is also a void that is filled by good will, projections and fantasies that are foreign to me. My real and tangible body is then emptied of its substance, of its flesh, feelings and desires, and I present only a meaningless external image in all respects, since it is not connected to my true - i.e. chosen - self-image. This refers, of course, to societies where strict religious rules are applied, and where it happens, as it does in Sudan, according to Article 152 of *The Criminal Code* adopted in 1991, that "whosoever commits an indecent act, an act that violates public morality or wears indecent clothing" is liable to forty lashes, most notably for having worn a simple pair of trousers (2). The law refers to "any person", but in most cases, it refers to women, since men are, of course, never indecent.

Let us repeat: those who choose and adopt clearly and knowingly the wearing of, in every sense of the word, forms and images of themselves through their social and cultural codes are fortunately free to do so. However, to authoritatively impose on others their forms and their images goes beyond the framework of a free and tolerant faith, freedom and the self-determinations of each and every person. To attack mundane forms of clothing, simple envelopes of signs that, by nature and definition, must circulate in order to freely make sense of duty and power, attacks the various forms of life. Having power over or thinking that one has some rights on the forms of life of others is therefore not only spiritual, mental or intellectual. Control wants to appear in a concrete form, and in order to do so, must itself take shape inside other shapes, even if it creates empty forms which it will fill according to necessity. In order to become that power and control, taking on a form is necessary, which proves once more that forms, all forms, are not neutral. By controlling the form it is already possible to enslave a large part of the container, thereby enslaving a being, a life, a psychophysical form. *Ghost* is an immanent critique - in the formed and forming object - a taking shape that can shift other forms of life which are by nature mobile, modifiable, changeable and which continuously escape a definite representation into submission.

Fixing a form consists in preventing the container from being able to modify itself, and in doing so, of modifying the external envelope. Hence a completely different reading could be made of *Ghost*, which the installation exposes literally: in order to prevent the external form from changing, the container is emptied out. This omits the fact that the formative form is correlated to the formed form; a form is always a form of something else or of a person. Without being formalistic, Kader Attia does not forsake this problem, which attracts even more attention because the hollow of each sculpture immediately leads us to ask of what or of whom is this form the form?

Every artist manipulates shapes practically, as is Kader Attia's case here with sheets of aluminum foil, which relates to forms of life which are reconfigured, sometimes in very different art forms. We are beings who take shape daily in order to live, and this recurrence of taking shape, which we might also call plasticity, can be found in the forms we produce, make and manipulate, in order for them to keep at varying degrees the traces of our own forms. All the objects around us are just the negative taking the shape of our bodies; they are our own inverse corporeal shapes. Architecture and urbanism, on which Kader Attia also works, are perfect examples of the complementarity of forms. If the forms of *Ghost* are the practical result of forms of life, practical in that the form must be accomplished, must be formed in the literal and metaphorical sense, life is essentially a practice of forms, by forms and with forms. In insisting upon the envelope and thereby highlighting the hollow, Kader Attia eradicates any formalist aestheticizing of the sculptures, so that their voids become, so to speak, their principal form. The void is that which enables what we see on the outside. From the void emerges the being of the forms. Since this void is also physically invisible and relates to non visible or present bodies, we might think about the proof of the visible by the invisible.

Generally speaking, everyday things, such as the air we breathe, our daily acts of freedom, are so present and obvious that they are no longer perceptible, and have become invisible. Speaking in strikingly plastically similar terms to Kader Attia's process, Gunther Anders comments on those things which form the basis of our existence through the voice of a character in his novel *The Molussian Catacomb* (3). Of those actions and facts which are the positive aspects of existence – contrary to sickness, for instance, which is a negative aspect immediately visible and perceptible – it can be affirmed that "the positive is invisible." The benefits of life, our individual and social freedom, our lives, are so evident that they are invisible to ourselves, and it is only when they are restricted or when we miss them that we become aware of their existence. In this way, the invisible, the loss and the void, revive their dynamic roles. Our carnal presence in the word is a primordial source of the fullness of our beings, and the positive in *Ghost* is the body which is both form and container of our life and our existence which is also invisible. If the body is lacking – because it may be stigmatized as guilty and guilt-making – our whole being lacks those hollows which are as many absences of the positive of corporeal interaction. The other is also lacking, but this lack is understood as a call to presence which highlights this positive character. The relative negativity, absence or obliteration which could be perceived in *Ghost* can thus materially reverse itself in the sculptural object because our carnal positive is so present that it becomes the invisible which has become visible through the void. An invisible and empty positive is the possible definition of the ghost of the other.

Translated from French by Vanessa Ackerman

Jacinto Lageira is a professor of Aesthetics at the University of Paris 1 Panthéon-Sorbonne and an art critic.

Notes

1. Karl Marx, *Capital* (1867), Volume 1 "The development of capitalist production", 1st section: merchandise and money. Chapter 1: Merchandise, IV The Fetishization of merchandise and its secret. Translation J Roy, reviewed by K Marx.

2. http://www.lemonde.fr/afrique/article/2009/11/28/
   http://www.jeuneafrique.com/Article/
   DEPAFP20091128T130142Z/
According to Amnesty, thousands of women are arrested each year: tp://www.amnesty.org/fr/node/18595
Read about a different perspective at: http://lecoran.over-blog.com/article-soudan-20-coups-de-fouet-pour-2-femmes en-pantalon-38571189.html

3. C. H. Beck, *Die molussische Katakombe. Roman* (1932-1936), Munich, 1992. Some extracts of the text, included the text quoted here, were used in Nicolas Rey's film, *Autrement, la Molussie*, 2012.

IN NO MAN'S LAND

There is no document of civilization,
which is not at the same time a document of barbarism. (1)

The term "No Man's Land" originally designated the area between two enemy trench systems which neither side could claim as its own: a strip of mud, gravel and barbed wire under gruelling artillery fire. During World War I, trench warfare resulted from the asymmetry between firepower and mobility, and quickly consumed many lives: more than 1,000,000 were wounded or killed in the Somme; there were an estimated 975,000 casualties in Verdun. Roughly one century later, the space separating trenches has expanded to include vast swathes of the planet. Like the ill-fated infantry on the Western Front, waves and waves of migrants and refugees perish while attempting to cross no man's lands such as the Sahara desert, the Sonora desert, the Indian Ocean or the Mediterranean Sea, across which they will face border fortifications, barbed wire and armed police. The in-between trenches are not an anomaly or an aberration, but an emblem for uneven development and asymmetrical power; the ever-recurring zone of abrasion between the human and the techno-economic complex.

As Theodor Adorno stated, suffering is a "fact of reason" it is an experience of harm that cannot be coded into a discourse on injustice, the part that has no part in our inconsistent totality. Suffering is everything and nothing simultaneously – the identity and non-identity between industrial exploitation and colonial terror; between empire and periphery; between the ever-increasing pile of consumer goods and products and the human lives they are made of; and the missing link between art and history.

In his work *Prisms*, published in 1982, Adorno wrote that "In the open-air prison the world is turning into, it is no longer so important to know what depends on what, such is the extent to which everything is one" (2). I understood the meaning of his words in October 2012, when I accepted an invitation to visit the Qatari capital, Doha. Our press trip itinerary started with a walk around the pier, which culminated in Richard Serra's 7. Seven massive steel plates arranged in a heptagonal shape, 7 is the greatest public art commission ever made by the Qatari Museum Authority. The sculpture was installed at the tip of the man-made pier adjacent to the Museum of Islamic Art, built by star architect I. M. Pei. As we approached the towering colossus, a journalist walking by my side confided, "I was here last year while they were building it, you should have seen the Indian workers, those poor folks, toiling under the blazing sun". As I looked into her eyes, she became apologetic. "I know it's an amazing artwork, but I'm only human..." she explained. Her expression betrayed genuine concern, yet she could not bring herself to disavow the sculpture. While circling around the metal edifice, I came face to face with another journalist who whispered, "After the HRW (Human Rights Watch) released a report condemning their labour policies, Qatari authorities issued a ban on outdoor work when the temperature rises above 50 degrees Celsius. But ever since, it has never officially been over 50 degrees Celsius!" He shrugged and kept snapping pictures. For all their qualms about labour rights, there are two things that my fellow travellers do not seem to question: that Richard Serra's 7 is an artwork, and that an artwork is a good thing.

Introduced into the philosophical lexicon during the eighteenth century, the term "aesthetic" is predicated on discontinuity; the aesthetic experience is somehow severed from usual conditions of sensible experience. From Kant onwards, detachment becomes the hallmark of aesthetics, which always entails a double negation: its object is neither an object of knowledge nor an object of desire (3). By introducing the notion of disinterest, Kant brought the concept of taste into opposition with the concept of morality. At the beginning of his *Critique of Judgment*, he illustrates his reasoning with the example of a palace, in which aesthetic judgement isolates the form only, disinterested in knowing whether a mass of poor workers toiled under the harshest conditions in order to build it. The human toll, Kant says, must be ignored in order to aesthetically appreciate an artwork.

But one could also say that, in the guise of a Hegelian totality, an essence manifests itself in its alienation, and any phenomenon is also defined by what it negates or denies. Kantian aesthetics mirrors British utilitarianism. Whereas Adam Smith bracketed out the sociological conditions that necessarily precede the contractual conditions in his parable about marketplace interaction, Kantian philosophy brackets the issue of power being out of the question of representation, and the command to "look but don't touch!" severs the eye from the hand, following the scopophilical logics of advertisement.

Either way, in Qatar, Kant acquires an unwitting materiality. Whether or not one chooses to ignore it, 7 stands at the unstable borderline between art history and labour history, at the tip of a vortex of transnational capital flows that relentlessly hauls bare life into the unyielding machinery of autocratic power. In the Gulf, social division of labour conflates with global division of labour generating such hierarchical hierarky that only a culture of terror can sustain it. Not the terror of chaos that rules in slums and shanty-towns all over the world, but the terror of absolute order. The man-made pier, the outdoor cafeteria protected by sailing canopy, the designer museum, Serra's sculpture: all exist inside what Michael Taussig would have called a "space of death", in the sense of the death of collective memory and communal experience – running parallel to the occasional death of migrant labourers or domestic aids, whose work is always external to the artworks they labour to erect.

The link between political and cultural representation was never straightforward, but nowadays, "a growing number of unmoored and floating images corresponds to a growing number of disenfranchised, invisible or even disappeared or missing people" (4). As a result, the term "art" has acquired two contradictory meanings; it can refer to ways of effectively claiming representation, or it can refer to a mode of expression, employing a set of formal tropes so as to limit ways of effectively claiming representation. This conflict is not a conflict between the art market and contemporary art, nor is it a conflict between art and politics, it is a conflict between two different sensible worlds and their political correlation.

Throughout modern history, the worker and the artist have always been kept in dialectical tension. As a consequence, art's ontology was never settled; art always divided into two. The Romantic ethos was built upon the opposition between art as a totalization of experience and labour as an alienation of experience. Hegel's "end of art" is not the end of art as such, but the end of one of its facets: art as a pedestrian activity engaged with mundane wishes and needs, which must be superseded so that the other side of art can be freed to "lay a claim to the absolute" (5). Because, in order for art "to be art at all, art must be something beyond art" (6).

In his essay *Modernist Painting*, American critic Clement Greenberg argued that Kant was the first real modernist. In his view, the essence of modernism, inasmuch as that of Kantian critical philosophy, lied in the use of a discipline's own methods in order to entrench it more firmly in its area of competence (7). The article achieved a canonical status and, in retrospect, turned "Modernism" into a synonym for artistic autonomy – a self-sufficient, abstract and hermetic form. Greenberg also implied another Kantian idea, that of progress. Modernist art seems to move forward in time, away from manifestations of extraneous content and towards a specificity of means, and, as such, becoming a purely aesthetic experience. In Greenberg's own words: "Nothing could be further from the authentic art of our time than the idea of a rupture of continuity (...) Modernist art develops out of the past without gap or break, and wherever it ends up, it will never stop being intelligible in terms of the continuity of art" (8).

Emerging out of the horrors of trench warfare, the early 20th century Dada movement wanted to be anything but art. Dada's emphasis on rupture was not an aesthetic gimmick, but the allegorical doubling of a material trauma, a gash literally inflicted on the surface of the picture reciprocating the lacerations on broken-faced soldiers' flesh and the craters scarring the land, gorging up the living. Around 1918-19 (9), the movement adopted the term "photomontage" in order to distinguish their politically oriented practice from the fantasist postcards and dioramas so popular during the Victorian and Edwardian eras. The Victorian fantasist postcards were typically the product of combination printing, a technique – albeit more complex – similar to the dual-negative photography invented by Hippolyte Bayard. Bayard had initially used the technique to achieve higher photographic realism – namely to solve the problem of overexposure which would cause the sky to appear like a blank slate, by juxtaposing a perfect cloud abode over his street photographs – but it did not take long for this usage to explode in a myriad of fanciful compositions. During World War I, it was popular amongst young soldiers' families or fiancées to copy and paste themselves onto the plane cockpit of the soldier they knew, in an illustration of the adage "always with you" – if not in body, at least in image. Another common habit would be to include juxtaposing photographic elements onto watercolours or creating fictional landscapes. But whereas the photographic montage used in traditional postcards created an illusion of continuity by artfully fusing all elements together, the Dadaist collage made the artifice visible by fully displaying the sutures and the cuts their images were subjected to; upon viewing, the illusion was shattered and the gap between sign and referent became apparent (10). The choice between photographic illusion and photomontage is not merely an aesthetic choice between kitsch and avant-garde. What is at stake is the insertion of a diegetic element onto the imagetic plate; recounting instead of just showing. That is, the commitment to a synchronic, rather than diachronic, understanding of art and life. Photocollages, Walter Benjamin noted, typically interrupt the context into which they are inserted (11), making it manifest that the present is composed of manifold irreconcilable states; that every actual thing is a concrete unity of opposed determinations.

The first ready-mades emerged out of the Dadaist assemblages, the three-dimensional counterpart to the collages and photomontages. Objects were nailed, screwed or fastened together in tortured makeshift compositions, exposing shards, knobs and wire mesh. The broken bones and incongruous experiences of shell-shocked soldiers were codified as fractured images and fragmented objects. Reminiscent of the concept of *bricolage* (patch-up job) introduced by Claude Lévi-Strauss, the assemblages make do with a universe of heterogeneous elements, which "bears no relation to the current project, or indeed to any particular project" (12). Instead of obedient objects, subservient to the designs of the people they are meant to serve, the assemblages confound and reverse the respective positions of dead materials and living beings. Whereas Greenberg proposes a neat historical chronology in which all fundamental antagonisms are solved by rearranging the conflicting terms into a temporal succession, Dada makes it plain that modernity never ceased to be a battleground, and that the present is constantly at war with itself.

In the pictures Henri Pierre Roché took between 1916-18, Marcel Duchamp's studio appears littered with industrial debris and everyday objects hung to the ceiling or nailed to the floor. The small porcelain urinal hangs over a doorway. Its origin is unclear. "One of my female friends who had adopted the pseudonym Richard Mutt sent me a porcelain urinal as a sculpture," Duchamp would later write to his sister, probably referring to Baroness Elsa von Freytag-Loringhoven. Either way, the choice of ready-mades, he claimed, "is always based on visual indifference and, at the same time, on the total absence of good or bad taste."

It was part of the political program of the avant-garde to "replace individualized production with a more collectivized and anonymous practice and simultaneously to evade the individualized address and restricted reception of art" (13), and, as Elena Filipovic noted, "Ultimately, Duchamp meets the museum's desire for precision with irony and approximation, its desire for totality with a fragmentary story, its desire for encyclopaedic coverage with *à peu près*, its desire for system and order with volatile taxonomy, its desire for the original with an ensemble of copies, and its desire for linear history with caesura, delay, and ungraspable logic" (14).

No object is a stable, univocal entity. To be clear, an object is not really something one owns or uses; it is rather a relationship into which someone enters. Fifteen years ago, while living in Congo, Kader Attia was given a piece of Kuba raffia cloth to which patches of Vichy (gingham) fabric had been carefully applied in order to mend a hole, possibly made by wear or by insects. At length, it dawned on him that there was an intention behind the stitching, that the usage of the Vichy (gingham) fabric was not accidental or arbitrary – simple raffia cloth would do, had the needle worker merely meant to hide the tear. Struck by the poignancy of this artifact, the French-Algerian artist initiated a decade-long research on the ontological status of repaired objects. The project's first iteration, *The Repair*, shown at the dOCU-MENTA(13), was an essay in comparative aesthetics written from the vantage point of the wretched of the West. In the darkened rooms of the Fridericianum, the disfigured faces of World War I soldiers were juxtaposed with broken fetishes, fractured African masks, and stitched-up pieces of loincloth, describing a narrative arc from the empirical notion of repair to the juridical realm of "reparation" as in the replenishment of a previously inflicted loss.

The project of *The Repair* points to a continuity, but this is the continuity of incision, which cuts across the rural landscape, the draftees' faces and tribal integration. As Kader Attia noted, drawing on Oswald de Andrade's concept of cultural anthropofagia, the repair is not a passive act but a sort of reappropriation of the self: the staging of a dialectic of destruction and healing, which aims at replenishing a previously inflicted loss. The act of repair as a cultural practice allows the people living in the periphery of Western Empires to appropriate the symbols of the colonizing powers into their own cultural order, and as such, it threatens the totalizing unity of the cultural icon. The repaired objects do not speak of syncretic abstractions, instead they articulate a new cultural idiom to address the arbitrariness of colonial power and the terror of slavery. But *The Repair* is not, strictly speaking, a research project. It is an artwork, and, as such, it doesn't just address the notions of anthropology, artefact or archive; it addresses the concept of aesthetics and the field of contemporary art. Though their sincerity seems at odds with the ironical stance of the ready-made, these objects do come to us as ready-mades, inasmuch as, and somehow ironically, the bullets or coins which compose them came to their makers' hands as raw materials. By placing the colonial otherness at the heart of the industrial revolution, *The Repair* makes it manifest that "formalism" and "dadaism", "modernism" and "postmodernism", are not historical moments but political positions (15). In the same way that colonies and manufacturing centers represent partial truths of the industrial whole, repaired anthropological artefacts and ready-made objects each represent partial attempts to reconcile social function and aesthetic form.

In spite of Duchamp's intentions, for almost half a century now the notion of the ready-made or found object has been heralded as the starting point in a long lineage of laboriously crafted conceptual distinctions, which sustained the transition from high modernism to so-called post-modernism. The original act of appropriation signified a rupture, a break with the tradition that preceded it. Mistaking the abstractions performed by aesthetics with a totally abstract aesthetics, the current acts of appropriation signify a continuity. They reclaim the tradition which precedes them, constituting a commercially viable mode of artistic production from whose perspective work is always external to the artwork, and it is not something one suffers; just something to be commanded at the click of a keyboard.

Or to put it differently and under the guise of a conclusion: much like the term "art", the term "modernism" came to acquire two diverging, even conflicting, meanings. The first, which became shorthand for artistic autonomy, sees history as the schematic process through which art rids itself of any reference to political life. The second one insists that there is a correlation between the modern regime of representation and the constitution of the political subject. From the perspective of the former, there is no historical dimension to contemporary art, just an explosion of stylistic eclecticism made possible by the demise of media-specific mandates: we are living in a post-critical and post-subjective era. According to the latter, however, modernity has barely begun.

Notes

1. Walter Benjamin, *Theses on the Philosophy of History*, VII (1940; first published in German, 1950, in English, 1955).

2. Theodor W. Adorno, *Prisms*, The MIT Press, Cambridge Massachusetts, 1983, p. 34.

3. Jacques Rancière, *Thinking between disciplines: an aesthetics of knowledge*, in PARRHESIA #1, 2006 pp. 1-12.

4. Hito Steyerl, *The Wretched of the Screen*, Sternberg Press, 2012.

5. Fredric Jameson, *The Cultural Turn*, Verso, London, 1998.

6. Id. p.83.

7. Clement Greenberg, *Modernist Painting*, reprinted in Modern art and Modernism: A Critical Anthology. Ed. by. F.Franciscana and Ch.Harrison. Harper and Row, London, The Open University, 1986.

8. Id. pp. 5-10.

9. The term is said to have originated with Raoul Haussmann whose work was influenced by Georgiana Berkeley's photo albums, composed between 1868 and 1871. Though Max Ernst used a similar technique, both he and Aragon used to refer to it as "collage" or "photocollage". Both terms were commonly used by the Dada movement around 1918-19.

10. Susan Buck-Morss, *The Dialectics of Seeing*, The MIT Press, Cambridge Massachusetts, 1991.

11. Id.

12. Claude Lévi-Strauss, *The Savage Mind,* The University of Chicago Press, 1962, p. 17.

13. Martha Rosler, *Take the Money and Run? Can Political and Socio-critical Art "Survive"?*, published in e-flux Journal #12, January 2010.

14. Elena Filipovic, in *A Museum That is Not*, published in e-flux Journal #4, March 2009.

15. Here I'm paraphrasing Susan Buck-Morss, *The Dialectics of Seeing*, The MIT Press, Cambridge Massachusetts, 1991, p.359.

Ana Teixeira Pinto is a writer from Lisbon currently living in Berlin. She is a PhD candidate and occasional lecturer at the Humboldt University, and a regular contributor to E-Flux Journal, Art-Agenda, Mousse, Frieze/de and Domus. Her work was also published in Inaesthetics (Merve Verlag), Renaissancen (Archive für Medien Geschichte, University of Weimar) and ISPS (International Studies in Philosophy of Science, Routledge).

LE VIDE / LE PLEIN (EMPTINESS / FULLNESS), 2008.
PHOTOGRAPHIC DIPTYCH, LAMBDA PRINT MOUNTED ON ALUMINUM,
66,5 X 100 CM EACH.

THE MORE WE KNOW THE SMALLER WE ARE, 2012.
SCULPTURE, TWO BOLTS, VIEW AT IZOLYATSIA
FOUNDATION - DONETSK, 2012.

UNTITLED (PLASTIC BAGS), 2008.
SERIES OF EPHEMERAL SCULPTURES, PLASTIC BAGS.
LEFT AND TOP: VIEW AT CENTRO DE ARTE CONTEMPORANEO HUARTE - HUARTE, 2008.
BOTTOM: VIEW AT HENRY ART GALLERY, FAYE G. ALLEN CENTER FOR THE VISUAL
ARTS, UNIVERSITY OF WASHINGTON - SEATTLE, 2008.

UNTITLED (NO WATER), 2009.
SERIES OF EPHEMERAL SCULPTURES, EMPTY PLASTIC PACKAGINGS OF WATER
BOTTLES, VIEW AT 1ST KIEV INTERNATIONAL BIENNALE OF CONTEMPORARY ART
KIEV, 2012.

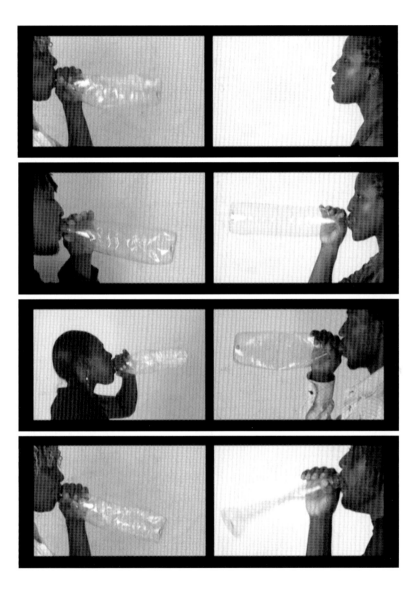

INSPIRATION-CONVERSATION, 2010.
VIDEO, 13 MIN 55 SEC, VIDEO STILLS.

SLEEPING FROM MEMORY, 2007.
INSTALLATION, WOODEN BEDS, FOAM, PLASTERBOARD, LIGHT BULBS, VIEW AT ICA BOSTON - BOSTON, 2007.

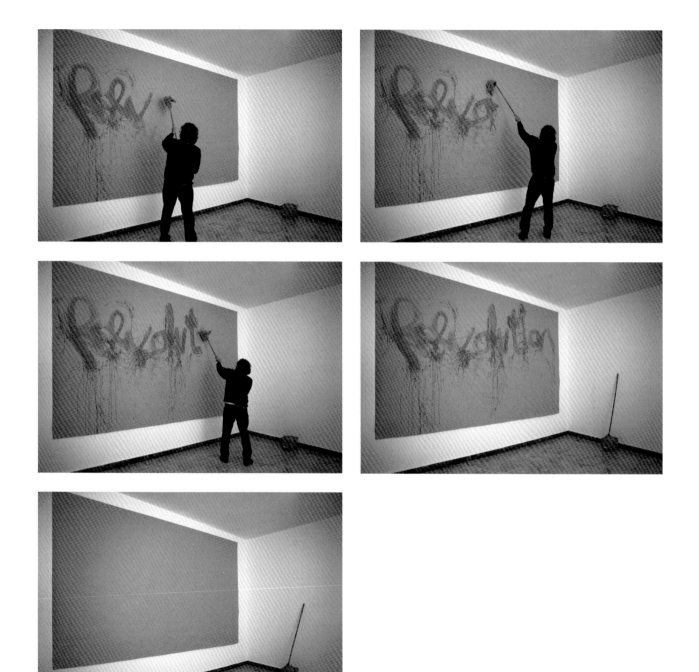

REVOLUTION, 2012.
VIDEO, 2 MIN 30 SEC, VIDEO STILLS.

BLACK HOLES, 2012.
FLOOR SCULPTURE, BLACK PIGMENT, RICE, INSTALLATION VIEW AT GALLERIA CONTINUA - BEIJING, 2012.

MIMETISM, 2011.
SCULPTURE, LEAD SHEET.

CONTINUUM OF REPAIR: THE LIGHT OF JACOB'S LADDER, 2013.
INSTALLATION, METAL SHELVES, WOODEN VITRINE, BOOKS, METALLIC STANDS, ARCHIVAL DOCUMENTS, LITHOGRAPHS,
TELESCOPES, MICROSCOPES, NEON LIGHT, MIRRORS, VIEW AT THE WHITECHAPEL GALLERY - LONDON, 2013.

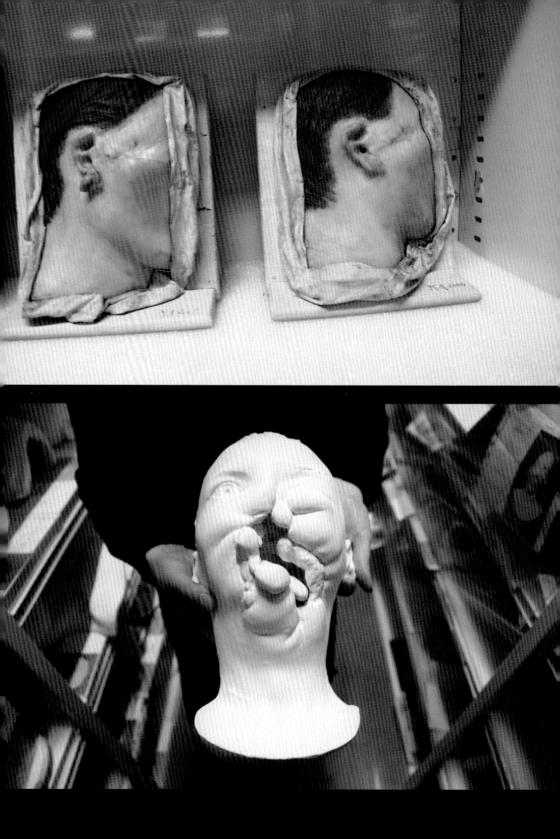

Top: World War I broken face wax moldings
Musée du Service de Santé des Armées, Paris
Bottom: World war I broken face plaster model
Musée du Service de Santé des Armées, Paris

Model of Auroville's utopist city. This city created in India in the late 1960s applied Indian philosopher Sri Aurobindo's precepts. French architect Roger Anger who was in charge of the town planning charter decided to mimic an intergalactic spiral.

Satellite image of the hurricane Katrina, USA, 2005

Talking about emptiness is talking about motion, circulation
and depth of field (that of perspective and Quattrocento)
and it is also talking about depth of time, meaning time
perspective, what is called the "high-speed train effect",
or acceleration. As an architect, an urban planner, talking
about the theory of emptiness is talking about quality and
quantity as well. Emptiness is not the same as nothing, it
is an area and a duration, what is called "a continuum" by
relativists. Empty spaces are a continuum, it is not only
space and atmosphere, it is a space-time. *Emptiness* and
fast are themselves both in relation with *alive*, meaning
the living and the life of whoever inhabits it. Hence the
ergonomic issue of the empty space: it's about distributing
rooms, places and it's also about distributing time.

"THE IMAGE GIVES DIMENSION TO CHAOS IN THE VISIBLE"
This statement is an introduction to the issue of geometry, for
the latter is an image that is the foundation of architecture.
Architecture is bound to Euclidean or non-Euclidean geometry.
We architects – who deal with the inhabiting man – face two
kinds of energies: that of emptiness and that of the fast,
inside the house and in the high-speed train as well. It is
kinetic energy and also what I call *cinematic energy of the
sensible.* I usually give one simple example of that: when you
are on a train, the landscape is passing by, it is cinematism,
the invention of cinema. It is no accident that one of the
first films ever shot was the Lumières brothers' *The Arrival
of a Train at La Ciotat*: trains have brought animation to
our vision of the world. The problem motion brings out is
that of speed and body motion, yet it also brings out the
issue of perception, and this does not only concern cinema.

CLAUSTROPHOBIA
The great confinement as mentioned by Foucault, especially
with prisons, turned into great confinement in a world
that – according to ecological signs – is too small for
our future. This is what causes city-dwellers to develop
claustrophobia, sedentary man's claustrophobia, which can
explain this tourism mania with people always travelling
around. There is collective claustrophobia in a world that has
become too small, that has been reduced by the acceleration
of both moving means and vision. Take Google Earth or
Google Street, the world is reduced to the instantaneity of
light. You get a suffocating feeling, a sort of suffocation
of sensitivity coming from that cinematic energy I talked
about earlier. The world is saturated, and not because it is
full, for there are still lots of empty spaces, but because

individuals are conscious of the world's narrowness with regards to progress: the world is too small for the progress of acceleration. We face geopolitical and chrono-topical issues (about the use of time and the use of space). Today the issue of empty spaces is a great political concern.

MODERN WASTELANDS

So, if I come back to my analysis, the inhabitability of emptiness is that of the lithosphere, meaning the empty space on Earth. However, something new has showed up since Fukushima: the possibility of new empty spaces which are uninhabitable not due to excessive cold or heat, but due to being contaminated forever. As a reminder, plutonium contaminates space for a duration of 24 000 years, iodine 129 for 15 million years… The issue of emptiness is not only about the great cosmos anymore, it is also about forbidden space. The Japanese are beginning to plan the North-South-East-West repartition of Honshu Island, and this is far beyond the 13 mile forbidden area surrounding the Fukushima nuclear plant. Because of the apocalyptic earthquake risks in Japan, we are already creating uninhabitable wastelands.

VERTICAL SATURATION

With metropolitan concentration being too high, towers come back to fashion, and the issue of empty spaces in altitude comes to light: There are 70 000 towers in Shanghai… Why not 700 000? With towers, you face the issue of emptiness in altitude and this brings the issue of population density in the sky, after the population density on the ground.
In the name of protesting against city sprawl (Mexico, Bombay, Tokyo), we turn to conquering empty spaces in altitude, and this is just as serious as horizontal saturation, I call it "falling upward". (…) And you can find echoes of this matter in current sciences, the search for exoplanets, inhabitable planets, with terra forcing, etc. The search for empty spaces, first in altitude, will then be sidereal. (…) Ecology, sustainable development to counter urban concentration is a good thing; however if it serves the proliferation of towers, it is an illusion.

THE CATASTROPHE OF PROGRESS

In the 60s, the issue of the uninhabitable was linked to the threat of total war and totalitarianism, while nowadays, it is linked to the threat of success and progress. Just like Hanna Arendt said, progress and catastrophe are merely two sides of the same coin. We are currently being threatened by the saturation that comes with progress. Let me remind you that at the end of the century, we will be nine billion and Malthus' interrogations will become reality. We are in a situation that can only be solved through movement, what I called inhabitable circulation. We are on the verge of a historical break in civilization, and it is unexpected, just like when men first became sedentary during the Neolithic era. But the world has become too small now, which obviously was not the case in the past. The world has become a tiny box.

A MINISTRY OF MOTION AND TIME
I'm working on speed and therefore on relativity. We need a ministry of time, not only of what time it is, but a ministry of what time is needed, a ministry of relativity. If the moment of inertia rules over inertia of spaces, then you need a ministry for organizing space-time, a chrono-topical ministry which would not only organize the territory or public transport timetables. Still, architects are not mature enough for that. They handle the tangible, inertia, they are not men of the abstract, nor motion. I may criticize speed but still, I understand it deep inside. Yet, if *emptiness* and *fast* are linked, then *alive* is inhabited.

Interview by Francis Rambert, following the Metropolis meetings on the occasion of the international symposium "Quand les architectes n'ont pas peur du vide", April 2011, Cité de l'Architecture, Paris.

SKYLINE

UNTITLED (SKYLINE), 2007.
INSTALLATION VIEW, AT SCAD - ATLANTA, 2008.

UNTITLED (SKYLINE), 2007.
INSTALLATION, OLD FRIDGES PAINTED IN BLACK, SMALL MIRRORS,
INSTALLATION VIEW AT BALTIC CENTER FOR CONTEMPORARY ART - NEWCASTLE, 2007.

KADER ATTIA: Looking at this photograph depicting one of Pouillon's buildings covered with satellite dishes in Algiers, I wonder how such accumulation should be interpreted. Although the satellite dishes reveal a certain cultural poverty, they are turned towards the outside world. During the 90s, they were turned to France or the United States, and since 9/11 they face the Gulf. News from *Al Jazeera* and all the soap operas produced in Arabian countries are really popular everywhere in Northern Africa. To me, each of these satellite dishes echoes an individual; they are like voices or mouths saying something. Eventually, this picture also helps us to understand that architecture is not only a static but also an organic thing, and just like a living body, it is an ever-changing entity. By the way, this concern about the body is the main focus of one major concept in architectural modernism: Le Corbusier's Modulor.

RICHARD KLEIN: At the time, the Modulor had a mission in relation to normality. Le Corbusier's idea was to adapt proportions according to the human body and not strictly mathematic data or measurements matching the industrial production of objects. This is why, despite everything that has been said, the Modulor embodied a form of resistance against a normalization in which only parameters were production means and that made the standards even more "prescriptive", if we may say so. There is a kind of humanist dimension to the Modulor: it is the human body that should dictate measurements to architecture. The dimensions of machines should not dictate the size of architectural items. Le Corbusier says: "Look, the navel of a man who is 1.83 m tall is at 113 cm, so 113 cm will be used as a reference." Noticing Roland Simounet's position towards the Modulor is interesting because he, just like other architects, adapted the Modulor to Muslim living conditions and drew his own conclusions. Since the body was positioned differently in space, he came up with new proportions and new mathematic relations to the ground.

K. A.: Therefore, according to you or people like Simounet, the body cannot be dissociated from architecture…

R. K.: Absolutely. Simounet even thought of body positions according to organization in space. The fact that he studied sitting positions is meaningful. Everything in his work bore the idea that what is accessory in architecture should be moved aside. He rather had what usually entered the finishing part included in the construction process itself: being able to sit on the edge of a window, where there is a view, close to where the body will be cooled… I think this is about this position of the body in space thing. Therefore this concern about the body inside the other body, meaning architecture, is closely linked to measurements: how are we supposed to establish the correct proportions in what we are going to build?

K. A.: Does it mean that he was looking for common sense ?

R. K.: He was…

K. A.: Speaking of "common sense", here I'm referring to André Ravéreau. He wrote a lot about Ghardaïa and the Kasbah, especially in a book entitled *Et le Site créa la ville*, in which he insists on the use of this notion of common sense by this particular architecture.

R. K.: Yes, not common sense in the debased meaning sometimes used. And Ravéreau, of course. Simounet also showed interest in what attracted Ravereau's attention. And then Simounet found interest in the Mzab, just like Ravéreau.

K. A.: He studied the Mzab.

R. K.: Right. One thing he was obsessed with were the pipe systems in buildings, even at latitudes where you don't at all face the same concerns as in the Mzab. You'll never see even the slightest soil downpipe in any of the buildings he made in France. He was looking for ways to drain water away. This, incidentally, brought him some trouble…

K. A.: Are the pipe systems hidden?

R. K.: They are. He included them in drainage channels, for example, or in shadow gaps. There's no gutter, no soil downpipe. And he truly owed this to studying vernacular architectures. But you see, the way the body determines architecture and the way architecture is determined by the environment are fundamental.

K. A.: I was thinking about Pygmy houses, which to me are the best example in matters of ephemeral houses, since Pygmy peoples from Congo, Central Africa and Cameroon live in shack-like constructions but they never stay more than three weeks in the same place. Plus, these constructions also illustrate the kind of preoccupation you talked about with Simounet: how to cope with water issues inside this ephemeral house in a tropical and equatorial area. You know, due to the heat and violent rain showers every evening, at the end of the day… So, in the end, things move on and yet always come back to the same place. Issues discussed by Simounet somehow fall under the field of architecture genealogy.

R. K.: Yes, in its fundamental and primordial aspects.

K. A.: Another topic I would like to discuss with you is that of social housing projects and their failure.

R. K.: I don't necessarily have such a negative opinion on social housing, even though some of them are a sort of treason in the sense that some principles established by Le Corbusier and others have been interpreted in an extremely poor fashion. Some structures, even those that look a bit plain, still possess a few qualities that deserve to be highlighted more often. Le Corbusier had to take full symbolic responsibility for the "failure of social housing". Similarly, we tend nowadays to reject concrete a bit too quickly. When you know about the history of this material, you realize the arguments against it are sometimes false.

K. A.: What do you mean by "when you know about the history" of concrete?

R. K.: It was invented to imitate stone. Even if its production enables industrialization, it's a material made of elements carrying very tight bounds to the ground, to earth. This can be seen with the textures of reinforced concrete used in France by Le Corbusier and others such as Auguste Perret. It is therefore a paradox. People are emotionally attached to the long-lasting character of stone and reject concrete, often due to its assimilation with industrialization and mass production.

But, back to Le Corbusier, he remains stuck between the assertion that his name means the failure of social housing projects and some sort of formalist worship from many of my fellow architects. In the 80-90s, neo-corbusianism chose white architectures from Le Corbusier's projects from the 20s, while at the time he hadn't yet shown interest in vernacular architecture in the way you mentioned earlier. Hence the fact that these projects from Le Corbusier received positive critiques from architectural and artistic schools of thought. Neo-corbusianism was considered a shield against the postmodernism of the 1970-80s.

K. A.: You mentioned interesting examples of social housing projects and two pictures came to my mind: the first one is the vertical city planned under Écochard's management in Casablanca, where you can see a vertical application of a medina with every balcony corresponding to the inside yard of a small house. The second one is Jean Nouvel's project in Nîmes conducted in the early 1980s which, to me, is a sort of replica or continuity, perhaps a reinterpretation, of something close to Le Corbusier.

R. K.: *The Nemausus.*

K. A.: There's the name. Still, successful cases remain seldom. The cynical paradox of the failure of social housing is that while colonial territory was an experimental field for young Western architects, the perfect place for building and coming up with new ideas and offering modern things, it's the people from this same colonial territory who came to live in Western housing complexes after independence movements (at least in France, Italy, Germany, Holland, Belgium, etc). And I find it important not to lose track of this history; from Le Corbusier's *The Voyage to the East*, Ghardaïa, and all architectural projects built in former colonies, to the construction of social housing blocks. I also wonder what it would take to revive an utopian project like the *Cité Radieuse* in light of the failure of social housing.

R. K.: I guess you're right to highlight this aspect. It is even more complex when you know that not only did people go to live there but also that architects who had been working in colonial territories came back to metropolitan France as well. They're the same people. Let's name Candilis, for example. He worked with Écochard in Morocco, then came back in the 1950s and kept on building in Île-de-France, Marseilles and other places.
Let's talk about the Parisian suburb of Sarcelles... It was designed by two architects with different yet academic styles: Boileau and Labourdette. When you have a close look at some buildings in Sarcelles, you'll find them very interesting on both a formal and material point of view: some areas there, especially the smallest buildings, make use of stone masonry. This is also why, despite all modifications, these buildings still show a bit of dignity: thanks to well-set stones and a good design. There are more experimental and also more formalist areas in Sarcelles, with a more pronounced technical aspect. In the 1950-60s, taller buildings with filling panels looked elegant in France. In the film *Any Number can Win*, you can see Jean Gabin take a train at Gare du Nord and get off at what would become the Garges-Sarcelles station. So he gets off and heads home where his wife is waiting for him, for he just got out of jail. Sarcelles is under construction and he walks around the

neighborhood. You have to have watched the first minutes of the film to picture the shock this place represented. I've always wondered why it's treated in such a negative way. Sociology played a part there, as well as changes in population; actually, a lot of things can explain it. Contemporary artists such as you and Cyprien Gaillard and Matthieu Pernot, who work on these matters, are constantly asking: did we even have a look at these buildings before condemning them?

K. A.: I lived for about five years (from my teens to early adult years) in one of those small stone buildings near Sarcelles station. You're right; they still have dignity. Yet, to me there's a great difference between those small stone buildings, structures by people like Fernand Pouillon in Pantin, and constructions by architects who asked the right questions, had a sense of space and saw things the right way... I remember moving from the social housing block in Garges-lès-Gonesse, that I left at the age of seventeen for my sister's flat in a small building in Sarcelles. It just changed my life. Every time I happen to pass by Garges, I go and check my old neighborhood: places like *Les Doucettes* or *La Muette* that are extremely poor despite plans for renovation or decorating. All of this never dragged *La Muette*, for example, out of poverty. I think one of the greatest problems is to have created mushroom cities in the middle of nowhere: they were isolated. When I grew up there, the Louvre was free one day a week; on Sundays, I think. To me, this meant more than venturing inside Ali Baba's cave, this place was like another world... When I began visiting the Louvre, I understood the necessity of moving. Plus, I soon realized I was considered the black sheep among my friends in the block; I was the one who didn't do things like others did, even though I didn't always see it at the time. Looking back, I would say one of the biggest failures of the housing complex plan was to create slums isolated from one another, where entire populations were verticalized and given an illusion of superiority. That, too, is the modern illusion. Whole cities have been piled up on limited areas just like in Goussainville (les Grandes Bornes) or Gennevilliers; these places are in the middle of nowhere or surrounded by fields. I don't know if you could quote people who constructed completely isolated blocks like those... I think social trouble in France, and in many other European countries, is mostly due to poverty in both material and cultural programs. And it's the isolation we're talking about that causes cultural poverty, the fact people are piled upon one another, yet out of each other's reach.

R. K.: You are right to find nuances, but I would like to come back to a few points. First, the serial attempts at rehabilitating, modifying and insulating the buildings. Nowadays, we scorn the concept of social housing without discussing how these projects were looked after. And often, what made some of them so awful is the way they were handled, more than their design.
I agree about the isolation. The urban point of view was a major problem considering how these areas were managed and what became of them. Nevertheless, one thing that is also criticized is their aesthetic and shape. This bothers me. They were built following the fashion of the time in the shapes people fancied then. These architects created shapes that matched the mood of the times, shapes you could also find in things people used every day. Repetition,

for instance, was a positive value, as it is present in kinetic art. When you see reproductions of these housing developments under construction, in popular press for example, you understand that they carried a positive image. I'm not saying it wasn't a mistake and a misunderstanding to confuse people's lives with such aesthetics – I'm simply taking these things into consideration. But I think we forgot these aspects a little too fast.

K. A.: To me, this is due to the fact that today, people almost systematically make the connection between the social failure of this modern project and its physicality. Architects who designed social housing complexes answered two kinds of needs: a political one and an economical one. In addition to that, the assimilation of cultures and populations inside these buildings happened through a grid system, which shaped the aesthetic of their facades, whether you fancy them or not. Once again, I follow you on this point, I'm quite sensitive to this style. But still, from an ethical perspective, what you should consider is that when you come from a village in Maghreb, Asia, Sub-Saharan Africa, and your name is Mamadou, son of so-and-so, and you move in a building where your identity is summed up to a mailbox (looking exactly the same as the flat and building you now live in), you suddenly drown; your subject is diluted in some sort of superior order turning you not into the subject but into the object of the environment you live in. I believe our society totally missed what matters in construction: the essential importance of not severing links, not separating populations. According to Levi-Strauss, "an isolated culture that never exchanges with another, cannot evolve", and this idea has been completely ignored in the town planning we are talking about.

R. K.: On that point I agree, of course. Meanwhile, I think it should be separated from responsibility issues, which lay on another level than the designer's. This question you are asking should also be a concern these days. Every current plan launched by the the French agency of urban renovation includes a magic phrase: to open up. And when you want to get rid of a housing project, you say it's locked. This has absolutely nothing to do with the isolation you talk about, since a given area could still be unsuccessful even with access and ways to connect. It's completely different. Perhaps I'm being too positive about that era and what was done thenin light of the present situation which, to me is blind doesn't handle incoming issues the way it should. We are currently bringing people to believe that demolition can settle matters, and I think this is seldom true. Nevertheless I do share your opinion about isolation.

K. A.: I guess the time in which we live, whose technical and technological innovation grants us fantastic ways of moving and sharing every day is, paradoxically, a time of great isolation, too. We are now living in an age of fast culture and the problem with everything being available is that we get isolated from the past; we lose the continuity of things and histories. And this notion of continuity enables us to understand and appreciate a lot of things. It might even let us find an aesthetic and ethical interest in the lines of some social housing projects, and see this architecture as a reflection of a given era. Still, no one ever talks about the symbolism of Écochard's project in Casablanca, in Morocco, but rather how his architects (George Candilis, Vladimir Bodiansky, etc.) tried to find new things while many social housing projects later ended up as failures or at least did not take the innovation of the vertical city into consideration. What was the matter then – was it economical? Did buildings under French Protectorate like the ones in Casablanca cost more than some blocks like *La Cité des 4000*, in la Courneuve? What really happened there? Was it due to a rupture between those times and places?

R. K.: There are still architects who kept on with this research and experimental practice in colonized territories. They came back with what they learned and tried to continue their work in social housing projects in the West. Candilis is one example. When he came back from Morocco, part of his work was really close to the experiments with ATBAT. His first achievements in metropolitan France were built with that knowledge. Architectural production then came under the influence of a sort of standardization, and so the possibilities for experimentation diminished. I'm currently studying an operation called "the million" for example. The goal was to build 50-square-meter two-bedroom apartements with less than a million francs in the middle of the 1950s. This standardization greatly reduced the potential of African experiments. Architects were forced to apply their knowledge to extremely restrictive standards. The few remains of African experiments in housing were hard to spot then. You have to know your trade to see all the tricks still used to be able to move around or enjoy views, but expression was far less pronounced. These experimental practices were finally overtaken by financial restriction and another reality that had to be dealt with: that of quantity.

Translated from French by Joël Mallet

Richard Klein is an architect. He also teaches Architecture History at L'École Nationale Supérieure d'Architecture et du Paysage in Lille, France.

UNTITLED (WALL PAINTING), 2006.
VIEW AT MUSÉE D´ART CONTEMPORAIN DE LYON - LYON, 2006.

OIL AND SUGAR #2, 2007.
VIDEO, 4 MIN 30 SEC, VIDEO STILLS.

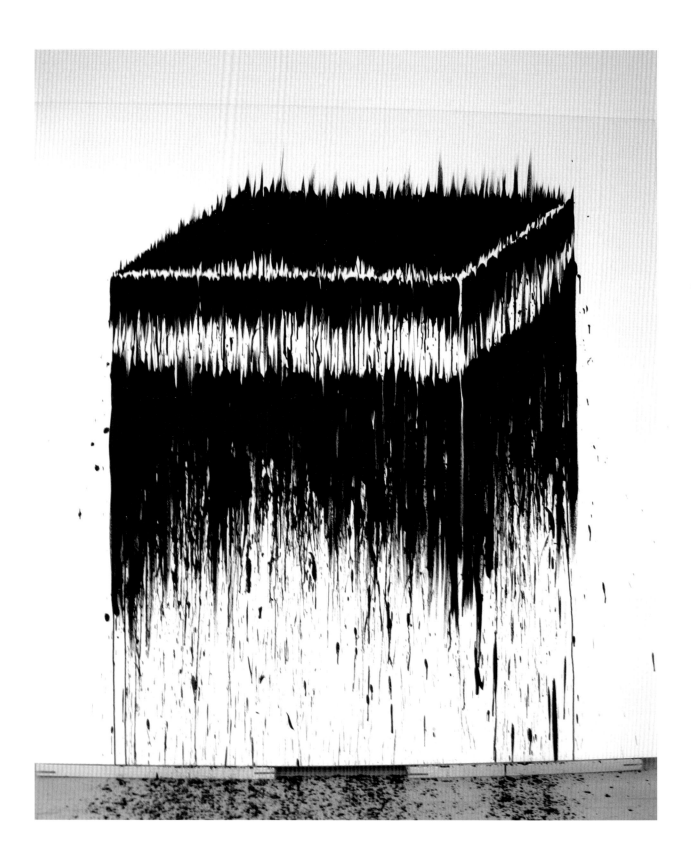

FROM THE SERIES **BLACK CUBE**, 2007.
SERIES OF PAINTINGS, BLACK ACRYLIC ON CANVAS, 2 X 2 M.

FROM THE SERIES **ROCHERS CARRÉS, 2008.**
PHOTOGRAPHIC SERIES, SILVER PRINT, 80 X 120 CM.

FRIDGES, 2006.
INSTALLATION, PAINTED FRIDGES, VIEW AT MUSÉE D´ART CONTEMPORAIN DE LYON - LYON, 2006.

INDEPENDANCE TCHAO, 2014.
SCULPTURE, METALLIC RACKS, WOOD, 115,5 CM X 288,4 CM X 59 CM,
INSTALLATION VIEW AT DAK´ART BIENNALE - DAKAR, 2014.

TOP : **THE HOTEL INDEPENDANCE - DAKAR, SENEGAL, 2014.**
BOTTOM : DETAIL OF **INDEPENDANCE TCHAO, 2014**

Manhattan is a city so hostile to the most fundamental needs of the human spirit that the dream of escape fixes itself in every heart. Get away! Avoid dissipating your life, the life of your family, in the midst of the implacable hardness. To be able to open your eyes on a patch of sky, to live near a tree, beside a lawn. And to flee forever from the noise, the confusion of the city. This measureless dream has materialized. Millions of city people have set out in search of an illusory country. Reaching it, living in it, they have killed the country. This enormous region, spread out so far around the city, is now suburban. Nothing remains except the dream, the desperate dream of being free, at least master of one's destiny.

Every day it means hours in the subway, on the bus, or in the train. And the loss of all collective life – the sap of a nation. And life has only a very limited liberty, with door beside door, window against window, the road in front of the door, the sky cut off by surrounding roofs, the few trees let after all that.

Le Corbusier, "What is the American problem?" in *American Architect*, 1936.

View of Manhattan, New York

Cité Confort planned by architect Fernand Pouillon, Algiers

WIRE WORLD

848

Early photo framing, archives from the newspaper *The Baltimore Sun*. Shibam, Yemen.

Model of low-rent housing project to replace 37 blocks providing 3816 dwellings for 13 500 persons. In the background are the director of the housing division and his assistant, Chicago.

HUGH FERRISS

THE METROPOLIS OF TOMORROW

LET US RETURN to the parapet which provided us with our original bird's eye view of the existing city. It is again dawn, with an early mist completely enveloping the scene. Again, there lies beneath us, curtained by the mist, a Metropolis – and the curtain, again, is about to rise. But, in this case, let us have it rise, not on the existing city, but on a city of the imagination. As the mists begin to disperse, there come into view, one by one, the summits of what must be quite lofty tower-buildings; in every direction the vistas are marked by these pinnacles as far as the eye can reach. It is apparent that this city, like those with which we had been previously familiar, contains very tall buildings and very many of them; indeed, we may assume, from their dimensions and their disposition over so wide an area, that here is an even greater center of population than anything we had hitherto known. At the same time, however, we are struck by certain peculiarities in the disposition of the towers now before us. In the first place, no two of them rise in close juxtaposition to each other; roughly calculated, they appear in no case to be less than half-a-mile apart. Also, there is a certain degree of regularity apparent in their disposal throughout; while they are not all precisely equidistant, and their relation does not suggest an absolutely rectangular checkerboard scheme, yet it is obvious that they have been located according to some city-wide plan. A little later the general clearing of the scene allows us to check up our first impressions. The tower-buildings rise to a height of a thousand feet from the ground – in a few particular cases, yet higher. And we now see that they spring from very broad bases, as well: their foundations cover three or four city blocks. In the particular cases mentioned, they must cover six or eight blocks. Yet, in the wide districts which lie between these towers – and which make up by far the greater area of the city – the buildings are all comparatively low. They average six stories; that is to say, they are no higher than the width of the streets which they face. Looking directly down upon the roofs of these buildings, we distinguish a color which suggests the presence of an abundance of planting. The first confirmed impression of the city is thus of a wide plain, not lacking in vegetation, from which rise, at considerable intervals, towering mountain peaks. This arrangement does not, indeed, embody any zoning principle which is altogether strange to us; obviously the zoning laws of this city, in so far as they pertain to heights and volumes of buildings, are reminiscent of other laws, previously encountered, which permitted a tall tower only over a certain percentage of a given area. In this case, the minimum area which may contain a tower is simply greater and the percentage of that area which the tower may cover is smaller. And yet, although no novel or difficult legal conception is involved and although this disposition of greater towers at greater intervals indicates simply an increase in dimensions, it is this very magnification in the scale which produces results – both practical and aesthetic – which are in decided contrast to cities previously seen. The cities with which we were previously familiar may, in a given area, compare as to total cubic content with the city now below us. In other words, a great number of typical, fairly large skyscrapers, set in very close juxtaposition, may have the same total cube, and house the same population as a few tremendous towers set at wide intervals with very low buildings in the intervening areas. In the former cases, however, the close juxtaposition of formidable masses – the monotonous repetition of similar bulks for block after city block – the close store of equally high façades across narrow streets – all combine to shut the human being away from air, light, and every pleasing prospect. In the city now below us – the same cubic content is so disposed, and high masses so dispersed, that a more humane environment seems possible. Let us now note, in the particular disposition of the masses at present before us, a possible aesthetic gain (not forgetting however, what has already been indicated more than once, that the psychological aspect is of interest because of its practical results). The fact is that in the general run of cities, the tall individual skyscraper, however, well designed can very seldom be individually seen. That is to say. juxtaposition is so close that only bits of the structure can be seen at one time by the pedestrian. Only by craning the neck does one see the whole of a tower; and then, of course, one sees only a ridiculous distortion. But in the city, now before us, each great mass is surrounded by a great spaciousness; here, we may assume, the citizen's habitual prospects are ample vistas. Without altering his upright posture, his glance may serenly traverse the vista and find at its end a dominating and upright pinnacle. Let us scrutinize the streets. The eye is caught by a system of broad avenues which must be two hundred feet wide and which are placed about half a mile apart. One notes that it is precisely at the intersections of these avenues that the tower buildings rise. We may conclude that here is a system of superhighways which carry the express traffic of the city and that the tower buildings are express stations for traffic. The half-mile-wide districts which are bounded by these highways are themselves traversed by streets of much lesser width – scarcely more than sixty feet; obviously, they are planned to carry only the traffic which is local to the district. On restudying these low-lying districts together with the occasional tower buildings, it appears that the latter

are not to be compared simply to mountain formations which
happen to have arisen, abruptly and at certain intervals in
a plain; rather, each tower seems to have a specific relation
to the low-lying district which immediately surrounds it. The
heights of the lesser buildings increase as they approach
the central tower; each peak, so to speak, is surrounded by
foothills. It would seem that each of these formations - each
peak together with its slopes and contributory plain - forms a
sort of unit. Those units may indicate that the city is zoned
not only as to height but as to use (which, again, would be a
familiar principle) and that some particular activity, some
specific function of the whole municipal body, is carried on
in each unit. A question arises, incidentally, as to these
tower buildings. They are very tall, and cover enormous
ground areas; each must house a multitudinous activity; each
stands in a considerable isolation from other buildings of
the same species; each dominates, and is, we may assume,
the center of control of a particular district. Is the word
"building" any longer sufficiently definitive? For the sake of
simplicity, let us adopt for them the term "center." Looking
off to the right from our parapet, we distinguish a group of
these centers which seem larger than the rest. They stand
together about a large open space; they seem to constitute
a sort of nucleus of the city - perhaps they are its primary
centers. Let us turn our binoculars in that direction.

THE FIRST CENTER to be seen is that structure, or complex of
structures, in which the control of the business activities
of the city is housed. Here is located the seat of government
of the city's practical affairs, including its three chief
branches - legislative, judiciary and executive. At this closer
view we can distinguish in greater detail the characteristics
of the tower-buildings. The tower itself rises directly over
the intersection of two of the master highways to a height of
1200 feet. There are eight flanking towers, half this height,
which, with their connecting wings, enclose four city blocks.
The center extends, however, over eight adjoining blocks where
its supplementary parts rise to a height of twelve stories.
We see, upon examining the Avenue, that more than one level
for traffic is provided. Local wheel traffic is on the ground
level; express traffic is depressed; pedestrians pass on a
separate plane above. Beyond the center, the lower districts
of the city are visible, together with the radial avenues which
lead to the other tower-buildings of the Business district.

THE SECOND STRUCTURE TO BE OBSERVED is the Art center. Situated
about a mile from the Business center, it is also one of
the group of major centers which first drew our attention.

By taking up a viewpoint nearer to the ground level, we see more definitely how the longer structures of the city tower above the great majority of the buildings. Presumably there is, in such an architectural landscape, a free access to light and air on the part of all buildings, whether high or low. A distinct advance has been accomplished in this imaginary city in the matter of smoke elimination: the roofs of all the lower structures have been developed into sun porches and gardens. The fact is, there is two feet of soil on these roofs, and trees are generally cultivated. Open-air swimming pools are frequent.

AT SOME DISTANCE from the two structures which have just been viewed we find the Science center. Here again is a very high central mass, supported by large wings, the whole extending over adjoining streets to embrace outlying structures. Here is housed control of the scientific activities of the city: these structures being planned on a large scale for laboratory work and scientific research. The traffic plane is wide and calculated to carry a great number of vehicles on more than one level. A waterway is carried down the axis of the main avenue.

THE THREE CENTERS which have just been seen constitute the nucleus, the group of primary centers, which originally drew our attention from our distant balcony. We must now note that each of these centers dominates a very wide district: that is to say, the city is divided into a Business zone, an Art zone and a Science zone. Let us descend into the Business zone. This, naturally, is the largest of the three districts. We find that its tower-buildings rise to greater heights; that they are closer together; and that the master highways have been developed for the maximum traffic.

THE BUSINESS ZONE is again seen in the accompanying view. In this case, we are looking west; the Business center is in the foreground, its relation with adjoining tower-buildings appearing from a somewhat different angle.

IN THE ART ZONE, as in the Business zone, we find tower-buildings only at considerable intervals. Here, however, more ground space is left open, and the main avenues are to a great extent parked.

BUILDINGS like crystals.
Walls of translucent glass.
Sheer glass blocks sheathing a steel grill.
No Gothic branch: no Acanthus leaf: no recollection of the plant world.

A mineral kingdom.
Gleaming stalagmites.
Forms as cold as ice.
Mathematics.
Night in the Science Zone.

THE POWER PLANT is located at the base of the Business
zone. In this city, coal is still being used; it is
carried aloft, from the cars, on the inclined elevators
and stored in the uppermost of the three levels of the
building. From here it is lowered to the boilers on the
second level. The structure is built of concrete.

THROUGHOUT EACH ZONE of the city, we find numerous tower-
buildings which are related, by master highways, to the major
center. These minor centers, or sub-centers, are each the
headquarters of some particular department of the general
activity of the zone. For example, we find in the Business
zone the rather large structure which serves as the Financial
center. Each of these tower-buildings houses all the facilities
for the day's work; containing, in addition to the offices
themselves, the necessary post office, bank, shops, restaurants,
gymnasiums and so on. Each is, so to speak, a city in itself.

THE RELATION OF TOWER TO STREET is shown in more detail in
the present view - which happens to be of the Technology
center. The ground level, practically in entirety, is given
over to wheel traffic; parking is all beneath the buildings.
The avenue has also a lower level, in the center, which
is used by express wheel traffic. We glimpse, through the
openings in the retaining wall of this lower level, the
right-of-way of the subway rail traffic. In the design of
this building, by the way, one may note an emphasis on the
horizontal lines, rather than the vertical lines, of the steel
grill. It may be questioned whether designers can, logically,
emphasize either, when both are essential in this system of
construction. The horizontal emphasis, at least, recognizes
and makes permanent the appearance which, in actuality, the
steel building itself always exhibits before the exterior
walls have been added. In this particular building, the
vertical members contain the elevator shafts and fire stairs.

A LOFT BUILDING, in the Industrial Arts district, is here
viewed just before the glass exterior walls have been
constructed. The latter will scarcely change the visual
impression produced by the steel grill itself: that is to
say, we see here the actual horizontals which were taken as
the cue for the finished design of the Technology center.

IN THE CITY which is momentarily before us, the many and varied religious denominations have achieved - for that moment - a state of complete harmony: the building now in view is none other than the seat of their combined and coordinated activities. Expressive of modern tendencies, this structure soars to great altitudes; if it has, at the same time, a slightly medieval cast, this is perhaps not altogether inexpressive of the institution which it domiciles. Even in the sharp perspective of the present view, one may surmise the presence of three outstanding towers - the two lesser being toward either end of the mass and the lofty central tower rising between. These stand, respectively, for the cardinal functions of this Christian host: one of the flanking towers houses the executive offices of the various Faiths; the other is more especially dedicated to their aspirational activities, or Hopes; in the third, which is the greatest of these, abide the Charities.

WHERE ART AND SCIENCE MEET - that is to say. where these civic zones contact with one another - there stands a tower about which are gathered the colleges of Arts and Sciences. Since this tower seems to stand somewhat apart, let us give a moment to examining the particular elements of its design. In plan it seems to show, at all levels, variations of a nine-pointed star - in other words of three superimposed triangles. Being planned, basically, on the equilateral triangle, the shaft rises - or, so to speak, grows - in what seem definite stages. For example, the vertical dimension from the top of the base up to the point where the vertical members break for the first time appears to bear a ratio to the dimension between this break and the break next above it, as well as to the total vertical dimension above the latter break. These three dimensions are to each other as three, one and three. (This could be actually measured, of course, only in a direct elevation and can be only inferred from this perspective presentation). This ascension in a total of seven units must perhaps be regarded as purely arbitrary; we can only affirm that this relationship which appears in the total form appears also in its lesser parts: for example, the last and uppermost of the three divisions just referred to, is itself broken vertically into three parts in which the original ratio repeats. Indeed this particular kind of "growth" appears to continue upward indefinitely. The real significance, if any, of a tower having, so to speak, a threefold plan and a sevenfold ascension, is obscure. And it is perhaps optimistic to say that here a number of separate parts aspire to be as one. In any case, this is the Center of Philosophy.

TO CONSTRUCT A DETAILED MAP of a panorama which is only
momentarily before us would scarcely be practicable: but,
as a result of even a brief bird's-eye view, we can sketch
a general layout of the city plan. It will give us a clearer
notion of how the traffic arteries are disposed and how the
buildings are zoned as to height and use. We may first note,
in this sketch plan, the black spots which indicate location
of the tower-buildings, as well as the broad light lines of
the main avenues: in short, the centers and the circulating
system which connects them. Let us take as a point of
departure, the structure which is upon the circumference of
the central circle. This is the Business center of the city.
The circular area upon whose edge it stands is the principal
open space of the city: the Civic Circle which, with its
parks, playgrounds and areas for open-air gatherings and
exhibitions, is the focal point to which the radial avenues
lead. It is likewise the fountain-head of the waterways
which distribute throughout the smaller parks of the city.
The district which lies below the Business center as well as
to the right and and the left of it - in other words, that
whole third of the plan which is penetrated by the avenues
radiating from this center - constitutes the Business zone
of the city. Here in close proximity to the center, are
located, in tower-buildings, the headquarters of the various
principal business activities and, grouped about them, the
chief industrial sub-centers. At a distance of a mile or so
from the Business center, the airports can be noted, located
on the main radial avenues, as well as the beginning of the
outlying residential districts. The latter appear as the
shaded areas which are pointed toward the center of the
city and which increase in width as they extend, fan-wise,
outward. It is apparent that both the business zone and the
residential districts which flank it may expand indefinitely
away from the Civic Circle. Such expansion, however, must be
along the radial lines which will, in all events, continue
to relate added outlying districts to the center. Returning
to the Civic Circle, we find indication of another large
structure upon the circumference. This is the Art center.
As in the case of the Business zone, radial lines extend
outward from this center, constituting the arterial system of
the Art zone. Here are located the tower-buildings in which
center such civic activities as the Drama, Music, Architecture
and so on. The third structure upon the circumference of
the Civic Circle is the Science center which, like the two
former, occupies a dominating position in relation to the
zone behind it. In addition to the radial avenues which
have been mentioned and which connect the various zones
with their respective centers, there is also a system of

circumferential avenues which connect the three zones with each other. These, doubtless, are intended to facilitate contact and communication between the principal activities of the city. As a matter of detail, we should find, if we followed the course of one of these circulating avenues such a progression as this: where it crosses the central radial avenue of the Art zone, there rises the structure which houses the Fine Arts; farther along the circumferential avenue, as it leads in the direction of the Business zone, we find, in turn, the headquarters of the Applied and Industrial arts. Similarly, had we moved in the opposite direction - toward the Science zone - we should find the structures which house the Liberal Arts. And, at the meeting of the two zones, the colleges of Art and Sciences. In other words, the Art zone is in direct contact, on the one hand, with the practical life of the city, and, on the other hand, with its scientific pursuits; and in it, presumably, the results of the latter two modes of activity are gathered and interpreted. We might also start from another point - the central radial avenue of the Science zone - whence, passing in the direction of the Business zone, we should encounter, in turn, the Pure Sciences, Technology, Engineering, and so on. However, let us not labor details but return again to the three major centers on the Civic Circle which first drew attention. It is at first glance somewhat puzzling to find that the two structures which are dedicated to arts and sciences are placed in positions as prominent as the Business center of the city. We must notice, moreover, that some very close affiliation between the three must have been really intended, since they are directly connected by the avenues which appear on the plan most prominently of all and which must have been calculated to carry a very large traffic between the three centers. Are we to imagine that this city is populated by human beings who value emotion and mind equally with the senses, and have therefore disposed their art, science and business centers in such a way that all three would participate equally in the government of the city? This might indeed seem a novel system of government. The plan indicates, at least, that the structures to house these activities exist, and that such a threefold system of government is regarded, in this city, as at least a potentiality; a potentiality which the citizens, whenever so moved, could fully actualize.

Hugh Ferriss, excerpt from *The Metropolis of Tomorrow*, 1929.
Ferris was an architect who influenced popular culture, for example Gotham City (the setting for Batman) and Kerry Conan's *Sky Captain and the World of Tomorrow*.

GHARDAÏA

UNTITLED (GHARDAÏA), 2009.
EPHEMERAL SCULPTURE, COUSCOUS, PORTRAITS OF LE CORBUSIER AND FERNAND POUILLON,
INSTALLATION VIEW AT TATE LIVERPOOL - LIVERPOOL, 2012.

UNTITLED (GHARDAÏA), 2009.
INSTALLATION VIEW AT TATE LIVERPOOL - LIVERPOOL, 2012.

LÉA GAUTHIER: The sculpture *Untitled (Ghardaïa)* was first exhibited at the Contemporary Creation Center in Tours. The piece, made of couscous, rests on the ground and represents the city in the Mzab Valley. Its walls depict the faces of two architects, Le Corbusier and Fernand Pouillon, and the official document registering Ghardaïa as a UNESCO site. What are the origins of this work?

KADER ATTIA: The piece, as well as the thought I developed about this place, is tied to a reality. This is important when speaking about genealogy, so we don't lose track of the connections between what is contemporary to us and this very peculiar city from the past. Ghardaïa was first built during the 11th century, and it later thrived because of the population of the Mzab region, the Mozabites. Their history is linked to Ibadism, a religious school of thought (certainly the first one) that emerged about 50 years following the Prophet Muhammad's death and inescapably attracted wrath from the dominant current of the time. Ibadism is a dogmatic life philosophy according to which spiritual wealth must be found on the inside while remaining absolutely abstract on the outside. Sunnites later considered it a hostile cult and tried their best to eradicate this kind of thought. Yet these ideas, which find their origins in Iraq, were adopted by Algerian Berber tribes. One of them eventually ended up settling in the Mzab, fearing extermination after being chased by Sunnites. There, in the heart of the Sahara, in the Mzab valley, an almost miraculous oasis spreads over several hectares, watered by a whimsy stream sometimes responsible for deadly spates and probably originating in some prehistoric groundwater inherited from a time when the world's biggest desert was a sea.

L. G.: What are the main characteristics of this school of thought?

K. A.: Ibadism is an Islamic school of thought characterized by staunch societal humility along with true religious fervor. Mozabites, Ibadism adepts, are people who speak very quietly and when they do, they do not express much. They rigorously see to freeing their relation to the world from anything unnecessary. Their whole existence is based on the idea that what you accomplish on Earth is done through outdoor labor and harsh spirituality. They are traditionally craftsmen and often great traders, however they reject any external sign of material wealth, which, in a country such as Algeria, causes them to be laughed at daily. When Mozabites arrived in the Mzab region, a few native tribes were already settled there. They were quickly integrated (even though some historians think they might have been forced to). The Mozabites soon had a kind of mystic fascination with the Mzab, the stream running along five desert hills. They built fortresses on each of these five hills in order to protect themselves. By the way, the name "Ksar", associated to these cities is based on military etymology, contrary to "Kasbah", which is more urban. Through their architectural style, the five cities (El Atteuf, Bou-Noura, Beni-Izguen, Meliken, Ghardaïa) embody a faithful extension of this religious austerity. After fleeing persecution to arrive in the Mzab valley, the faithful Ibadists considered the place as a gift from God they should defend against invaders outside the walls while sharing with the community inside the city. Obviously, the oasis would not exist without water. These people's spiritual austerity led them to develop a philosophy of life as well as an architectural style whose aesthetics and functionality find no equal in the world. Indeed, they built Ghardaïa following radical sketches and functionalism. When you understand why Adolf Loos' essay *Ornament and Crime* is one of the fundamental documents concerning modern thinking in architecture, you see how the discovery of this city by Le Corbusier represented a major influence in modern architecture. I give you this one example: Mozabite houses have practically no furniture, the walls themselves carry that functional purpose. In opposition to classical Western designs, including the furniture within the very architectural space states a rupture, and yet this same rupture finds its origins in tradition.

L. G.: Apparently, Le Corbusier was quite influenced by his stay in Ghardaïa…

K. A.: Le Corbusier was stingy when it came to sharing references about his influences, not only about Ghardaïa by the way, even though he quotes the city in several written works and conferences for his students. Three things fascinated him in Ghardaïa: the light ("architecture is light"), the people, whom he called the "desert Huguenots", and finally the architectural urban structure from which he kept three main elements to create his manifesto *The Athens Charter*.
But first, let me tell you this story: Le Corbusier gave a conference in Algiers during the early 30s. We know he'd been to the Mzab valley; at the time, the 370 miles you had to travel to go there represented quite a distance, plus Ghardaïa was not that famous. Alexander Gerber, a scholar, followed his hunch. He assumed that Le Corbusier had read one of the major essays in the history of vernacular architecture, Marcel Mercier's *La Civilisation urbaine du Mzab*, published in 1922. However, Gerber did not find this book, neither in Le Corbusier's archives, nor in the latter's bookshelves. According to most Le Corbusier "specialists", it seemed impossible for him to have even read such a volume. Gerber then had the idea to go and check where Le Corbusier used to work, the Government Library in Algiers. Not only did Gerber find out that Le Corbusier borrowed the book several times, but he also wrote quite a number of notes in it. If evidence about the influence of Mzab concepts on Le Corbusier's architectural style was needed, then Gerber managed to find it. In his book, Mercier talks about architecture but also adopts an anthropological approach regarding Mozabites. Le Corbusier therefore understood that Ibadist philosophy is very close to Protestant culture. When you compare Mozabite architectural rules and a manifesto such as *The Athens Charter*, the analogy is more than striking. The power of obscurity in Western culture just fascinates me. We are facing characterized cultural dispossession.

L. G.: You speak of dispossession, but could we not just speak about inspiration?

K. A.: On the one hand we can, and on the other we cannot, because you cannot just stick to mere inspiration when you know about the context and political dimension bound to architecture throughout the colonial project. Also, finding Le Corbusier's sources of inspiration regarding Ghardaïa is pretty close to hunting for treasure.

Hiding one's sources to such an extent corresponds to an act of appropriation, a true process of dispossession. Le Corbusier was used to appropriating other people's projects. While one can easily rise up against the way he did so with creations by Charlotte Perriand or Eileen Gray (the Irish architect who recently was the focus of a retrospective at the Centre Pompidou), why should one talk about inspiration when it comes to millenary Arabian-Berber vernacular architecture?

Le Corbusier designed the Ronchamp chapel after he came back from Algeria. It is inspired by Sidi Brahim's mausoleum in El Atteuf, in Ghardaïa. The entire Mzab valley has been a UNESCO site since 1982, that is to say about a hundred years after being discovered and studied by Western Europeans in the context of a modern, Western cultural model colonizing an extra-Western traditional otherness. Also, the last lines on UNESCO's official document state that the city might have influenced modern architects such as Le Corbusier or Fernand Pouillon. Lack of quotation is lack of acknowledgement. Even today, when Le Corbusier's work is the focus of a retrospective, Mozabite architecture is mentioned succinctly, in the best case. During a huge exhibition of his work in London, you could only see two postcards from Ghardaïa. We should try to imagine this conversation in another context, in Algeria or Congo for instance, so you can see how much Algerian or Congolese people could learn about the extent of their own heritage upon the world. Even though colonization is now over, it is still a fact that entire intellectual territories and areas have not been freed yet, or at least "reappropriated" by the traditional cultures representing the very origins of European "sources of inspiration" (thinking, for instance, about the massive contribution of African traditional arts, especially masks and sculptures, to modern Western art).

L. G.: Modernity stood as a rupture from tradition, imposing the fiction of radical innovation. So, as a contemporary artist you get to deal with this fiction in a piece like *Untitled (Ghardaïa)*.

K. A.: Yes, I do believe it is one of the meaningful aspects of this work. This is like reconstructing a chain, a necessary chain. When I use the word reappropriation in lectures, I sometimes face negative reactions for it seems to show some vindictive presupposition. This is not my point actually... what I'm truly interested in is the idea of continuity, the assertion of cultural circles inherent to each and every culture. I find it essential to reproduce and talk about connections. I act as a storyteller, architecture is my passion, but art is an amazing tool that enables me to stand up to Le Corbusier, and using couscous. While working on this piece, the first title I thought of was *Bon appétit, monsieur Le Corbusier*, because of course, this work is humorous, perhaps even ironic. It is a posthumous invitation to Le Corbusier, like

some sort of animist offering to these architects. This piece falls under reappropriation since I'm using an element that lies in the very "culinary DNA" of the region to recall a certain history: that of Ghardaïa inspiring the father of modern architecture so much, that when he established the fundamentals of his practice he somehow ended up devouring the city. So now I'm turning this dispossession into a dinner as a gesture of reappropriation. All in all, I invite people to some symbolic integration of dispossession, in some ways it is like cannibalism, in the way Oswald De Andrade, the Brazilian poet, defined it in *The Manifesto Antropófago*.

L. G.: Next to Le Corbusier's portrait is Pouillon's, another modern architect. What is the link between him and Le Corbusier, and more generally speaking, Algeria?

K. A.: The link between Pouillon and Algeria is essential in order to understand the revival of modern architecture in relation to the tradition of desert construction, and the failure of great modernists who blindly figured that concrete would match every specific cultural condition in housing. Fernand Pouillon's work in Algeria follows a "post-Corbusian" temporality. He developed a perennial relation with this country, considering he built there even after the Algerian revolution and the country's independence. Actually, Pouillon assimilated what Le Corbusier analyzed in Algeria, particularly in Ghardaïa and its urban structure... Nevertheless, Pouillon soon distinguished himself from his peers, whose experience was mainly inherited from Le Corbusier's work in Ghardaïa. First, he almost never used concrete for his constructions, but Algerian stone. Pouillon wrote in his memoirs: "The schools of thought in modern architecture always criticized this choice: living in your era means building with concrete and steel, if not then you are out of date." For someone who grew up in the south of France, the best material, the one that can seize the light and grows more and more beautiful as time passes, is stone. He praises it in *The Stones of the Abbey*. Was it stone that enabled him to build in Algiers what I consider to be one of the masterpieces in social housing architecture: the 200 columns housing development *Climat de France*, a 65-foot-high and at least 330-foot-long rectangular structure, held in the middle by 200-column more than 30 feet high? As far as Pouillon was concerned, social housing was a modern challenge: "The more modest the accommodation, the more monumental its architecture should be".

L. G.: The studies you did on the relation between Ghardaïa and modernism go way further than the making of this piece of work. You told me the archival research you carried sometimes only led to a positioning in space and a staging of the archives themselves. To what extent do you consider this reappropriation of archives and documents to be an artistic act?

K. A.: Each initiative generated by an artist within their work may come under their own praxis, which all in all makes it part of their creative field. Gathering archives or objects corresponds to an artistic exercise I've been developing for several years now as a way to get people to think. Images, written documents or objects have an intense relation to the archive due to their ambiguity. Michel Foucault warns us with the famous quote that continues to haunt me: "The archive stands as an authority, it shows what it wants to and as a result, conceals what it does not show". From this on, everything that can be expressed by using archives in a work that essentially consists of a collection of visual and/or written documents falls under some attempt at controlling what is out of control. However, isn't it the same for colors? While for centuries we believed they could be controlled, colors always turn out to be the masters of their own fate. Only people who are subject to synaesthesia are able to assimilate them according to standards that lie far from the wavelength transmitting their chromatic characteristics into our brain. This is the reason why I like to create physical proximity between original archive documents and the viewer in some of my works. The first time you get close to an old gelatine bromide silver print (from the late 19th century), a bird's eye view of Algiers's Kasbah, where endless roof decks spread down like a stairway to the sea, then a mysterious coming and going takes place in the mind of the spectator when he sees "what was". It comes and goes between what they see in the present and what comes from the past (on an iconographical and iconological basis) to the punctuation of contemporary thoughts about issues on the genealogy of modern architecture and its relationship to colonialism. The "simple" gesture of placing this old image within a contemporary creative context rejects any attempt at controlling it, but makes fun of its "authority" instead.

L. G.: Why did you choose couscous as a material?

K. A.: Couscous has been prepared in Maghreb for over 3000 years. Paradoxically, it embodies an organic ephemeral element as well as the cultural continuity you can find in the region like, for example, the Berber language spoken by Mozabites. So the piece carries its own temporality: it crackles, rots, disappears... Incidentally, when I installed it in the Tate, in Liverpool, I had to come up with something to slow the rotting process in order for the piece to "live" a little longer (until the end of the exhibition). I spoke with biologists who came up with chemical solutions that would stop the process instead of slowing it down. We had quite a number of tests, all in vain. It was stressful and a bit depressing. I was about to give up – I can remember it well, I was on my bed in my hotel room – but then I thought about salt caravans in the desert. As a matter of fact, adding salt to couscous, just like people did with meat for centuries to keep it fresh, allowed the rotting to slow down. The best solutions are sometimes incredibly simple... Le Corbusier was enthralled by the architecture of "non-architects" and the simple solutions they generated – in a time and space where tradition was merely common sense – and that proved to be eternal as centuries went by.

L. G.: Modernity in architecture imposed concrete, for example, as a material, and created a gap between construction and our hands. And couscous is also prepared with one's hands. Is this presence of gestural singularity also something you wish to reinstate through your work?

K. A.: It is, Physical gestures are the continuity of the "I" offering another approach to the traditional lines of human "creativity". The artist's hand movements are like a punctuation of his intellectual work. As far as I'm concerned, they are consistent with my intention, they make it alive and accurate. I sometimes design works and have them constructed by craftsmen, even though I always keep a close eye on the creation process, not to have absolute control, but just because I like it. The relationship you have with material, whichever it is, represents a condition to the reality of a work as a form of thinking. Of course, I tend to have preferences, such as wood and especially tropical species, food, stainless steel, etc., however no one can master everything. And there are times when the material physically stands up to you, so you need some helping hands...

L. G.: Here you're speaking of temporality and I would like to highlight this point. Your pieces are seldom perennial; you have to install them anew for each exhibition. Of course they are the same, but there's always a slight difference. You told me Mzab architecture was established about a thousand years ago, yet meanwhile, it is in a state of constant reconstruction. Architectural modernism aimed at destroying the old to replace it with the new, which would end up being destroyed too as soon as it became obsolete. Therefore, the temporality you are utilizing here is quite different.

K. A.: Regarding the nihilism of modernism when it comes to the past, perhaps I do, but I don't think I'm opposing such a different temporality than the one mankind has faced since the most ancient age of its existence. Do you really think that we create brand new things out of nothing because of independent thinking? Like Claude Levi-Strauss, I believe that the human mind is an immeasurable unconscious cognitive structure. Nothing gets to be invented, it is all repaired, constantly repaired... and that's what I bring to light in my in situ works, whether they be installations or sculptures. Each time they are displayed, they take shape in space differently. They are alive like a being I created that ends up living as its own subject – within a whole, yet whose singularity is autonomously expressed during each presentation. It is because everyone is different that everyone is the same.

L. G.: In order to deal with architectural issues, you place the spectator's body right in the middle of the installation. In Untitle (Ghardaïa) the scale establishes a relatively intimate bond between the viewer and the piece. One can also find genuine sensuality, as the smell of couscous is quite important. Where do you situate yourself within the reappropration process you wish to encourage?

K. A.: To tell the truth, it's not about my place, unless it's in terms of being an author who's but the carrier of a message between tradition and the contemporary. But, just like you highlighted, it is especially about the spectator's place as a physical body. Le Corbusier dealt with this issue in the Modulor. The human body is the greatest concern of architecture. This is what he generally saw in traditional architecture (exalted in Ghardaïa), and what he tried to focus his theories and work on. Many followed him on that path, even his "opponents", like Team X, for what is true within the field of architecture and art, is also true within the social field. The human body is at stake in every utopia. This is the question raised by Foucault in his conference *The Utopian Body*. It is due to the fact that we are inhabitants of our own body. I mean, the spirit inhabits the body, just like the latter inhabits a given space, an architecture.

Translated from French by Joël Mallet

Léa Gauthier is a philosopher and teaches Art Theory at The Royal Academy of Fine Arts in Brussels. She is also an art critic, a translator and a publisher.

MANUELLE ROCHE

LE M'ZAB

ARCHITECTURE IBADITE EN ALGÉRIE

ARTHAUD

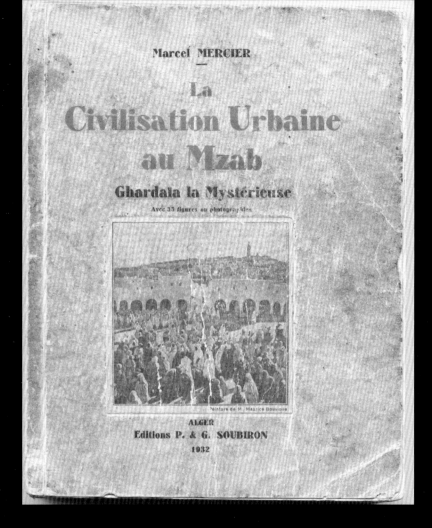

Marcel MERCIER

La
Civilisation Urbaine
au Mzab

Ghardaïa la Mystérieuse

Avec 33 figures ou photographies

Peinture de M. Maurice Bouviolle

ALGER
Éditions P. & G. SOUBIRON
1932

In his study entitled *Le Corbusier et le mirage de l'Orient. L'influence supposée de l'Algérie sur son œuvre architecturale* (1994), Alex Gerber proved how Le Corbusier had been significantly influenced by Marcel Mercier's book, *La Civilisation urbaine du Mzab*, first published in 1922.

19th century etching depicting Moroccan landscape.

Lithographs showing houses in Egypt from the late 19th century. These
influenced Hassan Fathy, one of Egypt's most important modernist architects

Top: Dogon architecture, Mali.
Bottom: Musgum hut in Cameroon.

Dogon architecture, house of the Ogon (the elder)

The mud constructions in New Mexico are called adobe buildings, a word originating from the
Arab term for "mud". The Spanish assimilated this technique in the 8th century while the Iberian
peninsula was under Muslim domination. The conquistadors have used a technical knowledge of mud
construction from their former colonial rulers the arabs, to then colonize the native culture of
building: the importance of covering the entire architecture to protect the exterior structure
of the house, for example, but also how to provide floor-level access by creating a door,

The Sidi Brahim mausoleum, in El-Atteuf (Ghardaïa), had an important influence on Le Corbusier's *Chapelle Notre-Dame-du-Haut* in Ronchamp, France, even though it was finished in 1955, 30 years after Le Corbusier's first trip to Ghardaïa.

ANDRÉ RAVÉREAU

LEARN FROM TRADITION

Third World countries are located in the areas where most ancient civilizations developed, certainly due to the quality of the climate – and mainly the heat. Thus, in their architecture, meaning shelter, you will find that closed spaces are always accompanied great outdoor spaces, both in terms of size and value, even though one could say that in some areas of Africa, it is the outdoor space that is always accompanied by a closed one. In such civilizations, you also notice that up to today the sitting position remained, with a number of subtle differences, on ground level. Finally, these areas often benefit from intense light, which determines certain ways of dealing with openings throughout centuries. Meanwhile, our part of the world, especially Northern Europe and America, is more or less deprived of such warmth and light. This is the reason why throughout time, the closed shelter had to fulfill all needs. Outdoor spaces are unused for long seasons, and in some cases, public social spaces tend to be closed as well. For ages, the difficulty in controlling temperatures pushed civilizations to come up with higher seats and their required supplement, the table, the piece of furniture that has the most influence on organization within the shelter. Finally, in these northern regions, light is most often mediocre and the issue of openings is one of the first preoccupations of construction (Gothic style is the best example of this search for light inside the shelter). Moreover, the development of glass production and its industrialization, along with heating technologies, had a major impact in those areas when it came to conquering comfortable closed spaces. During the industrial era, the Western world – which should rather be called the Northern hemisphere – fulfilled ancestral needs for comfort in terms of construction. Western architecture, through the different steps of its modernity, tends to meet the conditions that, throughout time, were imposed by the physical environment and the harsh climate from which it tried to isolate itself. However, since the most ancient times, Third World cultures have designed architectures in accordance with their physical environment in order to cope with it rather than to isolate themselves from it. It seems that in such societies, perhaps more than anywhere else, one seeks the qualities of a shelter, aside from the mere exploitation of constantly evolving modern production (materials, skills), in a sort of will to reclaim principles adapted to nature and established for many centuries. The haste and confusion in which most studies are conducted make it rare for such a synthesis to be achieved by a mind outside of isolation, and therefore of limitation. A few architects focus on recovering useful notions from cultural heritage, yet the research this requires is only feasible most of the time within the scope of student works; it consequently

remains unfinished, unused or uncollected and out of reach,
due to a lack of media - institutions - enabling it to be read
for objective use and teaching. A great amount of information
available in the writings of scientists, archeologists,
ethnologists, etc. is not used; their quest is too heavy a
task. From Sumer to 18th-century Maghreb houses, the evolution
of elements such as the Persian *iwan*, Greek *exedra* or Tunis-
style *K'Bou* in Grenada deserve to be studied in order to see
to which extent this favored living room element garnered
constant fortune along the same latitude, and to what extent
this same notion could be taken into consideration within
current creations. Erasing and forgetting values that can
still be carried on and are part of a heritage does not only
occur in the Third World. Certain areas of the so-called
developed world, like European Mediterranean countries, do
not apply useful knowledge for their own good; they lack the
time to take stock of old knowledge and new propositions.
In Maghreb, there are still permanent items and layouts
that have long been forgotten in southern Europe. Yet, an
enlightened search into the legacy of Antiquity would surely
bring profitable regulation to our Mediterranean culture.
Architectural teachings are too often subjected to the
universal aspects of modernity, which are especially those
of the Northern hemisphere chasing its own future. Because
we do not discern that a window in Maghreb or Yemen follows
objective motivations linked to a series of concrete factors
such as the height of our eyes in both sitting and standing
positions, and light control, we run the risk of assigning
their character to subjectivity, to the decorative styles
that are applied to them. While in fact, their character lies
in a clever, meticulous subjection to the well-appreciated
propositions and conditions of the physical environment. The
expansion of the North, through multiple forms of imperialisms
and influences since at least the 19th century, has disturbed
the Southern hemisphere to various degrees. The consequences
of industrialization first changed sociological behaviors in
the very world into which it appeared. Such changes are now
spreading to the entire globe. So, everyone building a shelter
is now subjected to their own doubts about social behavior.
In any case, the solution to such a matter will slip away from
builders as long as societies have not reached stability.
Nevertheless it should not be the same with the relation of
shelter to its physical environment. These days, architectural
thinking in Third World societies is utterly tricky and
complex to deal with, since these societies are subjected to
transformations that were first caused by a different climate
than theirs. For instance: laborious lifestyle, schedules
that ignore naptime, domestic appliances that must follow

norms dictated by European furniture standards (work-surface height), clothing influences, fashion that ignores traditional clothing which is adapted to the weather (abandoning sirwals for narrow-legged trousers that are not as practical for sitting), fitted shoes which can not easily be taken off so you tend to keep them on inside just like in the West, which brings people to forget ground-level seating and caring for the floor; the arrival of elevated seats, the chair and its complimentary object; the table. Nothing remains of ancient comfort, universalized items are actually out of their culture. Recollecting knowledge held in the heritage of a specific place or region and combining it with contemporary technical means can not only be taken on by one isolated builder. It would need institutionalization. A workshop including various trades and architects can gather, classify and make information available. This workshop, situated in a delimited geographic entity could test, within limited operations, the fruits of these acquired observations and knowledge. The first attempts at such a system took place in Ghardaia, with the Mzab in Algeria, in a roughly three-year-long experiment. Even though not every required trade was present, a permanent team of five to seven architects worked there with the help of a dozen student interns. With low-cost housing construction you can see an example of how elements of the local heritage work in harmony with new needs. In old Mzab houses, both levels, the lower covered one and the terraces, are equipped with a hearth for cooking. Indeed, in the summer you eat inside during the day and on the terrace in the evening; while during winter, it is the other way around. Moving around cooking utensils twice a day or serving a common dish on floor-level, with or without a table and with no were not problems then. With modern electrical goods that connect to pipes (water, gas), the kitchen can no longer be nomadic. Yet, although it cannot be by-passed, especially in an economical agenda, eating habits remained the same. The tendency (difficult to overcome in both the eye of the designer and that of the public) was to associate the kitchen with the lower level, that is to say a closed space, following the European model. In this model, the terrace is only a seasonal outdoor space used sporadically, and is not included within the primary relations of the house. However, during the summer in the Sahara, fresh nights make up for the overwhelming heat of the day. The night calls for us to experience it. The clarity of the atmosphere, which you will see nowhere else in the world, makes for an ambiance which includes the moon and the stars, this is a cultural factor. And this is also a space in the house. No house, no matter the class, can be deprived of it. In summer, besides having dinner, you linger there all evening and you sleep there with soft winds no air conditioning could match; in winter, you use it for daytime chores. In such an experience, the kitchen is therefore on mid-level in order to be linked equally and indifferently to both meal spaces, all while remaining unique. Without this solution, the notion and function of the terrace according to ancestral comfort would have been denied and then erased from behavior. Similar precious notions can not even be numbered. They risk disappearance. How many have already been lost? Preserving, rediscovering, and integrating such values into contemporary life is worth the establishment of this important system of local workshops.

André Ravéreau, "Learn from Tradition", in *Techniques & Architectures*, issue 345, December 1982–January 1983. Translated from the French by Joël Mallet.

THE REPAIR

THE REPAIR FROM OCCIDENT TO EXTRA-OCCIDENTAL CULTURES, 2012
INSTALLATION, MIXED MEDIA, VIEW AT DOCUMENTA(13) - KASSEL, 2012.

FROM HOLY LAND TO OPEN YOUR EYES

We remember *Holy Land* (2006), that beach on the Canary Islands that Kader Attia turned into a cemetery. It is on a similar shore that motorboats unload stowaways in search of the promised land, at least those haven't disappeared, swallowed up by waves. Like so many tombstones - seen from far away, one may mistake them for surfboards stuck in the sand - mirrors everywhere show the visitor his own reflection. It is an unsettling reminder of the missing in a memorial place without memory, haunted by disappearance and absence. The Atlantic shores seem quite far away from the World War I battlefields. *Open Your Eyes* carries our gaze toward the great theater of modern war. Attia's installation visits another memorial site endowed with all the visibility granted by official histories and remembrance rituals. Worlds away from Fuerteventura beach, World War I trenches stick out with their dismembered bodies, dead or alive. If Canary Islands stowaways leave no trace, and in mirrors the visitor sees only his own image reflected upon the blue sky, the mutilated of the Great War, at least on the French side, do not go unnoticed: photographed, listed, studied, they are also - as much as possible - "resurrected" and rebuilt. And therefore repaired. To the invisibility of the missing Africans in *Holy Land*, Kader Attia opposes the ghosts of the first half of the twentieth century whose image has been preserved because they were broken - we called them "les gueules cassées" - and yet they were likely to be repaired, hence reintroduced in the society of the living, and socially reusable in many ways. Medical prowess, humanitarian compassion, exaltation of good works and charity organizations, heroism of the suffering combatant, war damage sublimation... reparation allows for all of this and it is surprising that historians and anthropologists did not give it more attention in their works.

REPAIR or REWEAVE SOCIETY

Reparation, a modest operation often erased from the sources and, in theory, made to remain invisible, on reflection, soon appears to be ubiquitous. If we list its uses we soon realize that it appears as a major and constant reconstruction process or simply one of culture's and society's constructions. In history, both absolute innovations and total destructions remain the exception, since we wouldn't know how to start from scratch and that there will always be remnants to fix or things to redo. Thus we spend our social and intimate existence repairing: a wound that heals is a tissue that repairs itself and cell biology teaches us that eukaryotic cells are able to repair damages caused to their DNA. We repair our machines. These have increased since the end of the 18th century and rule the way we consider the coming centuries. So much so that reparation has become a leitmotif of Western and Asian science fiction. *Blade Runner* (1982) replicas along with all their Korean and Japanese descendants are fighting to repair organisms that are aging, defective or with limited life. Repairing the beloved becomes even a form of love, taking tragic, melodramatic and sometimes even humorous turns when WALL-E's little robot strives to revive his dear EVE (Extraterrestrial Vegetation Evaluator).

REPAIR RAMSCHAKLE SOCIETIES

However, reparation can be something else than an individual initiative or a mechanical problem. It becomes a collective endeavor when, after a defeat or a natural disaster, we must urgently repair battered societies. The case takes huge proportions when the shock involves societies who know nothing about one another. Under the Spanish invasion, Mexican society collapsed in 1521, a founding stage of Western modernity and barbarism. What to do after the fall of Tenochtitlan and the ruin of Native American societies? There remained, of course, entire parts of the defeated societies and the few thousand Europeans were unable to bring but snatches of "Western civilization" from the Old World to the New one. Failing to go back - to the pre-Hispanic world - or to have the means to reproduce Spain on New World ground, we had to build - voluntarily or not, whether spontaneously or deliberately - new forms of social, political and religious organization, in other words, build a colonial society. And therefore, an unprecedented society, under European domination thousands of leagues away from the Iberian Peninsula. Under these conditions, failing to innovate at every turn - because innovating implies a project, resources, time to think - we had to clear away the ruins, recover and repair all that could be repaired. When we mention societies, civilizations or again religions constructions, we paradoxically forget or we refuse to see that to construct means most of the time to recycle and to repair: in many fields, do-it-yourself is and will remain the norm. In a broken and colonized society, on each side, we repair at every turn. On the native side, we do not settle for pieces of walls as a shelter or simply tinker up ceramics to cook a scanty pittance. We must also learn to repair all that the invasion has damaged: the rituals, the stream of time, cycles of feasts and markets but also networks and alliances. On the Spanish side (hence the conqueror's), we also repair as a matter of urgency: all is missing, starting with weapons, guns, horse saddles, torn clothes, battered helmets, armors and chainmail pierced by Aztec darts or rusted because of the rain.

Learning to fix the things of others is also entering into their world. One of the first tasks of the Franciscan missionaries in America was to train Native American craftsmen to mold iron and leather the European way, craftsmen who, above all, were liable to repair what war and time had damaged. This apprenticeship, often neglected by historians, has played a leading role in the forced integration of societies. On the one hand, by establishing settlers' dependency on the local labor force, and on the other hand, by initiating natives into the secrets of European manufacturing of objets, such as locks, weapons or musical instruments. In young colonial cities and the New World countryside, where European imports are rare and extremely expensive, reparation is more than a survival mode, it's almost a way of life and for many a livelihood. When do-it-yourself becomes impossible and replacement as well, humanity, even European, must change or lose its habits: for a long time in many Brazilian villages, for lack of shoes to mend, Portuguese settlers walked around barefoot like the slaves and natives did.

REPAIR / CROSS-BREED

If these used materials come from the other side, DIY or reparation creates a never-before-seen object, leading to new practices, customs or beliefs. To repair fallen cults and try to give them a colonial extension, Native Americans tampered with names, places and images: in Mexico the Spanish Virgin of Guadalupe served for "repairing" the cult of the goddess Tonantzin, first by adorning it with a layer of Christian veneer, then by blending the old icon into the miraculous image that has prevailed to this day.

In all fields, repair rhymes with cross-breed and in all fields these proceedings disturb. The *Repaired* is opposed to the *intact* just as the *hybrid* is opposed to the *authentic*. Consequently, neither the repair nor the hybrid have their place in traditional museums. If we keep them instead of getting rid of them, these listed objects end up most often confined to storerooms, out of the general public's sight, who increasingly ask for purity and integrality. However, old, broken marble - and, in theory, unrepaired, and thus intact in its incompleteness - will have the honor of an exhibition and a catalog: we can be broken and classic, and so break away from patched-up or hybrid sub-worlds. The patched-up and the repaired draw unthought of middle grounds that art history but also anthropology and history in general have, for a long time, carefully shunned. Early-20th-century African American fine arts admirers have hardly done otherwise, as they were in search of pure, "authentically" African forms that were tirelessly liable to feed their creative process.

In fact to talk about reparation, rather than cross-breeding, most likely corresponds better to what the artist or craftsman might have in mind. No creator decides to yield "hybrid" works or "authentic" works. There are many modern categories resulting from a scholarly theory of origins or a reflection on mixtures that are hardly the deeds of busy hands in workshops. However, all reparations set the existence of a specific goal, of an urgency to fulfill, and their achievement must meet efficiency criteria or at least fit the intended purpose or effect. To repair is often the will to keep all or part of the thing, thus ensuring a semblance of continuity: it is therefore to grow a special connection with time while asserting a concrete, factual grip on it.

REPAIR / FOLD AWAY

The small Olmec mask conceived by Benvenuto Cellini and kept in Florence at the Palazzo Pitti - is it a reparation? Torn away from its pedestal, it has been through the hands of a famous Renaissance goldsmith so much that it became listed as the Florentine master's full-fledged creation. Presentable, because it has been repaired, it undergoes a metamorphosis that inscribes it in the glorious history of Renaissance arts. And its reparation will remain for a long time unspoken. When preparing the exhibition *Planète métisse* at the Quai Branly Museum, Paris, in 2007, I tried to get hold of antique marble to embody the idea of classical purity. There is nothing more difficult according to one of the curators at the Louvre, who was surprised at my ingenuousness: most ancient marbles are the result of several reparations that spread over centuries, from the heart of the Middle Ages to the 19th century and which consist of more or less significant parcels of work: an arm, a leg, a head, or even just a nose. Japanese temples - and many others on the planet - are subject to constant reparations that have the characteristic of remaining invisible, denying the European visitor the vital patina of centuries. They fold away time by folding into themselves.

Out of ignorance or unquenchable passion for the authentic, facing the Cellinian mask of Florence or the Louvre antique marble, two repaired objects and repaired with art, we agree to see only what appeals to us: the Greek purity, be it a Roman version, or the pre-Conquest exotic Mexican. Reparation is then so imperceptible as to drag the object from one world to another, wiping off its crafted and hybrid history. Florence or Greece thus become the exclusive origin of an object that actually saw the light of day in Olmec Mexico or which has continued to move from one European workshop to another. A number of art objects were thus created with the main intention to restore life to a damaged piece too curious or too beautiful to be purely and simply thrown away. It is no coincidence that in Spanish America and the Iberian Peninsula we speak of *"renovar"* whenever we restore and repair a statue, a painting or an altar.

REPAIR / REPLACE

In theory, reparation stops where substitution and replacement begin. To replace: a way to compensate for what can no longer be patched up. It is also a way to keep one's distance from what remains beyond reach: Natives in Mexico will quickly enough invent organs out of flutes, and these new kinds of instruments will produce sounds to delight the missionary's ear. In the second half of the eighteenth century, waves of neo-classicism submerged Latin American Folk and Baroque arts. The substitution is brutal. Baroque must be destroyed and no longer repaired. Giving up reparation leads to change and rupture. Unless, of course, this novelty establishes itself in the cycle of appropriations and reparations, and also unless these cycles become - as is the case today - increasingly rapid.

REPAIR / CONNECT

To repair is therefore also to connect - times, people, things - and that's why any global history of humanity must pay profound attention to this seemingly simple and commonplace gesture which often consists in inventing a way to insert one world into another, not in a gratuitous manner, but to yield meaning and social customs. Kader Attia's installation increases encounters and face-to-face meetings between worlds. As he explains, "It will consist of creating encounters between Western and extra-Western worlds, at emblematic times, cruel or glorious, of their history. However, beyond these juxtapositions, this work seeks to present a reading of existence through 'universalities', more than a bipolar confrontation between the Western and extra-Western world." What conclusion to draw from all these objects placed face to face? Perhaps the incentive to shift borders and viewpoints, in other words "to think globally." "To think globally" is a challenge that historians and anthropologists are trying to take up today, eager to get their old disciplines out from the rut of exotic monograph, the rut of national history or a eurocentric grand narrative. How? Since the end of the 20th century, contemporary art has opened us up to new paths: Alejandro Gonzalez Inarritu's camera, Pina Bausch's dance connect worlds and synchronize them in creative gestures that bear one or more globalities of meaning. With *Open Your Eyes: The Reparation*, Kader Attia turns into a historian, an archaeologist, an anthropologist and ethnologist in search of objects that can show us how societies rebuild themselves, face one another, intertwine and respond to one another. The effects of the European modern war *par excellence*,

World War I, the "restorative" progress in medicine and its laboratories, are all faced with the destructive assault of colonization and appropriation by the colonized. As if the modernity with which we are concerned today consisted of these parallel and opposite movements – African do-it-yourself crafts and cosmetic surgery – and it is these complex dynamics that we must try to think and identify first, for lack of not being used to watching them. Kader Attia sees and shows – "Open your eyes" – and the social sciences and museums are often too slow to recognize it. The result? A beautiful global history lesson that brings together seemingly unrelated worlds, as beneath appearances it detects the ground-swells that bind them together. It's enough to make us revisit the longstanding opposition between Occident and non-Occident that has constituted our lives for centuries and is now undeniably shaken by the meteoric rise of an Asia that has digested Westernization, by the vibrant existence of Latin America within the very heart of all major U.S. cities, and by the indispensable presence of new populations in Western Europe, bearers of the unexpected and unpredictable.

One would like to imagine other dialogues or extend them. When metal cartridges from the World War I turn into lumbering butterflies, we want them to fly alongside other creations such as Mexican artist Erika Harrsh's fragile paper butterflies. Dollar-butterflies ready to fly off this summer into the Manhattan sky toward a huge flying dragon with Mao's head, another way of speaking about entangled worlds, and not only about how they meet or just kind of mix on this narrow planet.

Translated from French by Hoda Fourcade Zeid

Serge Gruzinski is a researcher (CNRS, Paris), and teacher (EHESS, Paris). As a historian, he is a specialist of the Latin American colonial period.

"Appropriation involves more than the adoption of an old idea, theory, technique, or practice, in a new place and time. Whatever is appropriated is also changed in a way characteristic of its new historical location and perhaps alien to the preferences of its previous owners. All appropriation, then, changes what is appropriated." (Peter Barker)

METAXU

In Plato's Republic, the priestess Diotima teaches Socrates that wisdom, like love (eros), is a desire for that which one does not have. The daimon Eros, born of Poros (lack) and Penia (plenty), occupies an interstitial space between divinity and mortality, suturing humanity to that which exceeds it with a ladder of love, by which the lover ascends – rung by rung – from the basest form of love (the love of a singular, beautiful body) towards a "wondrous vision": the very form of Beauty, which is "of itself and by itself in an eternal oneness, while every lovely thing partakes of it". Mediating between humans and gods, immanence and transcendence, the finite and infinite, ignorance and wisdom, Eros makes the universe an "interconnected whole", conjoining the base reality (or shadow) of the thing sought to its form, or the essence of the thing itself. Eros, then, is *metaxu* (between) – an intermediary, a bridge linking two heterogeneous realms, a vector in a continuum. For Simone Weil, *metaxu* – which constitute at once a separation and a link – are "truly precious things [...] which form ladders reaching towards the beauty of the world, openings on to it [...] Numbered among them are the pure and authentic achievements of art and science."

RELATIONAL TRANSFORMATION

In a series of recent exhibitions; *The Repair from Occident to Extra-Occidental Cultures* (dOCUMENTA(13), Kassel, 2012), *Repair: 5 Acts* (Kunst-Werke, Berlin, 2013) and *Continuum of Repair: The Light of Jacob's Ladder* (Whitechapel Gallery, London, 2013), Kader Attia has explored the in-between as the site of a relational operation that mobilizes the evolution of nature, culture and being. It is precisely in the encounter between heterogeneous elements that the very event of becoming takes place. Becoming can thus be understood as the ceaseless and reciprocal transformation (what Attia deems the repair) of each of the elements brought together in the encounter. A salient example can be found in the exchange between modernist architecture and amateur building tactics in 1950s Algeria. Fernand Pouillon's designs for large-scale social housing projects in Algiers were deeply influenced by local vernacular architecture and largely respectful of the social functions made manifest in their form. As they were being built, local labourers reappropriated left-overs of the mass-produced and imported materials used in their construction to build their own informal settlements, thereby adapting their own building practices (and the forms they produced) to the materials they had at hand.

In cases such as these, the encounter between diverse subjects and their (self-)exposure to each other's cultures and practices is mutually transformative. The circle of ipseity collapses as each subject creatively adapts to its being-another, thereby re-making itself through its contact with that which it is not. This is what Judith Butler and Athena Athanasiou (2013) mean when they speak of "the heteronomic condition for autonomy", in other words, a fundamental "relational dispossession", an "injurious yet enabling" primordial vulnerability to alterity, which "marks the limits of self-sufficiency and [...] establishes us as relational and interdependent beings." The (always provisional) constitution of the self, the act of auto-poïesis, might properly be described, then, as metaxic, for it takes place in the space between self and other. It is both a creative leave-taking and a conjunction.

And yet we must not forget that this primary structural disposition to alterity is played out in specific and determining historical and political conditions. The mutuality of transformation is differentially produced, depending on the context in which it takes place, and this differential itself has been historically naturalized in order to legitimize what Butler and Athanasiou describe as "an abdication of political responsibility for social forms of deprivation and dispossession". Privative dispossession, which concerns the forcible expropriation of land, citizenship, labour and rights, or the enclosure of (and differentiated exclusion from) the commons, re-enacts and re-produces a prior differentiation between that which is considered legitimately human (which Butler and Athanasiou synonymize with the "proper(tied)" liberal subject) and that which is considered waste.

In *Act 4 of Repair: 5 Acts*, a sequence entitled *Nature / Mimesis as Resistance*, Attia projected a short video clip taken from the British naturalist David Attenborough's series, *The Life of Birds*. In it, we hear an Australian lyrebird mimicking with astonishing accuracy the human-made sounds it hears in the forest – the click of a camera, the piercing wail of a car alarm, the buzz of a chainsaw. The bird does not know, of course, that it is mimicking human sounds; rather, through its song, it is both making sense of the world it inhabits and re-producing itself as (orally) extraordinary in order to attract mates. Its reproduction of human sounds – while chiming with Derrida's account of mimicry as différance, a "productive freedom" contributing to "the profusion of images, words, thoughts, theories, and action, without itself becoming tangible" (Kelly, 1998), in other words representing the very process of becoming (in and through its encounter with the human world) – will not prevent or attenuate the destruction of the natural environment, nor will it intervene in the hierarchies inscribed in the anthropocene. The mutual transformation of subjects in an unequally differentiated world depends on a broader structural change, as Attia confirms when he tells the anecdote of Berber women who used French coins to make their traditional headdresses, but, during the war of independence, traded these in Tunisia in order to raise funds for the Algerian resistance.

RESTORATIVE AND TRANSFORMATIVE REPAIR

The genealogy of repair in Attia's practice can be further traced to early works such as *La Piste d'atterrissage* (1997-1999), a series of photographs of transsexual Algerian prostitutes working the Boulevard Ney in Paris. Forced to move to France through fear of violent reprisal in Algeria, these migrants – forcibly dispossessed of their homeland and living on the margins of mainstream French society – transform their bodies through plastic surgery, reappropriating – through the production of new forms – that which has been expropriated by discourses of sexual and gender normalcy. Their *karakou* (traditional Algerian dresses), poached from the culture that marginalizes them, and carefully re-worked and embroidered by hand, set in motion a complex series of meanings that cannot be reduced to the restoration of (or claim to) national or gender identity. Rather, they testify to the wearers' freedom to (re)interpret both. As they sculpt new forms and meanings from the materials they inherit, the subjects of Attia's photographs give what is anew. The Algerian transsexuals are not claiming their right to wear this item of feminine attire, but rather to participate in the production of its meaning; to make it again, another way.

A similar dynamic can be seen in the repairs performed upon the African artefacts, images of which were projected alongside photographs of "les gueules cassées" (the shattered faces of soldiers wounded in the World War I) in Attia's 2013 installation, *The Repair from Occident to Extra-Occidental Cultures*. The broken and damaged artefacts have been repaired and re-made by local artisans using a variety of extraneous and anachronistic materials, including staples and plastic buttons, to produce an overtly hybrid aesthetic, which shocks Western eyes, in their search for authenticity and intactness. The signature of the repairer, the repair itself, re-begins the object, mobilizing the difference that inheres in the same (as opposed to reinforcing the sameness of diversity that structures the expectation and reception of the integral artefact). That the will to repair is a commonality shared by occidental and extra-occidental cultures is demonstrated in the examples of trench art exhibited in a display cabinet as part of the same installation. These spent bullet cases and artillery shells, transformed by soldiers into decorative objects, resonate with a life purloined – quite literally – from death. They attest, like the obviously repaired African artefacts, to the heteronomy that is the (visible) condition of the existence of the repaired object in the present. As a counterpoint, the photographs of "les gueules cassées", taken before and after maxillofacial surgery (a procedure developed in response to the traumas occasioned by modern warfare) testify to modernity's desire to restore the subject – physically and psychologically – to the pre-traumatic state, leaving no trace of the damage occasioned or of the repair work undertaken. The modern reparative intervention (like the "quick fix" cognitive behavioural therapy used to address depression today) seeks to reintegrate, as efficiently and as swiftly as possible, the once again functioning subject in an order that remains unchanged by (because it largely produces) the traumas that beset its subjects. The repaired subject of modernity is presumed elastic, in that it is understood to have the capacity to return to its initial form following disfiguration or deformation. Plasticity, on the other hand, involves "not an infinite modifiability," as Cathérine Malabou explains, "but a possibility of displacing or transforming the mark or the imprint, of changing determination in some way". In other words, in the kind of transformative (rather than restorative) repair one sees at work in the African artefacts, or in the auto-poïesis of the Algerian transsexuals, the (ultimately impossible and deeply ideological) telos of origin is inflected and displaced by the re-beginning (or the re-giving) of what is and what has been. This second origin is the scene of a new point of departure. Retour (return) gives way to creative detour.

Transformative – or creative – repair amounts to a making or reading otherwise (the two are homologous) of that which is: a second, rather than a first beginning (the idea of invention ex nihilo is a modernist conceit); the creative actualization, or improvisation, of a future (one of the possible futures) always already latent in a present at once constituted by, but not identical with, the sedimentations and accretions of the past. (The future is irrefragable; it will be, as the past will be.)

ON THAT WHICH EXCEEDS US

In *Act 4 of Repair: 5 Acts, Nature / Mimesis as Control*, Attia juxtaposes stuffed wild animals, the hunting trophies so beloved of Western tourists to Africa both past and present, with African masks from Mali and Tanzania, the function of which was to channel the energy, faculties and intelligence of the animal they represent into the person who wears them. Both types of artefact speak of the human desire to control nature, to arrogate to itself the superiority of non-human subjects, or – through the prosthesis of weaponry – to subjugate those powers (of speed, cunning and strength, for example) and to reassert the superiority of the human. The Whitechapel Gallery in London occupies the site that was once home to a public library, one of the many founded by the Victorian philanthropist Passmore Edwards. In his recent exhibition at the Whitechapel, *Continuum of Repair: The Light of Jacob's Ladder*, Attia re-enacts the original function of the space, bringing together a vast collection of books that testify to the human will to know, order and understand the natural world. In the center of the installation, amidst the rows of shelving crammed with scientific and philosophical treatises, stands a large cabinet displaying artefacts and instruments that celebrate *cognitio ocularis*: a portrait of René Descartes, whose rationalist philosophy profoundly influenced the Enlightenment, the writings of Galileo, astrological maps and a variety of perspicilla: a magnifying glass, a pair of spectacles and a curious, hybrid instrument – a brass telescope that has been welded to a microscope. Above the cabinet, an ingenious construction of mirrors and strip lighting creates the illusion of a ladder of light, interminably reproducing the objects of knowledge below and suturing – albeit provisionally and imperfectly – the temporal and the infinite.

The installation fills the gallery space, rather like the Renaissance *Wunderkammern* that drew visitors into their immersive panoramas of objects appropriated from a realm beyond human cognition, at once inassimilable and awe-inspiring. And yet, in the equal attention it affords both the objects themselves and the achievements and victories of human knowledge, the installation also evokes the 17th and 18th century cabinets of curiosity, which gave equal weight to the exhibition and valorisation of the very tools and instruments that enabled the visual and cognitive apprehension of the objects on display.

In its conflagration of two historical modes of display, *Continuum of Repair* re-enacts, at one level, the triumph of reason over theology; of science over wonder and the domestication (through taxonomy and mathesis) of the mysteries of the natural world. And yet the disruptive detail, the grain of sand that gets in the eye, is surely the hybrid micro-telescope, an impossible object designed to yield to human perception (and therefore to cognition) both the infinitesimally small and the infinitesimally large; the particular that encapsulates the universal, and the universal that explains the particular. And yet, in its very pursuit of this "God equation", the arrangement of the two instruments means, in fact, that nothing at all can be seen through the lens.

The telescope was an exemplar of Baroque technology and human ingenium. For Alexandre Koyré, the instrument emblematized the spatial and epistemic transition from a closed world to an infinite universe – an exemplar, then, of a metaxic apparatus. But while it ostensibly enabled the human domestication of the celestial, allowing the human mind to explore (and assertively dominate) the unknown, at the same time it definitively ruptured the human worldview, disproving both the immutability and centrality of the earth in the cosmological system and disclosing the infinity of the universe. Baroque epistemology confirmed, then, a principle that still holds good in the quantum age: the more we know the world, the less, in fact, we can measure it. What we know about the world changes it, as it changes us. Cognition seeks to contain – but in so doing produces – its own supplement or excess. Nature escapes us; it remains, stubbornly, what Quentin Meillassoux describes as the "great outdoors" of pre-critical Cartesian philosophy.

Serge Haroche – the "photon tamer" – famously led a series of experiments that rely on capturing a light quanta between highly reflective concave mirrors, in order to actualize in the laboratory (as Galileo did with the telescope) that which had hitherto existed only as "thought experiments." And yet, the photon always escapes; no manmade box will ever be sufficiently perfect to contain it, or to prevent its entropic decay into the walls of the mirrors.

The difficulties we have today processing the counter-intuitive principles of quantum mechanics mirror, perhaps, the poetics of the sublime, a philosophy which emerged precisely in the era when the domestic users of the increasingly democratized optical technologies developed during the Baroque period were able to experience for themselves Galileo's stupefying discoveries.

THE PARALLAX VIEW (OR LIGHT REDUX AND THE METAXU OF EXPERIENCE)

Light enables us to see, but it cannot be seen. It is a medium that causes the object to present itself to us, gradually, through refraction. If light moved only in one way – and here is the nub of Kant's error – we would never see the object we wish to know. And yet Werner Heisenberg has taught us also that the world can never be wholly known, for our own point of view – our own perceptual and cognitive apparatus – is always already interposed between the real and us. Our perception of the world intervenes in and interrupts it. Light draws us, then, towards the world, but the world remains always still to come.

How, then, might we represent the world to ourselves (and also understand and account for the relational transformation and excess that this representation incurs in both the observer and the observed)?

In *The Order of Things*, Michel Foucault argues that our representations of objects are neither wholly cultural nor dependent on scientific rules. Rather, they are forged in our experience, that space between discrete or antithetic systems. More recently, Slavoj Žižek has pursued the creative valence of "parallax thinking", (from the Greek *parallaxis* – change) which precisely resists the totalizing reconciliation of incommensurable systems in favour of exploring the creative possibilities afforded by the spandrel spaces that emerge in between. As Fredric Jameson writes in his review of Žižek's work, "In parallax thinking, [...] the object can certainly be determined, but only indirectly, by way of triangulation based on the incommensurability of the observations". It is in this irremediable gap between desiring cognition and the present-not-present world, rather than in its closure, that Jameson locates the possibility of agency and crea-

tivity. It is here also, in this metaxic space, that we might locate the heterogeneous constellations that constitute Attia's artistic practice, this repair without synthetic resolution, a perpetual re-enactment of "an irresolvable dispute".

WORKS CITED

Judith Butler with Athena Athanasiou, *Dispossession: The Performative in the Political*, Cambridge: Polity Press, 2013.

Michel Foucault, *The Order of Things: An Archaeology of the Human Sciences,* London: Vintage, 1994.

Jacob Holsinger Sherman, *Partakers of the Divine: Contemplation and the Practice of Philosophy*, Minneapolis: Fortress Press, 2014.

Michael, Kelly, "Mimesis", in *The Encyclopedia of Aesthetics*, Oxford: Oxford University Press, 1998.

Alexandre Koyré, *From the Closed World to the Infinite Universe*, Baltimore: Johns Hopkins Press, 1957.

Slavoj Žižek, *The Parallax View*, Boston: MIT Press, 2009.

Amanda Crawley Jackson moved from Nottingham to Paris, where she taught at the École Normale Supérieure (Cachan) before taking up the position of Lecturer in French, then Chair of European Languages and Cultures, at the University of Wales, Lampeter. During her time in Lampeter, she served on the federal University of Wales Modern Languages Subject Panel and the Executive Committee of the Society for French Studies (UK).

KADER ATTIA: The issue of repair is now a major focus in my artistic research. I thought about it after watching a simple piece of raffia cloth a friend gave me in Congo, in 1997. The peculiar thing about this traditional loincloth is that it is scattered with small patches of Western fabric, reminiscent of Vichy fabric (gingham). For years, I thought these elements were just decorations with unexpected aesthetics, bits of modern Eastern material added like some sort of transplant on a traditional African piece of cloth. One day, I turned this ambivalent item around and discovered that behind each patch was a hole from overuse. The patches are actually signs of both an aesthetic and ethical act: it is a repair. From then on I spent my life looking for such signs. It enabled me to discover the complexity of fixing, in traditional extra-Western societies and in modern Western societies as well. Objects, masks, intentional or unintentional physical injuries all come from an intent to repair that changes from one culture to another. As a surgeon working in Paris, how do you understand this description of an inanimate, lifeless object – this loincloth mended by Kuba people in Congo with elements from a Western culture? You also worked in Africa, if I'm not mistaken.

BERNARD MOLE: The repair you're talking about is a passive one; it is the same as what we use in reconstructive surgery when we have to make up for a lack of skin with an auto-transplant (meaning a transplant from the same patient). The result varies quite a lot on a cosmetic level because the skin always keeps the characteristics of where it came from; even if it sometimes merges perfectly with the surrounding skin, it can also leave the impression of being an "imported part", which is obviously not the expected result for a patient, who always dreams of a restoration "ad integrum". The most elegant repairs often make use of what can be very complex scraps, which allows for true reconstruction of several tissues at the same time; these can perfectly mimic the original one. The most ancient repairs go back to 3000 years BC, in India, and to 15th century Italy, back when "traditional" punishment consisted of completely amputating one's nose.
The ultimate stage for this kind of operation was reached a few years ago in France with a complete facial homograft (transplanting the face of someone else), under the guise of a very intense anti-rejection treatment, which brought to light both technical and ethical issues: in fact, spending the rest of your life with someone else's face is not easy at all! However, after following up with the first cases several years later, it appears this integration is absolutely possible. Let us not forget that such patients are completely disfigured before the operation and have therefore already "lost their original face".
To some extent, mending a piece of clothing with bits taken from another eventually falls under the same process: you keep one alive thanks to the other and through your emotional attachement to the first. This reminds me of a Sicilian story I heard from Dominique Hernandez about a very poor woman who had owned an apron since her wedding day, and it had been sewn back up so many times that her husband ended up giving her a new one as a gift: as a reaction she did not replace the old apron with the new one but used the latter to cut new bits and complete her patchwork up until "the end" – in short, until her death!

K. A.: I always felt the polysemous characteristic in the concept of repair. For from the act to the result, there are infinite possible interpretations, as much for he who sees the repairing as for he who carries it out, and who/what is being repaired. Yet, a fixed-up cloth has no self-awareness of having been so, just like it is not conscious of being fabric. As for the viewer, can they think about the piece of cloth as repaired in itself? Impossible. What enables the human mind to a concept, like fixing fabric or a wound is the intellectual and experimental relation between the repaired item and its repairer, just like between the repaired item and the viewer. This relation, called "correlation" by modern philosophy, is what structures and rules over knowledge. What I find fascinating in this idea is the way the link established between two independent things is what distinguishes them, just like it unites them to create knowledge of the other thing by inference. Without correlation, knowledge would not exist.
Do you think correlation is a conceptual form of repair specific to intelligence, that it fills the abyss between intelligence and things? Speaking about modern Western thought, could we say that, up to our contemporary days, modern Western reconstructive surgery would be looking for the ethics of ad integrum restitution as the one and only standard for perfection, because it seems (according to your earlier example) to be the effect the patient wishes to see?

B. A.: I humbly admit my intellectual inability to answer such a question. Usually, surgeons are pragmatic, not to say down-to-earth people. They are artisans that interrogate themselves before, and sometimes even during, the operation. Yet, what distinguishes them from any other craftsman is that they absolutely must "finish the job" once they've started! Despite what can be said, even when the patient demands perfection, modesty should make us recognize the fact that the best result also comes from some personal part played by the person undergoing the operation. Ambroise Paré said something astonishingly humble and clear-sighted that proves to be a sort of guiding light throughout a practitioner's career: "I bandaged him, and God healed him." By the way, from a legal perspective, the final result matters less than what was done to get to it.

K. A.: I spent a lot of time watching the amazing formal analogies one could find between the reconstructed facial wounds of soldiers, such as the "gueules cassées", or broken faces, during World War I, and African traditional masks. I am particularly interested in the early years of the conflict because at the time, physicians like Hippolyte Maurestin in France or Dr J. Joseph in Germany were quickly overwhelmed by the increasing number of casualties. They had to fix fast and with rudimentary means because they lacked equipment, due to the war and certainly to the technology available at the time. What is striking in those reconstructions is their ethical and especially aesthetic dimension; their expression echoes traditional African mask repairs in which other constraints fashioned almost similar aesthetics...
This aesthetics is limited by the means at hand, which Claude Levi-Strauss even called a "patch-up job". In Europe, the expressive aspect inherent to reconstructed war injuries inspired expressionist painters like Otto Dix and Georg Grosz. By seizing it they condemned the horrors of war and gave birth to an important artistic movement: German Expressionism.
As I carried on my research, I discovered, especially with Dr J. Joseph from Berlin, that reconstructive surgery developed during World War I. A four-year conflict is long, for soldiers and for doctors as well. I was baffled by the physicians' talent: not only by their skill, but also their creativity that, sometimes within a single patch-up job, could do miracles...

Does your story about nose reparation fall under this kind of patch-up job? What are the results? Could a patient attempting to hide his outlaw past manage to do it?

B. M.: As terrible as the injuries were and as imperfect as the repairing was, a broken face led to a certain respectability (for it brought to mind bravery, sacrifice and self-sacrifice for your country, etc.). But things changed during World War II. After this conflict, priority was given to not showing signs of injury or to hiding injuries the public could not bear to look at. At the same time, the status of surgeons changed as well: amputation champions under Napoleon (the only chance of survival for soldiers with wounded limbs), claiming rightful status with the creation of the Red Cross by Henri Dunant, who had been horrified by the butchery in Solferino, benefitted from the shy but meaningful progress in anesthesia and the tottering surgery of the shreds seen during World War I, and later managed to establish real rules in how to care for serious injuries during World War II. I don't know if repairing amputated noses gave the operated victims a chance to change their social integration. We can assume it did whenever the result was skillful and discrete, but it must have been rare… Seeing the evolution in status for surgeons throughout history is funny: during Antiquity, they were respected for their knowledge and boldness, then they were despised and put down to the same rank as barbers up until the Renaissance (it is true they had intellectual power in colleges but what they knew was based upon absolutely crazy theories that surely took more sick people to the grave than the disease itself). It wasn't until surgeons finally cured Louis XIV's anal fistula that they regained a social position worthy of their talent!

K. A.: Retracing how some trades evolved in their social position throughout history is fascinating. Architects, too, have known various levels of acknowledgement depending on the time in which they lived. I remember an interview with Auguste Perret in which he complained about architects' status in the 20th century. They are not as praised as they used to be. In Ancient Egypt, the Pharaoh would greet them almost like demigods, while nowadays they are just employees for local elected representatives or company managers. Still, apart from this acknowledgement you are mentioning with Louis XIV and his doctor, Félix de Tassy, to me, architecture sometimes seems to share the same "raison d'être" as surgery. You can find some kind of repair work in building. I'm not only talking about reconstructing ancient ruins or renovating old modern buildings. It's about what truly animates the human mind, as both the factor and messenger in the evolution of its superiority over other species, through instinctive ethics that urge it to compete against the laws of nature: building, enhancing, transforming, recreating, etc. There are many possible analogies between the human body and architecture. According to philosophers like Michel Foucault, who expressed it in his lecture *Utopian Body*, body and mind are almost dissonant. The mind could inhabit the body the same way a body inhabits architecture. Bernard, Kader, your relatives, mine, people outside, all the people you assimilate to their earthly bodies, are something else in reality. What you can perceive, their shell, is only a puppet controlled by their mind. Every living person is above all a thinking mind. Your body is not you, but the shell inhabited by your spirit. This idea can be contradicted, and Michel Foucault himself does it in the second part of his lecture.
Nevertheless, I would like to come back to an example you quoted earlier. This story raised several questions I would like to ask you.
It was about a transplant on somebody who had been attacked by a dog, causing the person to be disfigured. The operation consisted of transplanting someone else's face. You said both body and mind could react negatively to such a graft, hence the necessity of complex medical disease prevention along with serious psychological follow-up. Is there a double consciousness of the repair by the body and the mind, or is it just a matter of medical ethics? I particularly recall a Cameroonian friend's father who had received an organ transplant from someone else. He never psychologically accepted having something he could not see but that seriously felt like some alien presence inside of him… Eventually, his body never managed to accept the graft and he died. Are there situations where the mind welcomes the graft while the body does not, or vice versa? Does this particular face transplant, along with what it implies in matters of "acceptation and reject" by body and mind fall under the umbrella of reparation, or is it pure creation? In other words, when you transplant a new face, or new hands, on a body that has lost its original parts, does the surgeon only fix it or does he create a new being?

B. M.: I would like to reassure you right away: there is no such thing as Pygmalion surgeon, or if there is, such a physician's behavior is clearly due to pathological perversion. Literature is full of these kinds of myths, from *Faust* to *Frankenstein*, where man thinks he can act like God. In this respect, I cannot resist telling you a joke: "do you know the difference between God and a surgeon? There isn't, except that God doesn't think he's a surgeon". There is a tendency to fantasize about our power as surgeons. Actually, we have none, we only have duties, and the most important one is to act properly for the sake of whoever gave us their trust. Everything else is just literature… We have been overwhelmed for several years now with so many fantastical visions – that tend to be more or less pathological – and they don't help in improving our image. No face transplant falls under creation, or maybe "recreation", meaning restoration/reparation. Nevertheless, this does not prevent one from wondering, of course, for our actions sometimes have an unexpected impact on a patient's behavior. We always hope it will be a positive one, but with experience, you get to learn it can also be deleterious, probably because we didn't really get what lay underneath this demand for reparation. Once you have more experience, such consequences are seldom, but one never knows! As far as I'm concerned, I also chose this specialty for the psychological support it implies, as well as the impossibility to cheat with the result.

K. A.: Perhaps the myth of Pygmalion surgeons comes from the fact that they walk alongside death, and most of the time, cast it back to where it came. They sometimes have an over-developed ego. Artists, too, have egos of varying sizes, the difference being that they do not save lives. Their works create a vanishing point on the horizons of thought and emotion, but it remains mere representation, staging. Mankind's superiority lies in the ability to bring science and art together both in harmony and dichotomy. Everything can be measured and then explained with mathematics – everything but art. Not only contemporary art, but all truly artistic initiatives without exception, from arts wrongly called primitive to the ones excessively considered as "major". This is the reason why I'm interested in the incursion of artistic process into the field of science. For example, when a sculptor reconstructing and imagining down to the last detail what a broken torn-up face looked like in order to inspire a surgeon to follow that lead and fix that face or order a resin prosthesis. I saw such prosthetic items from World War I at Val de Grâce Hospital in Paris.

What I find interesting here, is not only what you humbly mentioned as the artisanal part of your profession, but also the borderline between art and science, and honestly, between beauty and its opposite. All in all, the issue of beauty.

You work in Paris, but I heard you also go to Africa with an association that fixes children's smiles (or do you also perform all kinds of surgery on adults and children there?). Could you tell us a little more about this fantastic action you carry out alongside your Parisian activities? What does it mean to help people who do not have the means for facial surgery? I guess you involve your professional experience in both an ethical and aesthetic perspective.

And secondly – this question is a bit more sensitive – what can you say about beauty with the example I'm about to give you? For several years now, I've been working on what is called "sickness masks" in central, west, east and southern Africa, and Asia (from Tibet to Indonesia), and I would not be surprised to find some in Japan as well. A mask representing a sick person's face has a very meaningful place. Some of these objects had a real impact on the evolution of 20th century Western thought...

The Pende people from Congo even created the legend, and it might in fact be true, that such items directly influenced Picasso's *The Young Ladies of Avignon*, the iconic painting of Cubism's golden age. If extra-Western societies show sickness, it is surely in order to exorcise it, but especially to give it a noticeable position in public space: it is like acknowledging illness and giving it a social and material, as well as immaterial, almost divine value. The faces of sickness masks are misshapen, twisted and expressive, not to say expressionist. With this aesthetics, they mark what the modern Western mind finds asymmetrical, anomalous, almost repulsive. They remind me of aesthetic concerns and social issues that broken faces had to undergo in their postwar life. Jacques Derrida said that human physical beauty is certainly what is truly rare. Perfect facial symmetry is seldom, therefore it is beautiful... beautiful and rare, perhaps as much as a totally asymmetric face could be.

According to you, what is beauty in reconstructive surgery; is it primarily born from the surgeon's personal choices or from societal codification?

B. M.: Now, this is a delicate inquiry, and it questions the very notion of beauty: is it a gift from nature, a product of personal effort, a cultural footprint? Certainly a bit of each of these. Contrary to what people usually think, you must first approach the idea of beauty with a lot of doubt but nonetheless, some certitude. First, beauty transcends the ages: even when you want to bring into contrast Rubens' voluptuous Venus and Giacometti's ascetic ones, you soon realize beauty is immanent, it imposes itself throughout

history. Be it Nefertiti's famous bust exhibited in Berlin, Praxiteles' reproductions, faithful paintings of Agnès Sorel and so many others... who could possibly have a look at them and think "peuh, not that good"? Beauty is fascinating and repulsive, attractive and frightening, it is a grace one must use carefully, or a destructive weapon to whoever gets seduced (the devil's beauty).

Strangely, it is rejected by our Judeo-Christian society, and yet worshipped by it. To those who tell me "after all, nature made us the way we are, so we should not try and question God's work," I reply "our religion allows us to represent God, his son and his sanctified disciples in a glorified way: oddly enough, I never saw a painting of Jesus with his ears sticking out, a crooked nose, or as a fat person." And if you happened to be in such disgrace, would not you ask for a "reparation" (also meaning "redressing injustice")? Of course, as far as I know, there are several ways of showing appreciation in each civilizations. However, when you travel around the world, you soon realize beauty sometimes compellingly stands out by itself. Like a sort of masterpiece that is unfortunately temporary, but that you agree to behold without jealousy. I find it hard sometimes, but then I just play the part of the spectator who is simply happy to meet grace and exception!

I will conclude by saying that the purpose of aesthetic surgery is not to "bring beauty" (because what standards should we follow?) but harmony. By the way, such a demand is quite reasonable in France and only very few patients come with tabloid pages to use as a model! Plus, those kinds of needs are quite dubious because they can lead to dysmorphophobia, which cannot be solved.

K. A.: I always believed the apex of human civilization was prior to monotheism. As soon as the notion of a unique God appeared, human beings never stopped dogmatizing relations between people, from the social sphere to the intimate one, to finally control others through morality. Homosexuality, for instance, was stigmatized and demonized only after the advent of monotheism. Greco-roman civilizations left us obvious proof of that. As a humanist photographer, I found interest in people from all confessions and sexual identities. A few years ago, I directed a movie with a transsexual friend of mine who had been dreaming for years of going to India or Pakistan to meet with the Hijras. Originally, Hijras are men who enter an Ashram where they live with other men who decided never to live as males again, but as Hijras. When you don't know about them, they seem to live as women, but when you happen to spend some time with them, they will tell you "I'm neither male nor female, I'm Hijras".

Progress in plastic surgery does not only concern face, but body and genital organ transplants as well, it goes way further than the breast implants we all know about. What does it mean, to a surgeon, to graft elements that were not on a body, but that people want because they utterly need them for personal reasons? When Dr Joseph in Germany, or Dr Maurestin in France, fixed broken faces during the war, I guess their actions embodied some sort of an ethical mission, and also some kind of exhilaration, a technical challenge for them to take up. And especially, they mended something that had been destroyed by a bullet or shrapnel. Sometimes, the purpose of transplantation is for a missing part to be replaced. I really like your mentioning the artisan's thorough mind and I have one final question for you.

To you, and from the perspective of repair, what does it mean to take male genital organs off a man who always felt he was a woman deep down inside, or to add flesh on female genital organs on a woman who is convinced she is a man? Unless I'm mistaken, for I'm not really knowledgeable on the technical parts of the matter, it appears that on the one hand, the surgeon is taking parts off, and on the other hand, he is adding things. Could we say he is repairing?

B. M.: From a technical point of view, a man-woman transformation is relatively easy and often so well done that it can even deceive your most intimate relatives, even gynecologists. Meanwhile, the other way around is way much harder, even though complicated and bold tricks may give partial illusion... but hardly...

In France, this sort of surgery follows serious rules and the procedure takes a lot of time. Indeed, you need a collegial surgical-psychiatric-endocrinologist permission for the act to be taken into consideration; this requires years of patience, mostly because of the psychiatric expertise, which is actually the key in such a situation. Once you have this permission, a change in identity must be granted by the State administration before the operation. The operation proves to be a major part of the process, but when making a man a woman, it is common to perform a reversible act, such as breast implants or reducing the Adam's apple, in order for patients to get used to inhabiting their new personality beyond mere clothing. Also note that if you follow these official rules, the intervention is taken care of by healthcare services.

Outside of this "authentic" process, there are certainly less official operations with no psychological or psychiatric care. Those can lead to dead ends over which you have absolutely no control, to utter sexual misery and often suicide. So, as far as I'm concerned, it seems fundamental to wrap up this process with long and thorough follow-up care during which the surgeon, though he seems to be playing the most essential part, has no right to say anything about the actual decision.

As for saying we mend things, this is what a psychiatrist could say about our trade. At best, surgeons bring balance between a patient's personal convictions and the attributes they display. This enthralling issue inspired so many pieces of literature, and it obviously has nothing to do with what the public usually confuses with transvestitism. Then again, the box of fantasies is wide open and the technical surgeon must remain careful...yet open-minded!

Translated from French by Joël Mallet

Bernard Mole, plastic surgeon in France, is a founding member of the French Society of Plastic and Aesthetic Surgeons (SOFCEP). Formerly the intern in Paris Hospitals and later head of the Faculty Clinic, he conducts research and fellowships on several topics such as clinical applications for growing human epidermis. A precursor practitioner, he is the main IMCAS Paris Course Coordinator for plastic surgery teaching materials for several years. Today he is a renowned physician specialized in plastic and reconstructive surgery. He is the national secretary for France of the International Society of Aesthetic Plastic Surgery (ISAPS). He divides his time between his local practice and his humanitarian activities.

BIG BANG, 2006.
DRAWING, BLACK INK ON PAPER, 50 X 65 CM.

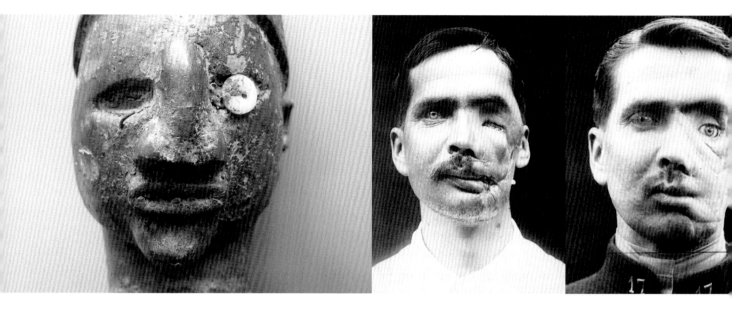

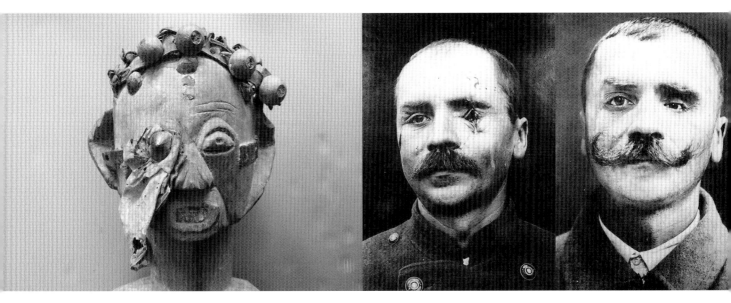

OPEN YOUR EYES, 2010.
DIPTYCH OF SLIDE PROJECTIONS, 13 MIN.

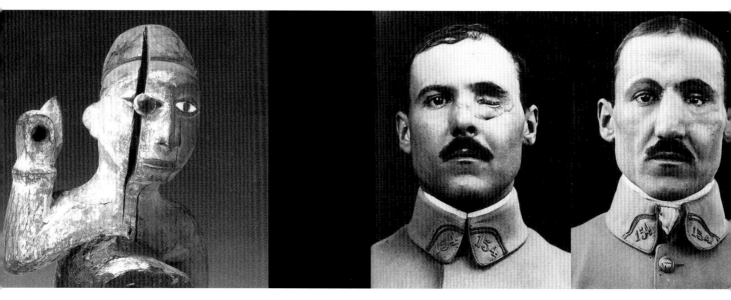

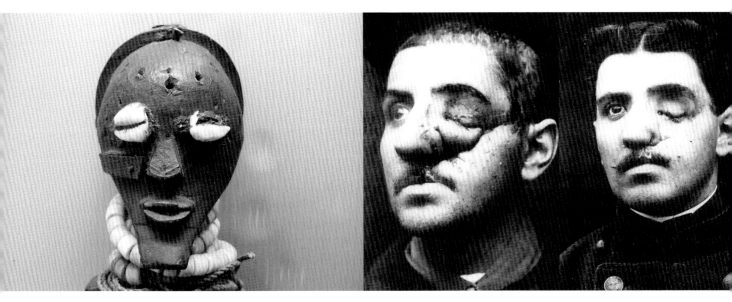

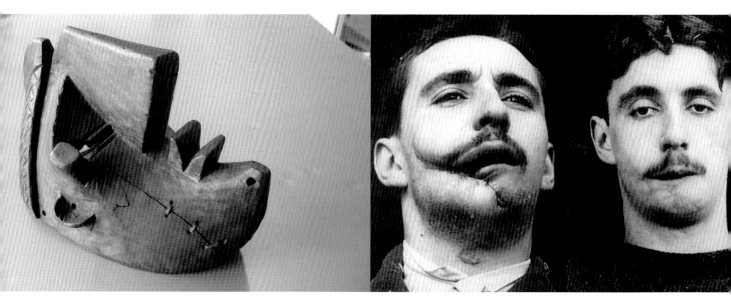

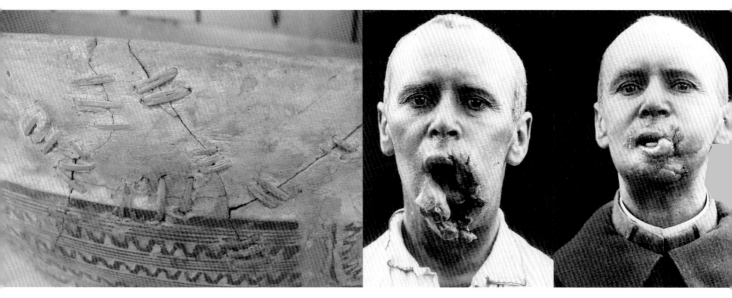

ARTIFICIAL NATURE, 2014.
INSTALLATION, 29 LEG PROSTHESES,
LEG PROSTHESES FROM WW1 AND WW2,
AND CONTEMPORARY ONES, IMAGE OF A PYGMY
GAME, INSTALLATION VIEW AT THE BEIRUT ART
CENTER - BEIRUT, 2014

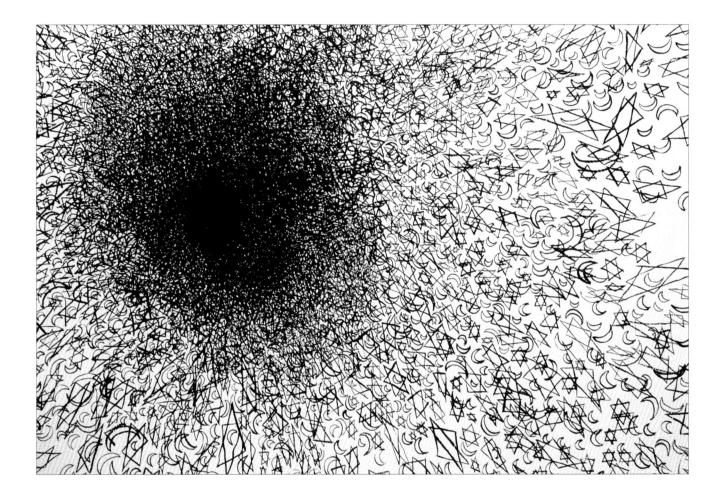

BIG BANG, 2006.
DRAWING, BLACK INK ON PAPER, 50 X 65 CM.

UNTITLED, 2006.
PASTEL ON BROWN PAPER, 50 X 65 CM.

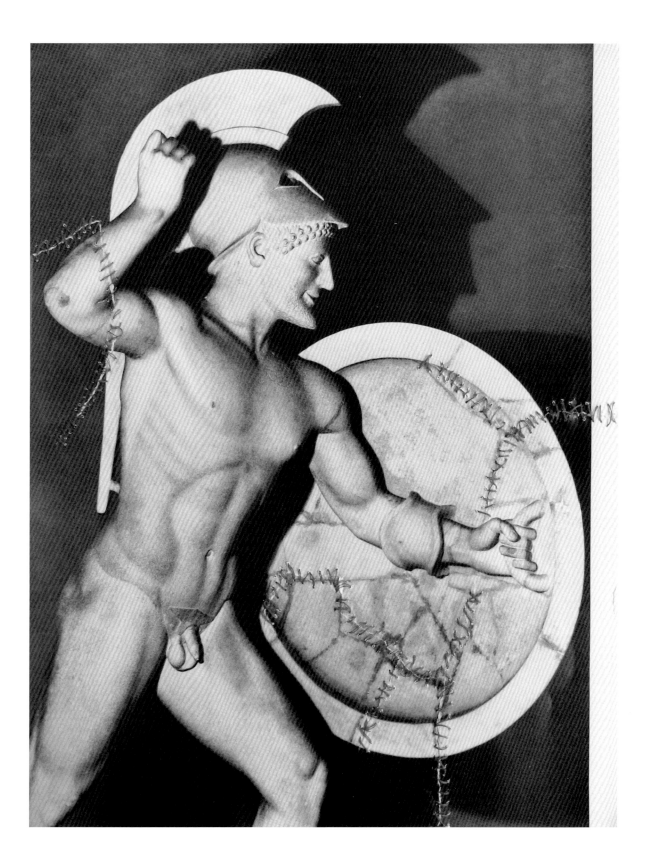

FROM THE SERIES MODERN ARCHITECTURE GENEALOGY, 2014.
SERIES OF COLLAGES AND DOCUMENTS, HELIOGRAVURES AND COTTON THREAD.

CLICHÉ CHEVOJON

PRAXITÈLE. TORSE DU SATYRE AU REPOS

B. TH. ÉLLER PARIS

Hofmer

Athen, Akropolis-Museum. Spätarchaische Marmorstatuen junger Mädchen (Koren) von der Athener Burg. Oben: sog. Peplos-Kore. Parischer Marmor mit farbiger Bemalung. Gesamthöhe (mit Plinthe) 1,21 m. Um 530. Rechts: sog. Kore mit den Sphinxaugen. Parischer Marmor mit Bemalung. H. 92 cm. Um 500.

Athens, Akropolis Museum. Late Archaic marble statues of young girls (korai) from the Athenian Akropolis. Above: the so-called Peplos kore. Parian marble, with traces of original colour. Total height (with plinth) 48 ins. C. 530 B.C. Right: the so-called kore with the Sphinx eyes. Painted Parian marble. Height 36½ ins. C. 500 B.C.

CLICHÉ CHEVOJON

A. CALAVAS, PARIS

IVᵉ SIÈCLE. TÊTE D'ARTÉMIS

TRADITIONAL REPAIR, IMMATERIAL INJURY, 2014.
IN SITU SCULPTURE, METALLIC STAPLES, WIRE, CONCRETE, VIEW AT THE BEIRUT ART CENTER - BEIRUT, 2014.

African mask helmet (Congo), broken then fixed traditionally. Here, the crossed repair echoes the engraved pattern. Traditional African repairs do not attempt at hiding the repair work like in the West. On the contrary, the repair work appears as an extra decorative item.

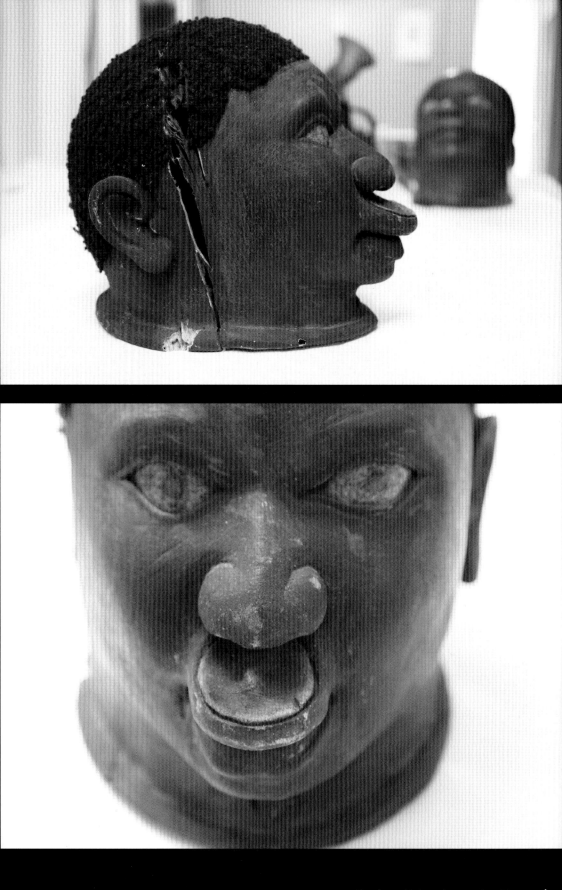

Broken Makonde mask, Tanzania.

World War I prostheses, Musée du Service de Santé des Armées, Paris

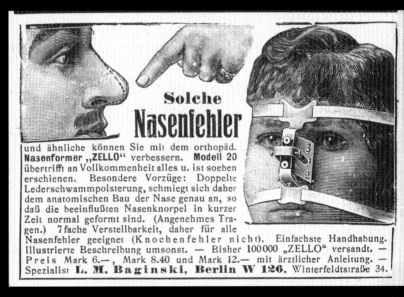
Prosthesis advertisement, excerpt from German newspaper *Die Woche*, 1903.

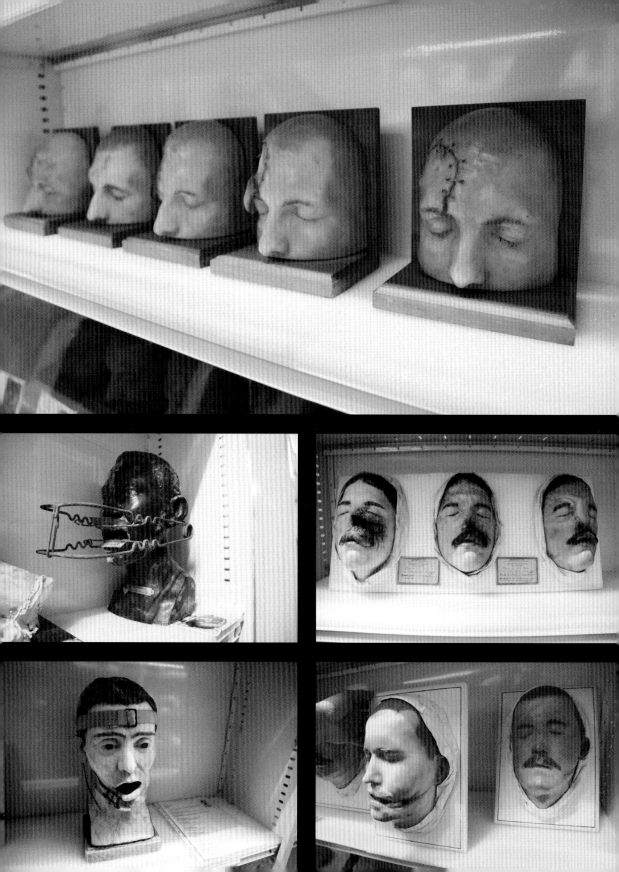

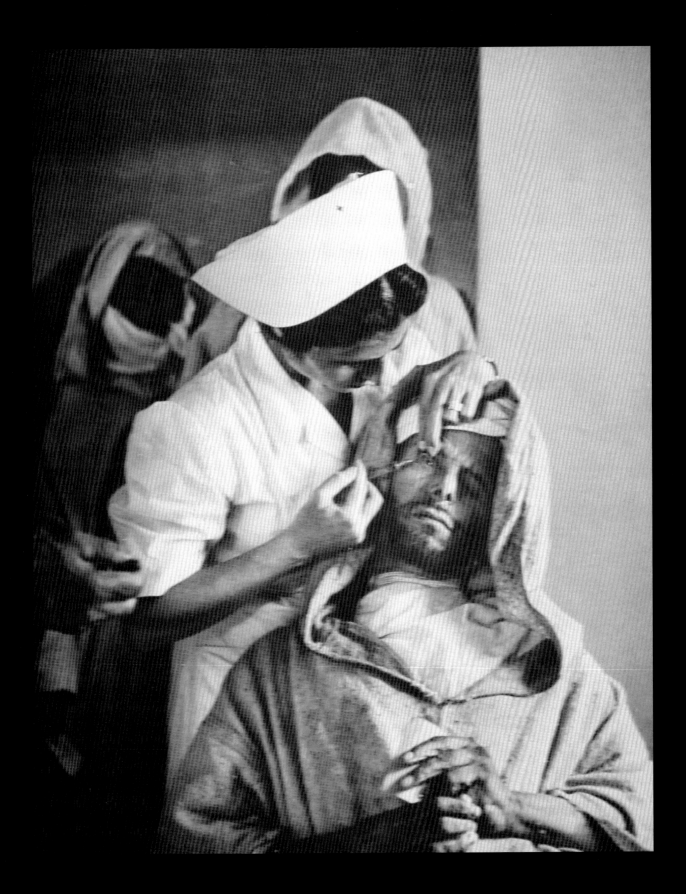

Left: Wax moldings and plaster models of World War I broken faces,
Musée du Service de Santé des Armées, Paris.
Top: French nurse treating a Berber farmer in Algeria during the 1950s.

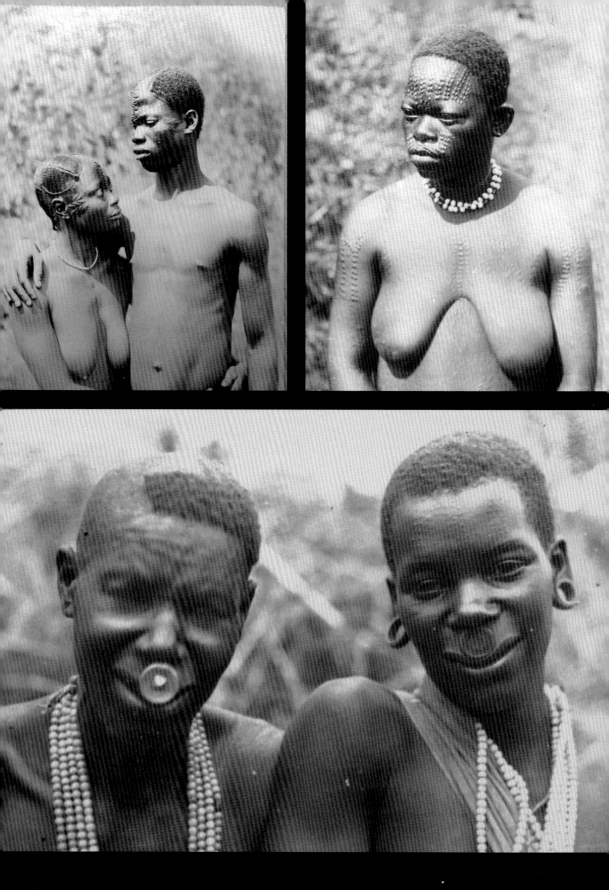

Intentional scarifications and mutilations in the Ngbaka tribe, Congo, Central Africa

Young man from the Bantu people, Africa.

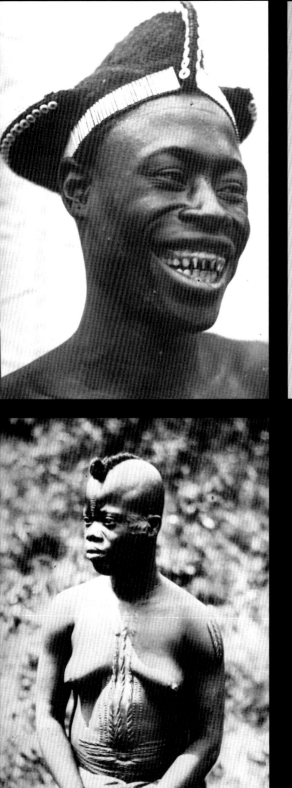

ERHARD SCHLESIER

DIE MELANESISCHEN
GEHEIMKULTE

Community repairing or building a hut

JEAN-PAUL SARTRE

THE COLONIZER AND THE COLONIZED

Only the Southerner is competent to speak of slavery because he alone knows the Negro; the puritanical and abstract Northerners only know Man as an entity. This fine line of reasoning is still in use: in Houston, in the newspapers of New Orleans and in "French" Algeria, since we're always Northerners to someone. The papers over there keep repeating that the colonizer is the only one qualified to speak of the colony. The rest of us that live in the mother country do not have his experience, so either we see the scorched earth of Africa through his eyes, or we won't understand a thing (…) In fact, racism is built into the system: the colony sells foodstuffs and raw materials cheap, and it buys manufactured goods from the mother country at very high prices. This singular trade is only profitable to both parties if the native works for nothing, or almost. This agricultural sub-proletariat cannot even count on an alliance with the least-favored Europeans: everyone lives off of them, including the "petits colons" [small colonizers] whom the big landowners exploit, but who are still privileged compared to the Algerians. The average income of a French Algerian is ten times that of a Muslim. Here the tension is born. To keep salaries and cost of living to a minimum, there must be great competition between native workers, so the birth rate must rise; but since the country's resources are earmarked for appropriation by the colonizers, the standard of living of Muslims continues to decrease for the same wages, with the population living in a chronic state of malnourishment. The conquest was achieved through violence; overexploitation and oppression need that violence to be sustained, hence the presence of the army. There would be no contradiction if terror reigned everywhere in the world, but the colonizer enjoys democratic rights over in the mother country that the colonial system refuses to the colonized. It is the system itself that promotes population growth to reduce the cost of labor, and it is the system again that forbids the assimilation of the natives: if they had the right to vote, their sheer numbers would shatter the system immediately. Colonialism denies human rights to human beings whom it has subdued by violence, keeps them by force in a state of destitution and ignorance that Marx would call a "subhuman" condition. Racism is inscribed in the facts themselves, in the institutions, in the nature of production and exchange; political and social regulation mutually reinforce each other since natives are subhuman and the Universal Declaration of Human Rights does not apply to them. Inversely, because natives have no rights, they are abandoned without protection to the inhuman forces of nature and the "iron laws" of the economy. Racism is already present, borne by colonialist praxis, engendered every moment by the colonial apparatus, sustained by relations of production that define two types of individuals:

for the one, privilege and humanity are one and the same. They become men by the free exercise of their rights. For the other, the absence of rights sanctions their destitution, chronic hunger, and ignorance, in short, subhuman condition. I have always thought that ideas take form from things and that they are already within man when he awakens them and expresses them to elucidate his situation. The colonizer's "conservatism" and "racism", his ambiguous relations with the mother country – everything is already given before he revives them into the "Nero complex". (…) There are neither good nor bad colonizers: there are colonialists. Among these, some deny their objective reality: carried away by the colonial apparatus, they perform every day what they condemn in their dreams and every one of their actions contributes to maintaining oppression; they will not change anything, or serve anyone and will find moral solace in their malaise, that is all. The others – by far the greater number – sooner or later accept themselves. (…) Conservatism begets the selection of mediocre men. How can this elite of usurpers conscious of their own mediocrity establish their privileges? By one means only: debase the colonized in order to exalt themselves, deny the natives their humanness, define them as simple privations. This isn't difficult, as it turns out, since the system already deprives them of everything; colonialist practice has engraved the colonial idea in things themselves; it is the movement of things that simultaneously designates colonizer and colonized alike. Thus oppression justifies itself through oppression: oppressors produce and use force to maintain the evils that make the oppressed, in their eyes, look more and more like what they would need to be to merit their fate. The colonizer can only absolve himself by systematically pursuing the "dehumanization" of the colonized, in other words, by identifying with the colonial apparatus a little more each day. Terror and exploitation dehumanize and the exploiter authorizes himself to pursue this dehumanization in order to exploit more. The colonial machine turns in a circle; it is impossible to distinguish idea from praxis and the latter from objective necessity. Moments of colonialism sometimes condition one another, sometimes blend. Oppression is first the hate of the oppressor for the oppressed. There is only one limit to this enterprise of extermination: colonialism itself. This is where the colonizer is faced with his own contradiction: "with the colonized, colonization disappears, and so does the colonizer". No more sub-proletariat, no more overexploitation: there would be a return to ordinary forms of capitalist exploitation, wages and prices aligning themselves with those in the mother country; it would spell ruin. The system wills both the death and multiplication of its victims. Any transformation would be fatal to it. Whether the natives

are assimilated or massacred, the cost of labor would continue
to rise. This laden machinery suspends between life and death
– and always closer to death than to life – those who are
compelled to drive it. A petrified ideology devotes itself
to regarding human beings as talking beasts. But it does so
in vain, for even to give them the harshest, most insulting
orders, it must begin by acknowledging them; and since they
cannot be constantly supervised, it must be resolved to trust
them. No one can treat a man "like a dog" if he does not first
regard him as a man. The impossible dehumanization of the
oppressed turns against itself and becomes the alienation of
the oppressor. It is the oppressor himself who restores, by
the slightest gesture, the humanity he seeks to destroy and,
since he denies it in others, he regards it everywhere as his
enemy. To escape this, he must mineralize himself, taking on
the opaque and impervious consistency of stone; in short, he
must dehumanize himself in turn. A relentless reciprocity binds
the colonizer to the colonized, his product and his fate. (…)
The colonial system is a form in motion, born around the middle
of last century, that will bring about its own destruction.
For a long time now, it has cost mother countries more than
it earns. France is being crushed under the burden of Algeria
and we now know that the war will be abandoned with neither
victory nor defeat when we will be too poor to pay for it. But
mostly, it is the mechanical rigidity of the apparatus that is
derailing it; the old social structures are pulverized, the
natives atomized, and yet colonial society cannot integrate them
without destroying itself. The colonized will therefore have to
rediscover their unity in opposition to it. The excluded will
assert their exclusion in the name of a national selfhood: it
is colonialism that creates the patriotism of the colonized.
Kept at the level of a beast by an oppressive system, they are
given no rights, not even the right to live, and their situation
worsens with every passing day. When a people has no choice but
how it will die, when it has received only the gift of despair
from its oppressors, what is left to lose? Its misfortune will
become its courage; it will make of its endless rejection by
colonialism, the absolute rejection of colonization. (…)

Jean-Paul Sartre, excerpt from the preface to *Portrait du colonisé,
Portrait du colonisateur [The Colonizer and the Colonized]* by
Albert Memmi, first published in *Les Temps modernes*, no. 137-138,
July-August 1957. Translated from French by Lisa Damon.

THE DEBT, 2013 AND THE CONTINUITY OF THE DEBT, 2013
DIPTYCH OF SLIDE PROJECTIONS AND INSTALLATION, VIEW OF THE EXHIBITION REPAIR, 5 ACTS,
KW – INSTITUTE FOR CONTEMPORARY ART - BERLIN, 2013.

Die Schuld Europas
gegenüber Afrika

170. La Grande Guerre 1914-15 — *Mise en batterie de pièces d'artillerie lourde de 155 court.*   A. R.

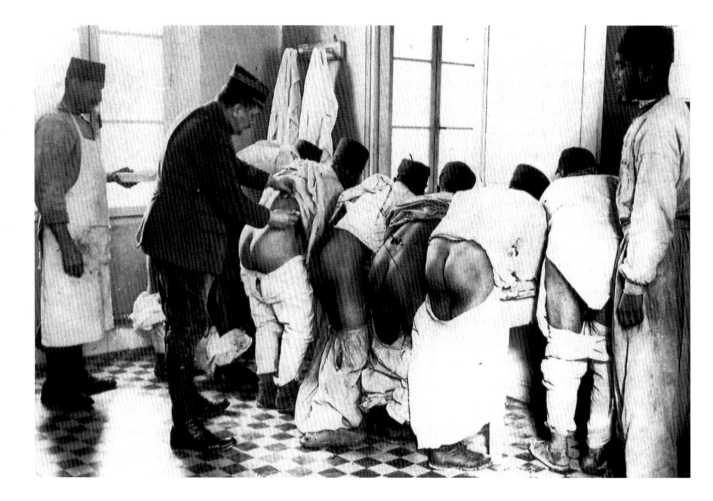

THE SOUND OF A RUMOR [1]

Never has the world been so rich and yet never has it been so out of joint. The gap between the remarkable accumulation of discoveries in technology and science in the fields of biology, neurology, reproduction, archeology, climate, astronomy, evolution and the difficulties faced by societies to resolve basic problems (access to clean water, to health, to food) is growing. We are simultaneously told that current globalization will bring a world of happiness for all and the planet cannot support what is presented as the desired way of life for all humanity.

The Promethean ideal of limitless growth and of Man's capacity to master all living organisms is more than ever with us. The push to colonize parts of the planet that had escaped human colonization or plans to colonize other planets on the old European model show how much the logic of colonization has become hegemonic. It is easy to trust science and technology. In recent decades they have opened new fields, comprehended areas that seemed impossible to explain, resolved problems that had remained unresolved for centuries. Who would not be excited and confident that humanity has a manifest destiny? Yet are technology and science not contaminated by Promethean thinking which promises that we, humans, will always be able to overcome the problems we create? Yet, the sound of a rumor is disturbing the scenario, the sound of discontent, of anger and frustration, of a desire for a post-Promethean way of life. At the entry of Chernobyl, an immense statue of a Prometheus now stands alone and forlorn. It is a monument to hubris and excess. The Promethean ideal has given the frame to the economy, science, governance and technology, it even stimulated them, as philosopher François Flahault has written (2). As humans, we do not like to have limits. Modernity opened the world wide to us, yet the "mechanisms that explain the extraordinary of modern society and thus its thirst for energy are the same that explain its tendency towards self-destruction" (3).

The current economic geography of exploitation and consumption is seeking to construct a seamless world, a "continuum of locations arrayed in a line from north to south and climate" producing an "equilibrium" rather than a specialization of nations (4). This project, which links climate, demography, geography and economy, ignores thanks to the neat clarity of numbers and the fascination brought by algebraic formulas, the materiality and immateriality of human lives, flesh, bones, language, dreams, hope, anger, joys and sorrows, conflicting passions and interests. In the world of numbers, the technologies of power erase the singularity of each life. Capital mobility and increasing freedom of trade suggest a model of a free place for everybody whereas the freedom of the few rests on the immobility of the many.

The world of the "free" throws a veil on the world of the billions held in bondage. Gender, race and class still constitute the nexus through which the global workforce is organized. The figures of the migrant and the refugee have become the figures upon which many of the problems of our age concentrate: new social inequalities, new wars, new forms of xenophobia and racism, new crises. They flee wars, dictatorship, poverty, desertification, floods. They disturb a global order based on national sovereignty and established borders. Yet, it must be said that their status as "illegals" benefits both the sending and receiving countries. They belong to the long history of the fabrication of precarious lives, of superfluous beings and to the long history of organization on the global scale of a mobile, gendered and fragile workforce.

They stand apart in a world of riches, in which a new market has emerged for the increased number of millionaires, exclusive spas, hotels, private jet companies, specialized travel companies and shops, and golf courses dedicated to the rich are multiplying. Parties are once again magnificent, the rich seek to outdo one another in lavishness, pomp and the flaunting of wealth. Palaces and chateaux that had become mere museums have now been reclaimed for balls and banquets. Everything must be sumptuous – diamonds and gemstones, silk, statin, cars, tables, dinners, yachts... Far away, kept from entering the grounds of lavish parties, young women and men stare at the sea and set out on flimsy boats; they hope to make the crossing that separates them from the bright lights of the cities. Their corpses litter the deserts of Africa, the coastlines of Europe, the mountains of Turkey, the waters of the Indian Ocean. New borders are being drawn to contain these pariahs, though wealth circulates freely.

The Charons of our neoliberal age are not carrying the souls of the dead across the Styx but living human beings. Yet they could cry, as the Charon of Dante's *Divine Comedy*: *"I come/To take you to the other shore across/Into eternal darkness, there to dwell/In fierce heat and in ice"* (5). Those who succeed in crossing the Styx are taken into the eternal darkness of the seas or into the fierce heat and ice of a life in the margins of society, in the shadows of society. The small boats sinking in the waters of Lampedusa and the *kwasa kwasa* (6) sinking in the waters of Mayotte are the coffins of those who do not make the crossing. The ones who manage to make the crossing camp at the gate of the rich cities. They glimpse the beauty of gardens and palaces. But the poor, the vulnerable are condemned to obscurity. "We do not disapprove of them, we do not reproach them anything but we do not see them", wrote John Adams (7). The lives of the oppressed are denied existence, their lives register when they die in mass.

There are the dead and there are the dead.
Ours are more easily forgotten.
Because they were born on a forgotten shore of the world.
The world of the powerful has no pity for the People of the Dhow (...) How can I be a foreigner or an illegal in the country of my ancestors?
Soeuf Elbadawi, *Comoros* (8).

What is needed to break the silence is what has always been needed: solidarity. In Tunis, Algiers, Dakar, Mayotte, Lampedusa, Calais and in other cities around the world, associations, artists, jurists, mayors and scholars are mobilizing to help migrants and refugees. This is why states have been criminalizing solidarity with refugees and migrants. European laws against refugees and migrants have hardened. The projects Eurosur and Frontex have been reinforcing the regulations protecting Fortress Europe. Italian fishermen who rush to save people on sinking boats are subjected to heavy fines (9); in France, in a 1991 interview, former president Giscard d'Estaing used the expression "immigration-invasion" and proposed to abolish the principle of *jus soli* whereby a child born in France is automatically a French citizen. Since then, conservatives and the National Front have lobbied to replace *jus soli* by *jus sanguinis*. A 2005 law made it illegal to feed, house or help the "sans papiers" (the law was repealed in January 2013) (10). In 2013, 15 000 Roms are said to threaten a nation of 62 million.

Though the transnational migrant has become the figure through whom fear and xenophobia are activated by political parties, migrants represent only 3% of the world's total population and only 1/3 of this 3% comes to Europe, the others are moving from southern to southern countries. States regulate migrations as harshly as Europe. The figure of the migrant and refugee challenges our certitudes and comfort. "One day, I may become that person", we think and the sentiment translates either into fear or into empathy. Fear is manipulated by political parties and corporate media and nowhere is this more glaring than in Europe, where the poor are encourage to wage war on other poor. The poor are always afraid to become poorest or to be confused with the poorest. This legitimate fear is instrumentalized by political parties and corporate media which seek to racialize rights.

If European policies about migrants and refugees have come under scrutiny, it is because on the one hand Europe represented itself as the land where human rights were invented, where inalienable principles about the individual were elaborated and on the other hand, because once Europe dominated three quarters of the planet, subjugated peoples, instituted regimes of exclusion and racial discrimination and pillaged the wealth of conquered countries. That Europe became "indefensible" (11). Colonization distilled a "poison into the veins of Europe, and slowly but surely, the continent proceeds towards savagery" (12). Europe must enter the process of its own decolonization.

In the 18th century, Europe's unsurpassed technology in weaponry, acumen to play on rivalry between indigenous groups and ruthlessness allowed a shift in the cartography of power. Despite continuous resistance, Europe's hegemony lasted until the independences in the second half of the 20th century. Yet, its hegemony never went without resistance, unexpected contacts and exchanges. Artists, writers and scholars challenged Europe's alleged superiority from the first moment of colonization. Their words and images constructed an alternative library. The long history of their critique culminated at the 1955 Bandung Conference. During this watershed event, leaders of the twenty-nine newly independent countries challenged the European cartography of power and provincialized Europe. "The despised, the insulted, the hurt, the dispossessed – in short, the underdogs of the human race – were meeting. Here were class and racial and religious consciousness on a global scale. Who had thought of organizing such a meeting? And what did these nations have in common? Nothing, it seemed to me, but what their past relationship to the Western world had made them feel. This meeting of the rejected was in itself a kind of judgment upon the Western world!" wrote Richard Wright (13). Africa and Asia reaffirmed their millenary connections interrupted by European colonialism and insisted on the role of culture

in constructing a new world. Though Bandung was also pregnant with tensions and contradiction, the final resolution mapped a multipolar world (14).

Europe is no longer the center of gravity. It has been further provincialized by re-emerging powers in Asia, South America and Africa, we are told. It may be interesting to wonder what has really been provincialized. European thought? Yes, to a certain extent but certainly not European banks or arms industry. European peoples? Perhaps. It depends which social class we are observing. The poorest are trying to survive, they attempt to migrate to the richer countries of Europe or to move to their former colonies now "emerging powers" (Portuguese in Brazil, Angola, Mozambique; Spanish in South America. The French still have their overseas territories where they receive susbtantial financial, cultural and social benefits and higher salaries than in France for the same job). Should we rejoice? There is certainly a comprehensible element of schadenfreude. Yet, if we look at the global economic and social model, we may want to hold our expression of joy. We observe the same Promethean model rooted in European thought at work in the world and if the axis of power is moving towards Asia, the accumulation of wealth still rests on forced labor, the organization of a mobile, gendered and precarious workforce, and the production of goods for global consumption based on the principle of obsolescence. The world has embraced the ideal of limitless growth and of man's capacity of mastering all living organisms. Post-colonial states adopted the politics of growth of the West (with the full support of the Western Left): industrialization, construction of huge infrastructures (roads, dams – "the new temples of India" according to Nehru), urbanization and production turned towards export. Nation-states are now following the European Bank, the IMF and World Bank policies. The manipulation of nationalism, tribalism or chauvinism that was connected to European colonialism is now common politics. Frantz Fanon's lesson about the pitfalls of national consciousness has been forgotten. Fanon wrote that the battle of colonialism "does not run straight away along the lines of nationalism". Otherwise, it will be an "empty shell, a crude and fragile travesty of what it might have been" and soon enough societies will "pass to ultranationalism, to chauvinism, and finally to racism." The "new humanism" invoked by Frantz Fanon, Amilcar Cabral, Aimé Césaire and others may then be neither "an emaciated universalism" nor a "walled segregation in the particular or dilution in the universal" (15).

The mobilization of anti-racist groups have made the criminalization of migrants more visible. But some of the borders where migrants are retained and sent back are not those we associate with Europe and they remain invisible. In the Indian Ocean, the border between the French department of Mayotte and the islands of the Comoros archipelago; in South America, the longest border of France with a foreign country, the border between French Guyana and Brazil; in the Atlantic, the coasts of the Canaries and the Azores; in the Caribbean, the coasts of Martinique, Guadeloupe and St Martin.

Yet Europe is far from being the only continent to criminalize migrants. In Africa, in the last ten years, more than eight million (8,000,000) Congolese left their country because of instability caused by armed conflict. So too did the Sudanese, and many people in the north of Mali with the Touareg group, Al-Shabab in Somalia and so on. They fled to African countries where they experienced discriminations and xenophonbia. In Asia, female and male migrants are deprived of rights. Moments of international festivity – the Olympic Games, the World Cup – are built upon the brutal exploitation of internal or external migrants. Rape, torture, humiliation belong to the structure of power. In South Africa, incidences of xenophobic violence are increasing and migrants and refugees speak of constant police harassment (16).

The contradiction between capital's need for a mobile workforce and a state's need for defending its borders against the "invasion" of refugees and migrants is always worked out for the benefits of neoliberal economy. In fact, "the transnational division of labor is shaped simultaneously by global capitalism and systems of gender inequality in both sending and receiving countries" (17). In many countries, the racialization of the growing care industry has led to a global trade in women which has been "immensely profitable to sending governments and entrepreneurs, and highly economical to the governments that recruit them and the elite who employ them" (18). The majority of migrant women are held in "conditions of debt bondage" (19).

The broken lives, broken bones, broken hopes of refugees and migrants have built an immense library of the intangible and of testimonies about the cruelty and brutality of the economy of predation. Recovering their voices and their words has long been the work of those who want to keep alive their existence. The world of migrants and precarious lives is caught between "opposite turns of the 'denationalization of economies' and 'renationalization of politics' (which) result in their conflicted incorporation as denied workers yet rejected citizens of receiving nations" (20). The current situation of female migrants reveals clearly the perpetuation of the racialization of the workforce. The new technologies of control (e-governance, biometric identification) contribute to diffuse microphysics of power that reinforce the process of racialization.

LIQUID CEMETERIES

Ya l-babur, ya mon amour
Kharrejni men la misère
oh boat, my love
take me out of misery
(rim-k) going far away
in my country I feel humiliated
I'm tired and I'm fed up
(rim-k) that's right.
Reda Taliani and 113, Algeria (21).

Among the great cemeteries of the world where disposable and superfluous people are buried, oceans and seas occupied a special place. Throughout history, they have received the bodies of women, children and men dead without a sepulture, their flesh food for the fishes, their names lost to History. Oceans and seas are the liquid memorials of a forgotten humanity, victim of predatory economy.

When was human life transformed into a good to be trafficked and sold, bought and killed according to the caprice of its owners? It seems that human society has long been familiar with enslavement. The fabrication of precarious and fragile lives has a long history. The World Heritage's list of monuments is the list of monuments built by forced labor, whose foundations rest on the crushed bones of thousands of slaves. The world has been crisscrossed by the routes of slave trade, the Silk Road, the Road of cotton, tobacco, coffee, sugar and spices. During the Axial Age, armies needed to be paid in coins, which came from mines worked by slaves, wars were needed to capture slaves needed in the mines, needed for producing coins to pay mercenaries (22). But slavery was not racialized. It was between the 16th and 19th century, during the colonial slave trade, that being a slave and being Black became synonymous. The invention of Blackness as a social, cultural and social status went along with the invention of Whiteness.

It started when capitalism had to resolve a conundrum: how to reconcile the immobility of land and labor and the need for mobility (bringing goods to consumers and seeking to lower the cost of transportation). The immobility of labor was partly resolved through the organization on a global scale of a mobile workforce which was gradually racialized and gendered. African women, children and men were enslaved and sent to lands chosen to produce goods (coffee, sugar, tobacco, cotton...) needed by a growing class of customers. The history of a racialized and gendered mobility has long been a history of murder and exile.

The Atlantic became a vast cemetery for the bodies of millions of enslaved Africans. Their last sight was the sight of a vast expanse of water, the ocean their sepulture. On the other side of the African continent, the Indian Ocean also received the bodies of enslaved Africans and Malagasy. Though one could think that a rationalized approach would have sought to bring down the loss of women and men as merchandise, their disposability was part and parcel of the economic system. In the wealthy port-cities of Liverpool, Bristol and Nantes, slave traders were careful to recover their loss using the same claims as those used for manufactured goods. The predatory economy of colonial slavery rested on a logic in which bodies were accounted along with donkeys, tables and furniture, and losses were covered by insurance. When in 1819, thirty slaves were thrown overboard from the French boat *the Rodeur*, "a ground was laid for a claim on the underwriters, by whom the cargo has been insured, and who are said to have allowed the claim, and made good the value of the slaves just destroyed" (23). The cost of transport of disposable people is today absorbed by the victims themselves, an advantage for both sending and receiving countries. As I have said, the need for a mobile workforce and the laws against "illegal migrants" are not contradictory. Both lead to precarious and fragile lives so that migrants and refugees remain dependant. The process of creolization that was at work in the plantations – the "seasoning" of new slaves, i.e. teaching them how to work, to act with other slaves or their owner, how to speak, by creolized slaves – and which was borne by slaves is still at work. Migrant communities bear the burden of labor market functions (recruitment, training) (24). They teach new migrants how to circulate in the city, where to go and what to do and not do.

"Sirens have changed since Homeric times, those who intone their lugubrious cants have dark skin and braided hair stuck on their skull, brown seaweeds that they tear away by handfuls," Nathalie M'Dela-Mounier, *France* (25). The Mediterranean and parts of the Indian Ocean are the liquid cemeteries of our Neoliberal Age. Women and men tell the story of a departure at night, of their dealing with the smuggler, of a boat carrying too many people, of babies and small children forced into silence so their cries do not attract the police, of men or women jettisoned to relieve the boat, of the lack of drinking water, of the fear and the stress, of the boat capsizing, of the panic, of the fishermen who tried to save the shipwrecked or those who continued their route deaf to their cries, of those who drown, of the search by the authorities, of the floating cadavers, of the cadavers found later in the fishermen's nets... (26). The small gestures of empathy, charging the battery of the cell phone for free, offering clothes, coffee, arms...

"In the public dump lies at the moment a small amount of boats, while more than 200 ships have been burned in September 2010. Someone burned all these boats, canceling de-facto the biggest contemporary evidence of the immigration phenomenon in the Mediterranean, in Lampedusa, and in Europe in general. It is still not possible to rescue nor to buy some of these boats: so they lie abandoned, waiting for destruction, under Lampedusa sun" (27).

Close to 20 000 women, children and men have died since 1988 in the waters of continental Europe. "As things stand we are just building a cemetery within our Mediterranean sea," said the Mayor of Malta when a boat carrying more than 200 migrants capsized on 11 October 2013 (28). The images of overloaded boats strike our imagination (29). They evoke exodus, women and men fleeing terror, misery, torture, seeking refuge, hoping that a feeling of common humanity will prevail. Yet, as we look at their visages, as we contemplate their gaze, realizing that they have seen and endured terrible things, we know that the reception is becoming increasingly hostile. The 10 000 to 30 000 arrivals in Lampedusa every year constitute and invasion for panicking Europe. The "cost" of migrants and refugees is always presented as the proof that they are a heavy burden on societies. We are told daily that they do no want to integrate, they have different values, they lie to authorities, they are not deserving empathy, they are not thankful enough, they should force their own government to resolve their problems of poverty, lack of health facilities, lack of jobs... Nothing is said of the asymmetry of power, of the routes of inequalities.

Studies show that it is the more educated who try to migrate. The journey tests their intelligence, their resourcefulness, their resilience and their courage. We should admire their bravery, and temerity. They go over mountains, survive in hostile countries, reconstitute communities. Their stories should be taught in school as lessons of indomitable courage and hope. We must listen to their incredible journeys, their tales of woe, their humor, their songs. Upon their arrival, the survivors are housed in terrible conditions. In Lampedusa, they often are a thousand in a place built for 250.

Details of the crossing are few. A survivor of the crossing between Anjouan and Mayotte tells that a smuggler will leave Anjouan once he has collected 1 500 Euros, the price per person is around 100 Euros, boats built to carry eight persons will carry between twenty to forty. During his own crossing, the narrator counted twenty five passengers, two pilots, luggage and two hundred liters of oil (30). Though many dead are not accounted for, the estimate in the waters of Mayotte is 150 dead per year, mostly women and children who cannot swim. We must be careful with the term "migrants" or "refugees," it tends to collapse under a unified category a myriad of experiences and it is necessary to remind ourselves that we are speaking of the experience of one woman, of one child, of one man, with their own singularity, their private thoughts and dreams *and* of a collective experience. Migrants and refugees often do not want to be considered passive victims. During the Lampedusa Festival held each year, their words can be heard breaking the clichés about their reasons to migrate which are diverse and complex (31).

The people and artists of Lampedusa have elaborated different answers to the increasing hostile Italian and European laws. Contemplating the wrecks that have accumulated a cemetery of small boats in the middle of their city, Giacomo Sferlazzo of the local association Askavusa suggested to create a Museum of the Immigrants with his friends. Scraping together the 400 € in monthly rent among themselves, they found a small place. They collected 800 objects on the beach and in the "boat cemetery." Others are items that less fortunate refugees were carrying with them when they died. The objects are displayed on wooden boards. They are what "the refugees have lost or left behind: a comb, a pot, an ashtray, a telephone book, a mirror, a single sneaker, Korans and Bibles" (32). They also "have a folder full of photographs they have collected. The pictures are washed out from the salt water and yellowed by the sun; only the outlines of faces are still recognizable. Here, a woman smiles shyly into the camera; there, a group of young, confident men flash victory signs." "The pictures are still beautiful," D'Ancona, another founder of the museum says, "they're memories of lost lives" (33). "These aren't just objects. They're clues that tell us something about people's dreams" (34).

"Yo pa renmen Ayisyen, men yo renmen konpa
yo pa renmen Ayisyen, men yo renmen Ti Payis."
Admiralty, Guadeloupe (35).

PROMETHEAN ENGINEERING

"Creative destruction" which recognizes change as the one constant in capitalism, has become the centerpiece for modern thinking on how economies evolve (36).

In June 2013, the New York Times reported that "China is pushing ahead with a sweeping plan to move 250 million rural residents into newly constructed towns and cities over the next dozen years.... The ultimate goal of the government's modernization plan is to fully integrate 70 percent of the country's population, or roughly 900 million people, into city living by 2025... The country's new prime minister, Li Keqiang, indicated at his inaugural news conference in March that urbanization was one of his top priorities" (37). The Chinese government declared that its plan was necessary if China wanted to keep its rate of economic growth: "If half of China's population starts consuming, growth is inevitable," said Li Xiangyang, vice director of the Institute of World Economics and Politics, part of a government research institute. "Right now they are living in rural areas where they do not consume" (38).

Chinese technocrats have adopted the ideology that links production, consumerism and growth: if more citizens lived in cities, consumption would rise, and raising consumption is considered the key to creating a sustainable economy over the long term because exports and investment-led growth are faltering. Already around 20 million Chinese are moving to the cities every year. It has been the greatest shift in human history with 150 million moving from the country to the city so far (39). An additional 300 million to 400 million people – more than the entire population of the United States – are expected to move from the countryside to the city over the next 30 years, according to China's Development Research Center, causing the China's urban population to rise from 47 to 75 percent. The Chinese government has well absorbed the old lesson of capital: wealth rests on the capacity to organize a mobile workforce kept in a precarious status. Indeed, as Kam Wing Chan has shown, "the success of 'Made in China' is inextricably meshed with the story of migrant workers toiling for subsistence wages to produce for exports" (40). The 155 million rural migrant workers have been, he said, the "backbone of China's export industry since the 1990s" (41). And more women and children participate now in migration to cities.

This formidable and unsurpassed plan of internal migration in a single country belongs to the Promethean ideal. However, this Promethean feat is not rooted in "Chinese" thought. Europe gave it birth. To European philosopher Immanuel Kant, the sublime "raise the forces of the soul above the height of the vulgar commonplace, and discover within us a power of resistance of quite another kind, which gives us courage to be able to measure ourselves against the seeming omnipotence of nature" (42). The "seeming omnipotence of nature," the expression says it all about the refusal to admit the interdependency between human beings and nature. The European idea that Man is a natural colonizer who has received the Earth to tame and colonize to its will and content contaminated modernity.

To Europeans, the colonization of the world meant bringing progress to unenlightened peoples. Nature was either untouched and virginal, to be preserved without the presence of indigenous peoples unable to appreciate fully the aesthetics of Nature, or savage and in need of being tamed. Nothing would stop progress, neither humans nor nature. The history of colonization was the history of devastation to the environment on an unprecedented scale. This is not to say that before the arrival of Europeans in countries of the "South" there had been no projects which required forced labor, deeply affected the environment and had not led to famines, migrations, or desertification. Certainly not. But environmental historians agree on the turning point operated by European colonization thanks to European discoveries in weaponry. Colonial environmental change started with colonial slavery (43). European colonial empires witnessed the greater exchange across continents of plants, animals and human beings. Post-slavery colonization pursued these policies supported by new technologies in agriculture and transportation.

The ideal was adopted by the Soviet Union and the postcolonial world, dominated global policies during the Cold War, and has found a new life today. And independent nations adopted the same policies (44). The Cold War (1945-1989), which was so important in shaping priorities in the economy for decades, (and whose legacies are still with us), led to similar policies around the world, shaped by a belief in technocratic solutions, by the links made between demography, agronomy, water management and botany, by the control of the environment, and by space technology. The "Cold War was the twentieth century's longest war, fought extensively on a global scale across a range of environments" (45). It was in the Soviet Union that these policies and practices led "to environmental degradation on a scale that may be exceeded only by current practices in China" (46).

The Soviet Union fully embraced Promethean thinking. Stalin invited writers to become the "engineers of the soul." Literature should service industrialization and identify those who resisted, the "enemies of the people" (47). Nothing would resist the will of the people, "Soviet rivers will flow/where Bolshevik will dream them to flow," said a popular song. And deserts would be "liquidated" (48).

These policies, whether in the North, South, West or East have had similar consequences: reinforcing the power of science and technology (hence of business) over politics. They have perpetuated a form of killing that has become "commonplace undertaken through degrading environmental conditions to affect quality of water, hygiene, nutrition and healthcare" (49).

IF GHOSTS COULD SPEAK

In *Nostalgia for the Light* (*Nostalgia de la luz*, 2010), Chilean filmmaker Patricio Guzman traveled to the Atacama Desert. In the vast lunar landscape, high altitude and dry climate have made it the ideal site for a huge new observatory opened in 1977. Astronomers could start to peer deep into the cosmos in search for answers concerning the origins of life. Nearby, lay the remnants of the Chacabuco Mine prisons, the concentration camps instituted by General Pinochet for political opponents. Bodies were buried in secret mass graves in the desert. For years, wives and sisters of the disappeared have sifted through the sand searching for body parts of loved ones, dumped unceremoniously by Pinochet's regime. They will continue their daunting task in the colossal desert, they said to Guzman, until death overtakes them. One interviewee suggested that Chile needs an observatory that can look at its own landscape, find the missing bodies, uncover and root out all its unresolved agony. The contrast between the infinite far away, galaxies of dying stars, and the infinite fragments, bits and pieces of bones mixed with the desert's sand, powerfully evokes the power of human imagination and need for mourning, for giving the dead the sepultures they deserve. The women's search for a memory of a memory is poignant. It finds an echo in the certitude of a Tunisian mother convinced that her son did not die in a shipwreck but rather that he has succeeded in reaching Europe but cannot call her. She worries for him, she imagines his loneliness, she prays for him (50).

Wandering souls and ghosts are haunting our planet. If they could speak, the words of those fabricated as disposable and superfluous would tear the veil of hypocrisy and reveal the cruelty and brutality of an economic system based on predation.

Françoise Vergès is currently a Consulting Professor at the Center for Cultural Studies, Goldsmiths College, University of London, and president of the Comité pour la Mémoire et l'Histoire de l'Esclavage (France). Françoise Vergès has written on vernacular practices of memories, on slavery and the economy of predation, the ambiguities of French abolitionism, French republican colonialism, colonial and postcolonial psychiatry in the French colonial empire, Frantz Fanon, Aimé Césaire, French postcoliolnality, postcolonial museography, and the routes of migration and processes of creolization in the Indian Ocean world.

Notes

1. Derek Walcott, "The Sea is History," from *Selected Poems*, 2007, Farrar, Straus and Giroux. http://www.poets.org/viewmedia.php/prmMID/19972. All websites consulted 23 October 2013.

2. Françoise Flahault, *Le crépuscule de Prométhée. Contribution à une histoire de la démesure humaine*. Mille et Une Nuits, 2008, p. 25.

3. Jean-Pierre Dupuy, *Retour de Tchernobyl. Journal d'un homme en colère*. Le Seuil, 2006, p.99.

4. Masahisa Fujita, Paul Krugman and Anthony J. Venables, *The Spatial Economy*. MIT, 2000, p. 309.

5. Dante, *The Divine Comedy, Inferno, Canto III,* The Harvard Classics, http://www.bartleby.com/20/103.html

6. "Small boat" in shi mahoré.

7. Quoted by Hannah Arendt, *Essai sur la Révolution*, Paris, Gallimard, 1967, p. 97.

8. From the poem by Comorian writer Soeuf Elbadawi, *"Un dhikri pour nos morts"*. http://www.la1ere.fr/2013/04/23/un-dhikri-pour-nos-morts-le-drame-des-kwasa-kwasa-entre-les-comores-et-mayotte-30745.html

9. Bossi Fini Law, 2002; www.eurofound.europa.org , www.errc.org

10. "Sans papiers, le délit de solidarité supprimé" RFI, 3/01/2013, www.rfi.fr

11. Aimé Césaire, *Discourse on Colonialism*, translated by Joan Pinkham. Monthly Review Press, 2000, p.32.

12. Ibid, p.36.

13. Richard Wright, *The Color Curtain*, http://www.spunk.org/texts/pubs/lr/sp001716/bandung.html

14. http://www.fordham.edu/halsall/mod/1955nehru-bandung2.html

15. Letter by Aimé Césaire to Maurice Thorez, 24 October 1956. Translated by Chike Jeffers.

16. http://www.cormsa.org.za

17. Rhacel Salazar Parrenas, *Servants of Globalization. Women, Migration and Domestic Work*, Stanford University Press, 2001, p. 72.

18. Chang, op.cit. p. 151.

19. Ibid.

20. Ibid, quoting Sasskia Sassen, p. 247.

21. "Partir loin" written by Algerian rappers Reda Taliani and 113 whose first recording dates back to 2005: http://fortresseurope.blogspot.fr/2006/02/immigrs-morts-aux-frontires-de-leurope.html

22. See David Graeber, *Debt. The First 5,000 Years*. Melville House, 2011.

23. James Walvin, *The Zong. A Massacre, the Law and the End of Slavery.* Yale University Press, 2011, p. 201.

24. See Zygmunt Bauman, *Globalization. The Human Consequences.* Columbia University Press, 1998; Pheng Chea, *Inhuman Conditions.* Harvard University Press, 2006; Grace Chang, *Disposable Domestics. Immigrant Women Workers in the Global Economy.* South End Press, 2000; Pun Ngai, *Made in China. Women Factory Workers in a Global Workplace.* Duke University Press, 2005; Rhacel Salazar Parrenas, *Servants of Globalization. Women, Migration and Domestic Work.* Stanford University Press, 2001; Saskia Sassen, *Globalization and its Discontent. Essays on the New Mobility of People and Money.* The New Press, 1998 and *Losing Control? Sovereignty in an Age of Globalization.* Columbia University Press, 1996.

25. Nathalie M'Dela Mounier "Rivage Atlantique," October 2013, www.africultures.com.

26. www.malango-actualite.fr/.../mayotte-interception_de_kwassa_kwassa-;reunion.orange.fr/.../naufrage-d-un-kwassa-kwassa-plus-d-une-vingtaine-de-victimes;mjamawe.skyrock.com/3148815472-Immigration-clandestine-Naufrage-d-un-kwasa-kwasa.html; Migrants.outremer@rezo.net.

27. http://www.mariotrave.com/projects/civilians/2011/10/16/aska-vusa-lampedusa/

28. www.bbc.co.uk/news/world-europe-24499890

29. http://askavusa.blogspot.fr/

30. www.malango-mayotte.fr/immigration_clandestine/traversee.htm

31. http://fr.scribd.com/doc/154299567/LampedusaIn Festival2013-English

32. http://askavusa.blogspot.fr/

33. http://askavusa.blogspot.fr/

34. Ibid. Also, Charlotte Bonzonet, "Lampedusa, seule au monde," *Le Monde*, 14 October 2013.

35. "They do not like Haitians but they like their music; they do not like Haitians but they like Ti Payis" (Haiti). Declaration by Admirality, the singer from Guadeloupe, about anti-Haitian racism in Guadeloupe. http://www.migrantsoutremer.org/La-dispora-haitienne-en-Guadeloupe

36. A term coined by Joseph Schumpeter in his work entitled *Capitalism, Socialism and Democracy* (1942) to denote a "process of industrial mutation that incessantly revolutionizes the economic structure from within, incessantly destroying the old one, incessantly creating a new one."

37. www.nytimes.com/.../chinas-great-uprooting

38. Ibid.

39. "Invisible and heavy shackles" *The Economist*, 6 May 2010. The author invited the Chinese government to "unleash the buying power of its people." It seems that the 2013 decision is going in the direction of unleashing the buying power.

40. Kam Wing Chan, "Chinese Internal Migration," forthcoming in Immanuel Ness and Peter Bellwood, eds. *The Encyclopedia of Global Migration*. Blackwell Publishing. www.faculty.washinton.edu , p.1.

41. Ibid.

42. Immanuel Kant, *The Critique of Judgment*, The University of Adelaide Library, http://etext.library.adelaide.edu.au/k/kant/immanuel/k16j/part8.html

43. Joachim Radkau, *Power and Nature. A Global History of the Environment.* 2009; Alfred W. Crosby, *Ecological Imperialism. The Biological Expansion of Europe, 900-1900.* Cambridge University Press, 2004.

44. The critical literature about the politics of development is important and I cannot list here all the titles and still do them justice.

45. J.R. McNeill and Corinna R. Under, eds, *Environmental Histories of the Cold War.* Cambridge University Press, 2010, p. 235.

46. McNeill and Under, 2010, p. 21.

47. In 1933, Maxim Gorki led a group of one hundred twenty writers to a visit to a gulag, more precisely to the camps built for forced laborers constructing the canal of Bielomor between Leningrad and the White Sea, a canal 227 kilometers long.

48. See Frank Westerman, *Ingénieurs de l'âme.* Translated from the Dutch by Danielle Losman. Paris: Christian Bourgeois, 2004.

49. Eyal Weizman, *The Least of All Possible Evils. Humanitarian Violence from Arendt to Gaza*, Verso, 2011, p.86.

50. Tunisie: les limbes des rapatriés, http://fortresseurope.blogspot.fr

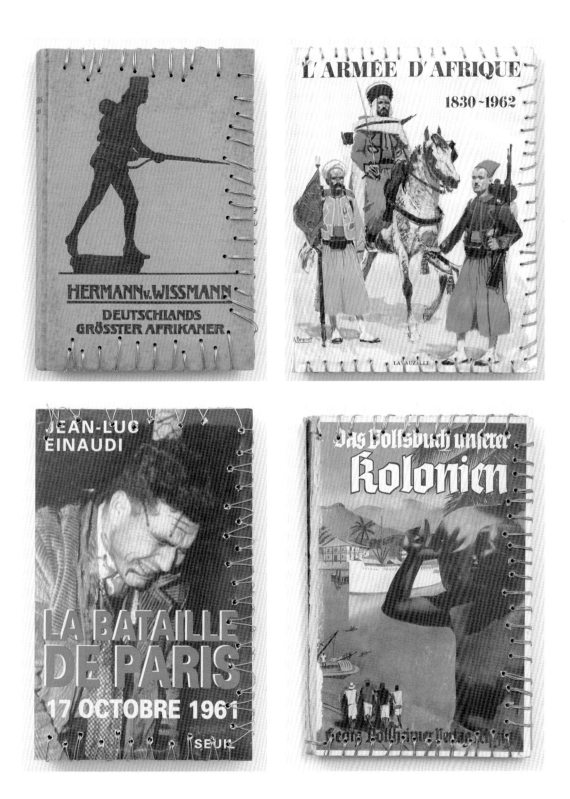

THE CONTINUITY OF THE DEBT, 2013.
INSTALLATION, METAL SHELVES, BOOKS SEWN WITH WIRE, PRINTS AND NEWSPAPERS FROM THE 19TH CENTURY,
BROKEN CERAMIC BUST OF A SENEGALESE INFANTRYMAN, LOGO OF THE BANANIA CHOCOLATE BRAND, TOTEM
MADE OF BANANIA METAL CANS AND OF THE HEAD OF A SOLDIER OF THE FRENCH COLONIAL ARMY.
LEFT: VIEW OF THE EXHIBITION REPAIR, 5 ACTS, AT KW, INSTITUTE FOR CONTEMPORARY ART - BERLIN, 2013.
TOP: DETAIL.

J'ACCUSE, 2012.
INSTALLATION, PHOTOGRAPHS, COLONIAL POSTCARDS, BANNERS, VINTAGE NEWSPAPERS, BOOKS, ARCHIVES,
VINTAGE BANANIA BOXES, SENEGALESE INFANTRYMAN'S JACKET, VIEW AT NEWTOPIA EXHIBITION - MECHELEN, 2012.

HARRAGAS, 2009.
205 X 300 X 5 CM,
RECONSTRUCTION OF GÉRICAULT'S PAINTING
LE RADEAU DE LA MÉDUSE WITH THOUSANDS
OF IMAGES OF ILLEGAL IMMIGRANTS,
INKJET PRINT ON CANVAS AND FRAME.

Top: 19th century etching showing three people blowing up a landmine.
Bottom left: 19th century etching showing a slave begging his master.
Bottom right: 19th century etching showing negotiations

19th century etching showing a white explorer crossing a swamp with the help of natives.

19th century etching showing a white
man shooting a talisman to destroy it.

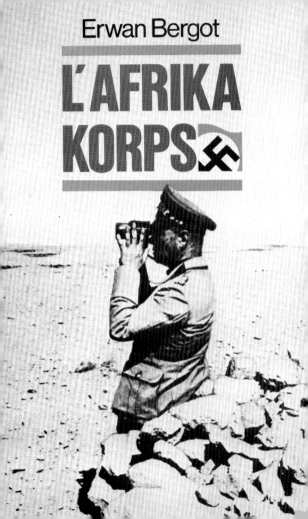

Great figures of German colonization (explorers and
influential men), excerpt from a Nazi propaganda book.

Hauptmann Hermann Wißmann mit seiner kleinen

uppe befreite Oſtafrika vom Menſchenraub der arabiſchen Sklavenhändler wie z. B. Tippu Tip

Captain Hermann Wissmann releasing East Africans from abduction by Arabic
slave traders, for instance Tippu Tip, with his small Askari troop.

Carl Peters, der Begründer von Deutsch=Ostafrika. Das erste Expeditionslager von 1884.
Unten das 1934 zu seinem Gedenken vom Dritten Reich in Hannover errichtete Ehrenmal

Carl Peters, founder of German East Africa. First expedition camp, 1884. Below his
picture, the memorial raised to his memory by the Third Reich in Hannover in 1934

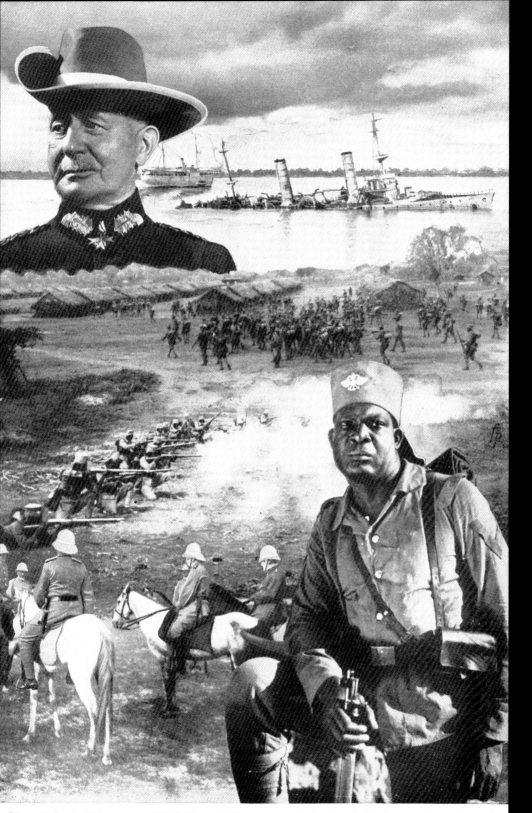

Die unbesiegte Schutztruppe Ostafrikas mit ihren treuen Askaris und ihr Kommandeur General von Lettow-Vorbeck. S. M. S. S. „Königsberg" im Rufiji-Delta und „Möve" im Hafen von Daressalam

East Africa's undefeated protection force with their loyal Askaris and their commander, General von Lettow-Vorbeck. S. M. S. S. "Königsberg" in the Rufiji delta and "gull" in the port of Dar es Salaam

Typen aus dem Gefangenenlager in Zossen

(Links beginnend) Araber, Senegalschütze, Indier, Turko, Marokkaner (2) Zuave.

Imprisoned infantrymen in a German camp near Berlin during World War I

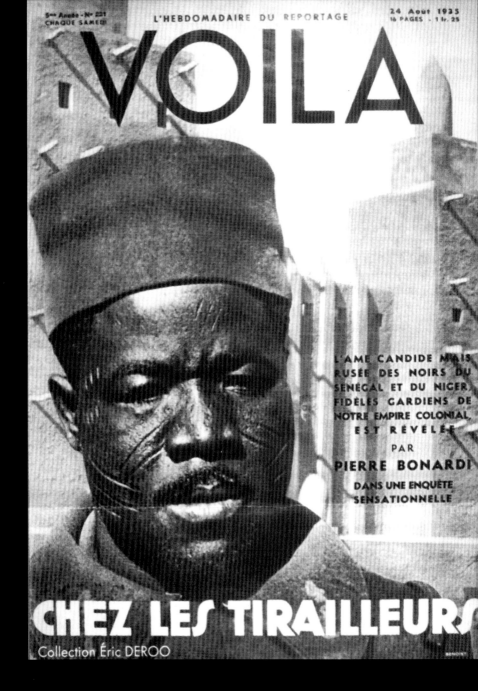

5ᵐᵉ Année · Nº 231
CHAQUE SAMEDI

L'HEBDOMADAIRE DU REPORTAGE

24 Août 1935
16 PAGES · 1 fr. 25

VOILA

L'ÂME CANDIDE MAIS
RUSÉE DES NOIRS DU
SÉNÉGAL ET DU NIGER
FIDÈLES GARDIENS DE
NOTRE EMPIRE COLONIAL,
EST RÉVÉLÉE

PAR

PIERRE BONARDI

DANS UNE ENQUÊTE
SENSATIONNELLE

CHEZ LES TIRAILLEURS

Collection Éric DEROO

Voilà weekly news magazine, 24 August 1935.
Founded by Gaston Gallimard and directed first by the Kessel brothers, then
Fels, the magazine was published up until the beginning of World War II.

4ᵉ RÉGIMENT
DE TIRAILLEURS MAROCAINS

CERTIFICAT
DE
BONNE CONDUITE

_Le_ ....

commandant le 4ᵉ Rég. de Tirailleurs Marocains

certifie que le ....

_né le_ ...., _à_ ....

département d ....

a tenu une bonne conduite pendant tout le temps
qu'il a passé sous les drapeaux et qu'il a constamment
servi avec honneur et fidélité.

_A_ ...., _le_ .... _19_ ....

A. M. CHOTEL · PARIS

Certificate of good conduct given to soldiers
in the French 4th regiment of Moroccan
infantrymen during World War I.

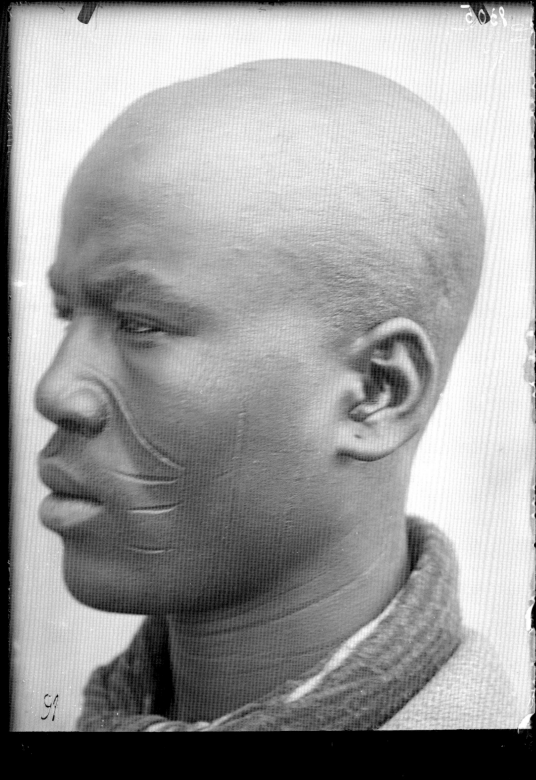

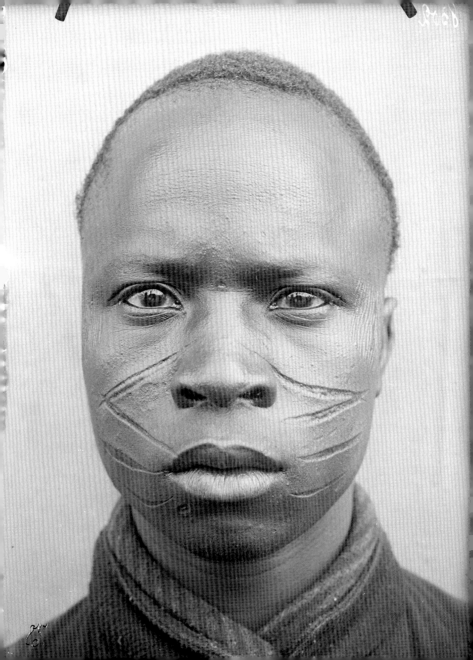

Clandestine immigrants approaching European borders.

JACQUES DERRIDA

VIOLATIONS OF THE RIGHT TO JUSTICE

(…) I do not know who invented the locution "sans-papiers" [without papers], nor how the terrifying expression "sans-papiers" took root little by little only to become legitimate recently. It is a whole process, sometimes slow and insidious, sometimes explosive, brutal, accelerated like a police raid in a church. The terrifying habit that allowed this word to acclimate itself to our lexicon deserves ample analysis. What we call, in one word, a "sans-papiers", is thought to be missing something. He is "sans" [without]. She is "sans" [without]. What exactly is he missing? He must be found wanting what the said papers represent. The law; the right to appeal to the law. We imagine that the "sans-papiers" is in fact "without rights" and virtually outlawed. By challenging his normality and civil identity, we are not far from challenging his identity itself. It seems as though he lacks more than just a determinate thing, one among many: he is naked and exposed, without rights, without recourse to the law, wanting of the essentials. With nothing. In reality, what he lacks, the lack we impute to him and that we want to sanction and punish, why hide it? I would like to reveal it by using a very precise term: worth. What worth? Of what is a "sans-papiers" unworthy? And why is a "sans-papier" considered unworthy? Why, and in the name of what is he refused a sense of worth? For French law and the French police do not simply mistreat the "sans-papiers", forcing them to squeeze into barely inhabitable spaces before amassing them in detention camps, "transition" camps, hunting them down, expelling them from churches and the country, often treating them with no regard for human rights, by which I mean the rights guaranteed by the Geneva convention and the European convention of human rights (art. 3), with no regard for the so-called rights of man and without regard for human dignity – which they are literally denied, explicitly refused, and I am weighing my words here. We deny dignity to those we accuse (…) of showing themselves "unworthy of living on our soil". (…) Let me therefore repeat my question: are we beginning to grow accustomed to the expression, a human being "sans-papiers"? To the situation, to the [legal] status "sans-papiers" that is an absence of status? The expression is French, purely French. It is an idiom. Someone in the newspaper the day before yesterday rightly pointed out that we now belong to a society of "sans" [withouts]: those who are "shelterless", "jobless", "homeless", "diploma-less", SDF (sans domicile fixe/without fixed abode) which we prefer to abbreviate as S. these days. A "sans-papiers" is not Musil's "man without qualities", but we must ask ourselves what happens to a society when it defines the source of all its problems as the "without" of others, of those who are deprived of

what society thinks we should have (for that is what we are
asked to believe today). If the expression "sans-papiers"
is undoubtedly a French idiom, we must nevertheless note two
things about it: one, the symptom is universal and first and
foremost European; it is the ill of all "rich" "neoliberal"
nations that, depending on the needs of its economies, welcome
or allow in from economically less well-off countries – most
often ex-colonies – a work force that is exploited until the
day that another situation, at once economic, political,
ideological, electoral, brings on a different calculation and
organizes a policy of racist, protectionist xenophobia, of
manhunts and deportation, with no regard for the principles
proclaimed high and loud by politicians and rhetoricians – on
the left and on the right. There is no country or nation-
state in the world today, especially among the rich capitalist
ones, that is not closing its borders, placing in hibernation
the principles of asylum and hospitality to the foreigner
– only good for times when "all is well" and "it is
useful" (between efficiency, service and servitude). After
several decades of an unprecedented crisis of the nation-
state, when millions of displaced people have taken to the
roads, what is left of the nation-state cramps up under
nationalist-protectionist, identitarian and xenophobic
convulsions, and produces a figure of racism both well-worn
and renewed. There is a word for "sans-papiers" in every
nation-state culture. In the United States for example,
we say "undocumented", and hunts for "illegal immigrants"
are organized. To speak seriously of the problem of French
"sans-papiers", to effectively fight against what is, let
us not forget, a singular human tragedy where every case is
singular and effects men, women and children in distress –
and is simultaneously a general phenomenon, the exemplary
symptom of what happens to the geopolitical sphere with what
we call neoliberal market globalization – we must therefore
take into account singular situations and the particular
case of France, and also the European political context
(what has been made or what we wish to make of Europe, of
the Schengen Agreement, for example, which is still not
applied in France) and a world supposedly in the throes of
"globalization". Besides, this concept of globalization is
quickly becoming the latest platitude, depository of the
worst confusions, not to say calculated mystifications.
(…) In terms of what is happening, of course, we must
understand, without forgetting the singularity of the
wrong, that analysis and struggles must be simultaneously
worldwide, European, national and local. Serious scholars
have demonstrated it: it is pointless to believe that certain
migratory flows can be stopped, but it is also pointless to

believe that these flows will surpass certain limits and especially, that they are dangerous; it is stupid and shocking to ignore, even from the point of view of the national interests of France and francophone culture, that we not only have responsibilities – the responsibility to recognize those who choose our country, our culture and our language (often for having already helped us while harshly colonized by France, and for example during the two world wars) – but that their choice is an opportunity for us. Some of our neighbors have been intelligent enough to understand this opportunity and take it: for example, close by in Europe, the Portuguese, the Spanish, the Italians have recently undertaken massive "regularization" programs. Against the backdrop of these analyses and worldwide struggles, we must never forget that the present policy of repression in France is not only a failure to live up to a tradition of honor and rights, not only an ignominious betrayal, it is also a lie and a gross mystification, the response to an imaginary threat that only serves as a convenient alibi to profound political failure. This failure, it must be said, does not only belong to the current majority government. Whether in terms of increasing unemployment, the market economy or speculation – the deregulation of which is an engine for destitution and marginalization – whether in relation to a horizon for Europe driven by simplistic calculations, by a false economic science and a mad monetarist inflexibility, etc., by power abandoned to the central banks; from all these standpoints, we must understand that the policies regarding the "sans-papiers" and immigration in general are an electoral diversion, a "scapegoating" operation, a pitiful maneuver to scrounge up votes, a small and ignoble one-upmanship to beat the Front National on its own turf. And let us never forget that if the first victims of this bankrupt strategy are our friends, our guests, the immigrants and "sans-papiers", what is put in place by the government is a system of police inquisition, recording, surveillance and quartering (on French and European soil). This machine threatens all liberties, the liberties of all, those of the "sans-papiers" and those of the "non-sans-papiers". (…)

Jacques Derrida, *Violations of the Right to Justice*, excerpts from a transcription of an improvised talk given on 21 December 1996 at the Théâtre des Amandiers (Paris) during a demonstration of support for the "sans-papiers," in *Marx en jeu*, editions Descartes et cie, 1997. Translated from French by Lisa Damon.

SELF-MAKING

LA PISTE D'ATTERRISSAGE, 2000-2002.
DIPTYCH OF SLIDE PROJECTIONS, MUSIC.

KADER ATTIA: Do you remember when we first met?

HÉLÈNE HAZÉRA: I remember a phone call to the newspaper office where I was showing off my marginal notability: "I would like to show you my work on the Algerian transsexuals of Boulevard Ney." I knew that transsexuals had paid a toll during the Algerian civil war and that the warm and resolute voice over the phone was that of my guilty conscience. Yes, I can remember your small apartment not far from that bar the Zorba (at the time it was the National Work Confederation headquarters), in Belleville. Yes, I can remember that huge slap in the face that sent me back to my transsexual prostitute past. Yes, I recall the beauty in those pictures about forced exile, the photograph of a small tray, a glass of tea and a biscuit, that brought a whole culture back to life. Pictures of transsexuals holding candles, wearing traditional dresses to celebrate a friend's birthday, confirmed my intuition: we are the guardians of traditions. The attention you brought to female "bledlings", to country girls (in contrast with city girls who always cope better in big cities) echoes one of my worries about the supression of farming cultures in France.
I had to find a newspaper willing to publish my investigation (they were scared of it), and then for two weeks, I didn't quit knocking from door to door. I spent entire nights in the cafes where these girls gather, I tamed a couple of them so they would tell me about their lives. I'd had Algerian friends before, and I even met the younger brother of one I knew very well who, after being deported back to Algeria, was murdered. Strangely enough, what I liked most in your work took shape in that search: the human. In your work, I saw the underlying power of that humanity: I also caught up with a friend from Pigalle I'd had no news of, and we haven't lost sight of one another since.
When I saw your slide show, tears often filled my eyes without me being able to distinguish sadness from the emotion born from beauty. And I cried a little about me, I must admit.

K. A.: What slowly started to interest me in my relation to boulevard transsexuals is the intimacy they share. I'm not talking about sexuality here, but their domestic lives interior. Where do they live? And how? Is it a frugal lifestyle? A comfortable one? What do they eat? French or Algerian food? Actually, what first attracted me was some strange desire for ethnology; an objective form for interpreting their personal worlds following the interpretation that I, the son of an immigrant, had been trying to reach for years. Uprooting, you know what it is, especially with this passion of yours for "rooted" music.

H. H.: German writers who couldn't go into exile invented the term "internal exile". In an article I wrote on Arabian (and Kabyle) scopitones in Barbès Boulevard, I said that in my youth, I would go rub my own "internal exile" up against those beauties. I just had to enter one of these Algerian cafés, face the scopitone machine and feed it with one franc coins in order to get my fill. I wouldn't dare compare the misery I felt at the time to that felt by the men who left their families to go looking for a job in France. Because I'd compared one of his writings on the racket of time passing to a poem by a poet from Texcoco Nezahualcóyotl, Guy Debord said that I was an "exocentric".
When Oum Kalsoum performed at the Olympia in 1967, I asked my mother if I could go. She said ok but the tickets were too expensive. I couldn't explain why I wanted to go, but there was an advertisement for the concert on Europe 1, the radio, and it appealed to my curiosity. It's one of the first records I bought, a 45-rpm vinyl record. My own rebellion wasn't through rock music but through Arabian music and French 78s.
You know I had to prostitute myself. We all mingled, we didn't really have a choice. Being friends with Karima, the Algerian transsexual, made me discover new things, especially Fadhela Dziria, the Arabian-Andalusian haouzi. But "the Andalus" reminded me of Pérotin the Great's French medieval music… because sure, I might be an executive's daughter (who grew up in the countryside for some time), but I'm still fascinated by what comes from the land, because of its power, its roughness and its grace. From an old Breton farmer lady singing a "gwerz" to a Bedouin lady singing and playing her bendir, it's a short path for those who open their heart and ears. The world changes really fast. Soon those with only one culture will be considered the true poor (but far less than those who only know superficial, universal media culture). I show the deepest respect to Edward Said, but nowadays, as soon as someone says they LOVE Arabian culture, they're called orientalists, and I think this is being excessive. Dinet is no orientalist at all, he's a passionate man. He's a convert, he's completed the Hajj. There again, a political vision overrides cultural vision. Because what is a culture? It's a photograph of a glass of tea on a tray and a gesture of the hand bringing an entire world back to the surface. The same way you can build a prestigious edifice with archeological stones.
I was a little Proustian there, wasn't I? However, I do find meaning in that… actually, yes, you're right. A culture is especially about some order or disorder that's urging to just climb back from the depths of history. As if this order/disorder was just expecting some reactivation to be performed again indefinitely. Without being nostalgic, which too often equals praising tarnished colors as some other truth, I always liked the way tales and stories were being passed on through generations, social layers, borderlines… even when they are quite improbable…

K. A.: I remember a friend of mine who lived on the boulevard. I introduced him to you, he was named after some chic perfume from the 80s, "Rochas", I think. I really liked him because he hadn't forgotten the storyteller tradition from where he was born, the Aurès Mountains. One day he told me about how, to "practicing" Muslims in his village, meaning those who seriously follow religious texts, anal penetration was more or less serious according to whom did what. In fact, the one penetrating is master of his actions and should be punished for that, while the one who gets penetrated is forgiven for he's feeling a pleasure only anal penetration can let you experience. He said that in Muslim culture, the penetrated is seen as irresponsible… but let's not linger over such unverifiable stories.
What I tried to translate through my own way of seeing the world, with a camera and sometimes a microphone, is the storytelling dimension of the transsexual world. And aren't Hijras from India, Bangladesh and Pakistan great story-tellers too? Then, I gradually started to wonder whether there was a given specific transsexual culture.

H. H.: It was Wladimir Horowicz who wrote, "Pianists? There are jews, homos and the bad ones…" I'm convinced you can find good heterosexual pianists, yet to me it's obvious that minorities tend to develop particular cultural attitudes. For someone who is being discriminated against, culture isn't mere entertainment. It's strictly survival. In the documentary

I directed for *La Piste d'Atterrissage*, I asked the girls I met what kind of music they listened to, and their answers were quite interesting. With Doriana, it was incredible; she would listen to all sorts of music, from Western classical to Arabian popular music, without mentioning her taste for "little Kabyle singers no one has heard of." To me, she was a true music lover. You once told me Arabian musicians tend to say that "the only ones listening to what we do are Sephardi Jews and transsexuals..."

When in Bombay, I asked Mahini which female singers she liked, and she answered: "I don't like contemporary singers that much, I prefer singers from the past" and I couldn't help laughing. I work in the music world in Paris and one of the greatest specialists on songs from the 50s is a woman who used to work at the Carrousel cabaret...

The first transsexual to undergo an operation when Magnus Hirchfeld found refuge in France was a painter named Marie-Joseph Le Poulain (1906-1991). In Montparnasse in the 30s, there was also a Hungarian transsexual sculptor, Anton Prinner (1902-1983). I have lots of friends who are artists, but usually what's being shown is the way cisgenders see transgenders, and not transgenders themselves. Is there a transgender culture? There's a culture of the memory of social and familial rejection, which you'll find in many societies. There's some common experience, an experience of going from one gender to another, of the obsession with this change. We still have to find some room in culture and though I may be a miscreant, I also believe there's some kind of spirituality waiting to develop... in some distant relation to shamans.

During the 80s, I ended up on Bugis Street, Singapore's transsexual street. There were Chinese, Malaysians and Indians; we would talk with each other. We all came from seemingly different cultures. Yet, it was clear we all had some really significant common points. How we would laugh! So when the queers would come and tell us it was neo-colonialist to say there was a relationship between "Western" transsexuals and Hijras, it made me giggle. I had a book by a French amateur writer telling about his stay with Hijras (though without stating he was intimate with them, of course). I lived in a "women's home", and one of them had this young transsexual she'd picked up in Marseille with her. She'd stumbled onto this book and left for India, to whatever town. Later, the Hijras heard about her and came in delegation to look for her, so that she would move in with them! This is just so wonderful... the fact we can be so distant yet so close to one another. This echoes Michel Foucault's sophism: "Homosexuality did not exist during the 19th century because the word did not exist." Still, there was a whole vocabulary, "mandrake", "sodomite", "he's playing in both teams" and as for "tribads"... people used to say they "played the Game of Flats." There sure are differences of course, according to which country you live in. Tahitian girls, Rae raes or Mahus for instance, give the impression their culture is less bothered by that, they have less trouble on the matter. But when you turn things around, there are a lot of similarities. As far as I'm concerned, I see some sort of unity crossing cultures in there.

K. A.: As an artist, I'm tired of being constantly associated to a given community, and I have transsexual friends who feel exactly the same. I think they just want people to stop bothering them about their identity, and that their only

wish is to be considered, appreciated, or perhaps not, for the artists they are. All in all, I understand them.

Nevertheless, artists always talk of what they know. Perhaps what they are on the outside, on the inside, or even both, why not. As you know, I have a passion for non-Western traditional arts. Do you know that in Dogon culture, in Bandiagara (Mali), it's quite common to see androgynous effigies depicting both male and female sexual attributes on one human-shaped body? It always reminded me of Aristophanes' story in Plato's *Symposium*: at first, men were made of two united bodies, woman-woman, man-man and woman-man. Then, because of the gods being jealous of their happiness, men were split into two, each half struggling all throughout life to find its missing part. It's a metaphor for a kind of love whose magnetic finality leads to the survival of the species. *The Symposium* is about politics but also, and this is essential, about a politics of love.

I once asked Pamela, who came from Algiers, if she believed in love. She'd just been dumped by her boyfriend who was stolen by some transsexual who was just as beautiful as her and had immensely slender legs. Pamela answered: "*Hanouni*, love is a show... a show in which you are the artist. When it's over, it's only for a new performance to start. This is what it means to be an artist: always on stage!" What my camera failed to catch was this astounding resignation for life. It was as if in every one of us, this desire for happiness sounded like some sort of "void", and that to all appearances, you had to take part in some social organizational system where you have to fake being happy. With her, it was impossible to have coffee or even take a single picture between 13:45 and 14:45. Facing her small color TV set, she piously watched each and every episode of her soap opera, *The Young And The Restless*. This habit enabled her to chat later in the day with the residents of her small building, which stood in one of the streets near Clichy Avenue. She would gossip with the concierge or cleaning ladies who lived in more chic flats, and they would tie, untie and retie the easy plot line of *The Young And The Restless* over and over again. "Everybody is allowed to dream, you know," she told me...

H. H.: Kader, what transsexual artists are facing is the fact that their works are not being exhibited, just like for a long time there was no room for female painters in museums, or the same way women's poetry was left out of poetry anthologies. The radio recently refused one of my works on Marceline Desborde-Valmore, the great 19th century poetess, just because she was "not famous enough." The woman Verlaine included in his "Poètes Maudits", the woman Baudelaire and Rimbaud adored... she was "not famous enough!"

My community is mostly a community of rejection. And here I'll paraphrase the Black Panthers: "There is no transgender problem, there only is a cisgender one." You know, I admire artists who show interest in transsexuals. I was the first to write about Stromholm's photographs of Paris' transsexual pioneers, which was as brave a work as *La Piste d'Atterrissage*. But again, I have girlfriends whose work simply isn't taken into consideration.

My friend Karima translated beautiful Algerian songs. I recall one day when I brought a Fedhila Dzirita tape from Barbès, just for the sleeve where she was dressed in a saroual and a turban. Karima had just lost her companion then, so I pressed the play button and the lyrics of the song were: "Long legged stork, have a walk to my lover's mausoleum..." Karima translated it for me as the song played, and it was the story of her life. You know how I love this work, *La Piste d'Atterrissage*, where on the occasion of a birthday, they put on traditional dresses and stand holding candles. I always felt something intensely magic, intensely serious in this picture... and also a strong link with cultural heritage.

(...) Dear Kader, these are sad days. Some political sewage is flowing back into the streets and the government is now making concessions. Transgender activism has become really violent. The violence we've suffered is now even being reproduced among us. I feel depressed, but still, I'm always ready. I also learned about Peter Seeger's death on the Internet (I used to sing *We Shall Overcome* when I was younger and I just loved the way he played the banjo), and Miklos Jancsos' death too. I used to go watch his films which were so pure... I never lost my passion for Magyar culture, this isolated small area inside Indo-European Europe. How terrible... (...)

I would like us to talk about poetical image. When I was twelve or thirteen, I read an old edition of *Les Orientales* by Victor Hugo (1829). Oh! The virtuosity of Hugo's lines on Djinns... At the end of this collection, there was a section with a short file on Arabian and Eastern poetry, along with translations from the era. It started in the ante-Islamic era up to today. The use of imagery was incredibly powerful. An ante-Islamic poem that had been translated by Ernest Fouinet remained in my mind, it was dedicated to a she-camel: "Her legs split up when running, like buckets from the well to his tent the man is carrying." In a few pages, Hugo delivered an overview on Arabian, Persian and Turkish poetry – up to Djellal Eddin Roumi – he even quoted a Malaysian pantoum: "Butterflies sport on the wing around/They fly to the sea by the reef of rocks/My heart has felt uneasy in my breast/From former days to the present hour." (1) The first and third lines in the first stanza become the second and fourth in the second stanza, and so on. Baudelaire later adapted the pantoum for French poetry, and it is one of his most beautiful poems : "The hours approach when vibrant in the breeze, A censer swoons to every swaying flower; Blown tunes and scents in turn enchant the bower; Languorous waltz of swirling fancies these! A censer swoons in every swaying flower; The quivering violins cry out, decrease; Languorous waltz of swirling fancies these! Mournful and fair the heavenly altars tower." (2)

Installations kind of annoy me. Once more, they are copies of surrealism. The puerility of the fashion world (the only good I could say about it would be to praise window dressers' work in department stores). When you started with that, I couldn't help but frown. Without even seeing your installations, I would rather look at your humanist photographs. I was suspicious to tell the truth. What I have against installations (because I've seen some grotesque ones) is how they belong to pure concept. Yet I went to the biennale in Lyon in order to actually see *Flying Rats* and I must admit that, face to face with this piece, facing this schoolyard with children made of seed paste being pecked by pigeons, it was an epiphany. Just like the release of the doves giving rhythm to the death of an old man in Stajyt Ray's *Pathar Panchali*.

In the same fashion, a pile of fridges can become a whole... a plastic bag flying in the air gets tied to the ground... it becomes like a Lois Fuller, or even Samia Gamal. A "fountain in love with itself," it becomes perpetual motion. Image and motion.

K. A.: Things take shape without us noticing it and then one day, someone names them. I was always suspicious of words, and even more of work titles. Words can be prisons and the terminology inherent to contemporary art hasn't improved with time, I must say. I prefer the word "sculpture" to "installation", because it is second to none, and "installation" is being used for anything and everything: you have installation programs, you install central heating, you install representatives, etc. This term, which is falsely contemporary, is actually a modern ghost.

Translated from French by Joël Mallet

Hélène Hazéra is a journalist, actress, radio show producer and director. Transgender woman, she notably worked for the newspaper Libération *where she became a music specialist until 1999. She is in charge of France Culture's radio show "Chanson Boum." A committed activist, she is the transgender committee manager for Act Up. She also writes documentaries about Algerian transsexual prostitutes in Paris or gay Iraqis who found refuge in England for the magazine* Têtu.

Notes

1. *A Grammar of Malayan Language*, with an Introduction and Praxis. Translation William Marsden. London, 1812. Google Book Search. Web. 04 May. 2014.

2. Charles Baudelaire, *Flowers of Evil*, New York: Ives Washburn, 1931. Translated by Lewis Piaget Shanks.

FROM THE SERIES ALTER EGO, 2002.
PHOTOGRAPHIC SERIES, SILVER PRINT, 110 X 180 CM.

COLLAGES, 2011.
3-CHANNEL FILM, 67 MIN, VIDEO STILL.

THE BODY AS A TARGET AND OBJECT OF POWER, 2010. SLIDE PROJECTION OF EROTIC POSTCARDS OF ALGERIAN WOMEN TAKEN BY FRENCH SETTLERS ON VINTAGE MAPS OF ALGERIA DURING COLONIZATION, VIEW AT GALERIE CHRISTIAN NAGEL, ART BASEL - BASEL, 2012.

FROM THE SERIES MODERN ARCHITECTURE GENEALOGY, 2014.
COLLAGES AND DOCUMENTS, CARDBOARD, SILVER PRINTS, GRAPH PAPER, PHOTOCOPIES, ENGRAVINGS FROM
VINTAGE BOOKS.

Méquinez (*Fig. p. 167*). — Dessin de G. Vuillier, d'après un croquis de M. Ch. Tissot.

Lili Elbe (1882 – 1931) was the first identifiable recipient of sex reassignment surgery. Elbe was born in Denmark as Einar Mogens Wegener and was a successful artist under that name. In 1930 Elbe went to Germany for sex reassignment surgery, which was experimental at the time. The first surgery, removal of the testicles, was done under the supervision of sexologist Magnus Hirschfeld in Berlin. The rest of Elbe's surgeries were carried out by Kurt Warnekros a doctor at the Dresden Municipal Women's Clinic. The second operation was to remove the penis and transplant ovaries, which were taken from a 26-year-old woman. They were soon removed in a third then fourth operation, due to rejection and other serious complications. She stopped painting, believing it to be something that was only done when she was Einar. The fifth operation was to transplant a uterus and was intended to allow Elbe, then nearing the age of 50, to become a mother. She soon after died of transplant rejection.

Dawn Langley Pepita Simmons (1922-2000) was a prolific English author and biographer. Born "Gordon Langley Hall", Simmons lived her first decades as a male. After sex reassignment surgery in 1968, Simmons wed in the first legal interracial marriage in South Carolina

(PAR-5)PARIS,March 27-(AP) - PROSTITUTES PROTEST - Prostitutes wearing masks go past policemen as they demonstrate near the Place de la Concorde, in central Paris, Wednesday over plans to close 270 apartments in the red light district's Rue Saint-Denis. The group of about 100 women were prevented by police from nearing President François Mitterrand's Elysee Palace, their main objective. (AP WIREPHOTO) (gk 41540photo/pascal baril)1985

Prostitutes protest, Paris, 1985.

In the reality of things, architecture and urban planning answer the essential functions of modern man. And who is this modern man? It is an immovable entity (the body) endowed with new consciousness.

Le Corbusier, *The Radiant City*, 1924.

Le Corbusier painting in the nude at Eileen Gray's villa, summer 1939.

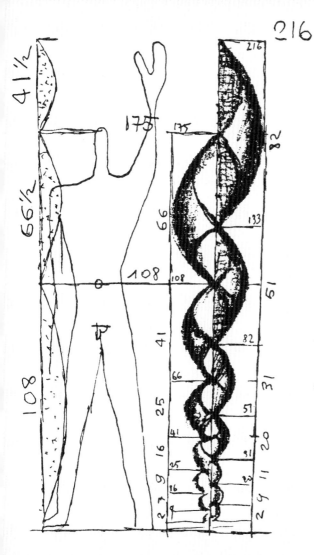

216

à bord du Cargo
" Vernon S. Hood "
Le 6 janvier 1946
LC

Une Beauté de Polynésie

Une Beauté Géorgienne

Une Beauté de la Terre de Feu

Cl. Andrew-Apia.

Cl. Reutlinger.

Cl. Ellis and Valéry, London.

Cl. Neurdein.

Une Beauté Noire

Beautés

Blanches

Une Beauté Arabe

Cl. Bourne et Sheperp, Bombay.

Beautés

Jaunes

JEUNE FILLE BIRMANE

UNE OUEDDA DE L'ÎLE DE CEYLAN

JEUNE FILLE JAPONAISE

EGYPTIENNE VOILÉE

Types de beautés orientales

(*Voir texte p. 95*)

It is certain that the representation, or to
be more specific, the act of representing (and
therefore reducing), implies in most cases
a form of violence towards the represented
subject; you can find true contrast between
the violence in the act of representing and
the inner peace of the representation itself,
the image (be it verbal, visual, or any other
form) of the subject. Whether you call it a
spectacular image, an exotic image, or even a
clever representation, there will always be
the paradoxical contrast between what lies
on the surface, seemingly under control,
and the process producing it, the latter
inevitably implying some degree of violence,
decontextualization, miniaturization, etc. The
representing action or process implies control,
accumulation, confinement; that implying a
certain kind of estrangement or disorientation
from the person doing the representation.

Edward Said, "In the shadow of the West",
interview with Jonathan Crary and
Phil Mariani, *WEDGE*, 1985.

SCIENCES CULTURISTES

Juillet-Août 1964

PRIX : 2 F

SOLEIL

★

N° 72

&

★

VACANCES

Serge
NUBRET
M. UNIVERS
(Photo STAN)

Tu braveras deux fois la mort
En faisant un petit effort

Revanche
103

Pour la Patrie, pour l'Humanité

9330

PORTE-BONHEUR
POUR LES TRANCHÉES

75

REX
584

Sachant combien la femme est douce, tendre et bonne.
Il confond le remède, et la main qui le donne.

EM
12

French propaganda postcards advertising war
effort and patriotism during World War I.

EDWARD W. SAID

ORIENTALISM

(...)

I have begun with the assumption that the Orient is not an
inert fact of nature. It is not merely there, just as the
Occident itself is not just there either: We must take seriously
Vico's great observation that men make their own history, that
what they can know is what they have made, and extend it to
geography: as both geographical and cultural entities – to
say nothing of historical entities – such as locales, regions
geographical sectors as "Orient" and "Occident" are man-made.
Therefore as much as the West itself, the Orient is an idea
that has a history and a tradition of thought, imagery, and
vocabulary that have given it reality and presence in and
for the West. The two geographical entities thus support and
to an extent reflect each other. Having said that, one must
go on to state a number of reasonable qualifications. In the
first place, it would be wrong to conclude that the Orient
was essentially an idea, or a creation with no corresponding
reality. When Disraeli said in his novel *Tancred* that the
East was a career, he meant that to be interested in the East
was something bright young Westerners would find to be an all
consuming passion; he should not be interpreted as saying that
the East was only a career for Westerners. There were – and
are – cultures and nations whose location is in the East,
and their lives, histories, and customs have a brute reality
obviously greater than anything that could be said about them
in the West. About that fact this study of Orientalism has
very little to contribute, except to acknowledge it tacitly.
But the phenomenon of Orientalism as I study it here deals
principally, not with a correspondence between Orientalism and
Orient, but with the internal consistency of Orientalism and its
ideas about the Orient (the East as career) despite or beyond
any correspondence, or lack thereof, with a "real" Orient.
My point is that Disraeli's statement about the East refers
mainly to that created consistency, that regular constellation
of ideas as the pre-eminent thing about the Orient, and not
to its mere being, as Wallace Stevens's phrase has it.

A second qualification is that ideas, cultures, and histories
cannot seriously be understood or studied without their force,
or more precisely their configurations of power, also being
studied. To believe that the Orient was created – or, as I
call it, "Orientalized" – and to believe that such things
happen simply as a necessity of the imagination, is to be
disingenuous. The relationship between Occident and Orient
is a relationship of power, of domination, of varying degrees
of a complex hegemony as is quite accurately indicated in the
title of K. M. Panikkar's classic *Asia and Western Dominance*.
The Orient was Orientalized not only because it was discovered

to be "Oriental" in all those ways considered commonplace
by an average nineteenth-century European, but also because
it could be - that is, submitted to being - made Oriental.
There is very little consent to be found, for example, in the
fact that Flaubert's encounter with an Egyptian courtesan
produced a widely influential model of the Oriental woman; she
never spoke of herself, she never represented her emotions,
presence, or history. He spoke for and represented her. He
was foreign, comparatively wealthy, male, and these were
historical facts of domination that allowed him not only
to possess Kuchuk Hanem physically but to speak for her and
tell his readers in what way she was "typically Oriental." My
argument is that Flaubert's situation of strength in relation
to Kuchuk Hanem was not an isolated instance. It fairly
stands for the pattern of relative strength between East and
West, and the discourse about the Orient that it enabled.

This brings us to a third qualification. One ought never to
assume that the structure of Orientalism is nothing more than
a structure of lies or of myths which were the truth about
them to be told, would simply blow away. I myself believe
that Orientalism is more particularly valuable as a sign of
European-Atlantic power over the Orient then it is as a veridic
discourse about the Orient (which is what, in its academic
or scholarly form, it claims to be). Nevertheless, what we
must respect and try to grasp is the sheer knitted together
strength of Orientalist discourse, its very close ties to the
enabling socio-economic and political institutions, and its
redoubtable durability. After all, any system of ideas that
can remain unchanged as teachable wisdom (in academies, books,
congresses, universities, foreign-service institutes) from the
period of Ernest Renan in the late 1840s until the present
in the United States must be something more formidable than
a mere collection of lies. Orientalism, therefore, is not an
airy European fantasy about the Orient but a created body of
theory and practice in which, for many rations, there has been
a considerable material investment. Continued investment made
Orientalism, as a system of knowledge about the Orient, an
accepted grid for filtering through the Orient into Western
consciousness, just as that same investment multiplied -
indeed, made truly productive the statements proliferating out
from Orientalism into the general culture. Gramsci has made
the useful analytic distinction between civil and political
society in which the former is made up of voluntary (or at
least rational and noncoercive) affiliations like schools,
families, and unions, the latter of state institutions (the
army, the police, the central bureaucracy) whose role in the
polity is direct domination. Culture, of course, is to be

found operating within civil society, where the influence of ideas, of institutions, and of other persons works not through domination but by what Gramsci calls consent. In any society not totalitarian, then, certain cultural forms predominate over others, just as certain ideas are more influential than others; the form of this cultural leadership is what Gramsci has identified as hegemony, an indispensable concept for any understanding of cultural life in the industrial West. It is hegemony, or rather the result of cultural hegemony at work, that gives Orientalism the durability and the strength I have been speaking about so far. Orientalism is never far from what Denys Hay has called the idea of Europe, a collective notion identifying "us" Europeans as against all "those" non-Europeans, and indeed it can be argued that the major component in European culture is precisely what made that culture hegemonic both in and outside Europe: the idea of European identity as a superior one in comparison with all the non-European peoples and cultures. There is in addition the hegemony of European ideas about the Orient, themselves reiterating European superiority over Orental backwardness usually overriding the possibility that a more independent, or more skeptical, thinker might have had different views on the matter.

In a quite constant way, Orientalism depends for its strategy on this flexible positional superiority, which puts the Westerner in a whole series of possible relationships with the Orient without ever losing him the relative upper hand. And why should it have been otherwise, especially during the period of extraordinary European ascendancy from the late Renaissance to the present? The scientist, the scholar, the missionary, the trader, or the soldier was in, or thought about, the Orient because he could be there, or could think about it, with very little resistance on the Orient's part. Under the general heading of knowledge of the Orient, and within the umbrella of Western hegemony over the Orient during the period from the end of the eighteenth century, there emerged a complex Orient suitable for study in the academy, for display in the museum, for reconstruction in the colonial office, for theoretical illustration in anthropological, biological, linguistic, racial, and historical theses about mankind and the universe, for instances of economic and sociological theories of development, revolution, cultural personality, national or religious character. Additionally, the imaginative examination of things Oriental was based more or less exclusively upon a sovereign Western consciousness out of whose unchallenged centrality an Oriental world emerged, first according to general ideas about who or what was an Oriental, then according to a detailed logic governed not simply by empirical reality but by a battery of desires, regressions, investments, and projections. If we can point to great Orientalist works of genuine scholarship like Silvestre de Sacy's *Chrestomathie arabe* or Edward William Lane's A*ccount of the Manners and Customs of the Modern Egyptians*, we need also to note that Renan's and Gobineau's racial ideas came out of the same impulse, as did a great many Victorian pornographic novels (see the analysis by Steven Marcus of "The Lustful Turk").

And yet, one must repeatedly ask oneself whether what matters in Orientalism is the general group of ideas overriding the mass of material – about which who could deny that they were shot through with doctrines of European superiority, various kinds of racism, imperialism, and the like, dogmatic views of "the Oriental" as a kind of ideal and unchanging abstraction? – or the much more varied work produced by almost uncountable individual writers, whom one would take up as individual instances of authors dealing with the Orient. In a sense the two alternatives, general and particular, are really two perspectives on the same material: in both instances one would have to deal with pioneers in the field like William Jones, with great artists like Nerval or Flaubert. And why would it not be possible to employ both perspectives together, or one after the other? Isn't there an obvious danger of distortion (of precisely the kind that academic Orientalism has always been prone to) if either too general or too specific a level of description is maintained systematically?

My two fears are distortion and inaccuracy, or rather the kind of inaccuracy produced by too dogmatic a generality and too positivistic a localized focus. In trying to deal with these problems I have tried to deal with three main aspects of my own contemporary reality that seem to me to point the way out of the methodological or perspectival difficulties I have been discussing, difficulties that might force one, in the first instance, into writing a coarse polemic on so unacceptably general a level of description as not to be worth the effort, or in the second instance, into writing so detailed and atomistic a series of analyses as to lose all track of the general lines of force informing the field, giving it its special cogency. How then to recognize individuality and to reconcile it with its intelligent, and by no means passive or merely dictatorial, general and hegemonic context? (…)

Edward W. Said, excerpts from *Orientalism*, 1978.

EXPOS

White women posing amongst natives in the colonies

Abluis Aethiopem quid frustra: ah desine, noctis
Illustrare nigræ nemo potest tenebras. *Andr. Alciat.*

I. Sadeler sc. et ex

19th century etching depicting the Mbunza king dancing in front of his wives. The Mbunza kingdom was at its height. Mbunza had strengthened its supremacy in the area, defeating Arab leader Mohammed Abou Qorn in 1867. In about 1880, the latter succeeded in dividing the kingdom into a number of sultanates all under his authority. Then, soon after its arrival, Belgium took control of Haut-Uele. By 1895, the ancient kingdom of Mangbetu was completely conquered

Androgynous fetishes are believed to be related to the Dogon creation myth, according to which there was nothing at the beginning except the god Amma. He designed the world and brought it to life with his words and saliva. This world made of air, earth, water and fire was not perfect, so Amma decided to start again. Using his words and saliva once more, he created "the world egg", containing the seeds of the very first beings: two couples of androgynous twins, one male and the other female.

Lip-plated women from Congo. These women's lips are pierced when they are ten or eleven, usually by their fiancé. He pierces the lip with a wooden needle, then passes a couple of thin straws through it. After a few weeks, it is replaced by a dowel that is regularly changed. Slowly, a large hole develops into which in which a circular plate is set.

Mangbetu mother and child. In Mangbetu culture, there are several reasons for voluntary cranium lengthening. Sometimes a mere expression of beauty, the sugarloaf-shaped head enabled easy identification with one group. Mangbetu people thought men with flat skulls were weak, believing lengthened foreheads to be a sign of intelligence and wisdom. From a technical perspective, the operation consisted of wrapping the baby's skull with a raffia or giraffe hair cord that would be tightened progressively throughout one year until the skull bones were fully set. The slanted skin gives almond-shaped eyes. This tradition continued until the 1950s.

MICHEL FOUCAULT

THE UTOPIAN BODY

This place that Proust slowly, anxiously comes to copy anew every time he awakens: from that place, as soon as my eyes are open, I can no longer escape. Not that I am nailed down by it, since after all I can not only move, shift, but I can also move it, shift it, change its place. The only thing is this: I cannot move without it. I cannot leave it there where it is, so that I, myself, may go elsewhere. I can go to the other end of the world; I can hide in the morning under the covers, make myself as small as possible. I can even let myself melt under the sun at the beach – it will always be there. Where I am. It is here, irreparably: it is never elsewhere. My body, it's the opposite of a utopia: that which is never under different skies. It is the absolute place, the little fragment of space where I am, literally, embodied. My body, pitiless place. And what if by chance I lived with it, in a kind of worn familiarity, as with a shadow, or as with those everyday things that ultimately I no longer see, that life has grayed out, like those chimneys, those roofs that line the sky every night in front of my window? Still, every morning: same presence, same wounds. In front of my eyes the same unavoidable image are drawn, imposed by the mirror: thin face, slouching shoulders, myopic gaze, no more hair – not handsome at all. And it is in this ugly shell of my head, in this cage I do not like that I will have to reveal myself and walk around; through this grill I must speak, look and be looked at; under this skin I will have to rot. My body: it is the place without recourse to which I am condemned. And actually I think that it is against this body (as if to erase it) that all these utopias have come into being. The prestige of utopia – to what does utopia owe its beauty, its marvel? Utopia is a place outside all places, but it is a place where I will have a body without body, a body that will be beautiful, limpid, transparent, luminous, speedy, colossal in its power, infinite in its duration. Untethered, invisible, protected – always transfigured. It may very well be that the first utopia, the one most deeply rooted in the hearts of men, is precisely the utopia of an incorporeal body. The land of fairies, land of gnomes, of genies, magicians – well it is the land where bodies transport themselves at the speed of light; it is the land where wounds are healed with marvelous beauty in the blink of an eye. It is the land where you can fall from a mountain and pick yourself up unscathed. It is the land where you're visible when you want, invisible when you desire. If there is a land of fairy tales, it is precisely so that I may be its prince charming, and that all the pretty boys there may turn nasty and hairy as bears. There is also a utopia made for erasing bodies. This utopia is the land of the dead, those grand utopian cities that the Egyptian civilization left behind. What is a mummy, after all? Well,

a mummy is the utopia of the body negated and transfigured.
The mummy is the great utopian body that persists across
time. There were also the golden masks that the Mycenaean
civilization placed over the faces of defunct kings: utopia
of their bodies, glorious, powerful and solar, of a terror
disarmed. There have been paintings, sculptures, tombs, those
reclining statues that, since the Middle Ages, prolonged in
immobility a youth that can no longer pass away. Nowadays
there are those simple marble cubes, bodies geometricized
in stone, regular figures of white on the great blackboard
of cemeteries. And in this utopian city of the dead, suddenly
my body becomes solid like a thing, eternal like a God. But
perhaps the most obstinate, the most powerful of those utopias
with which we erase the sad topology of the body, has been,
since the beginning of Western history, supplied to us by the
great myth of the soul. The soul. It functions in my body
in the most marvelous way: it resides there, of course, but
it also knows how to escape. It escapes from the body to see
things through the window of my eyes. It escapes to dream when
I sleep, to survive when I die. It is beautiful, my soul: it
is pure, it is white. And if my body – which is muddy, or in
any case not very clean – should come to soil it, there will
always be a virtue, there will always be a power, there will
be a thousand sacred gestures that will reestablish my soul
in its primary purity. It will last a long time, my soul, more
than a "long time", when my old body comes to rot. Long live
my soul! It is my body made smooth, neutered, rounded like a
soap bubble. There you have it. My body, by virtue of these
utopias, has disappeared. It has disappeared the way the flame
of a candle is blown out. The soul, the tombs, the genies
and the fairies have taken it in an underhanded way, made it
disappear with sleight of hand, have blown out its heaviness,
its ugliness, and have given it back to me, dazzling and
perpetual. But to tell the truth, my body will not be easily
reduced. It has, after all, itself, its own phantasmagoric
resources. It, too, possesses some placeless places, and places
more profound, more obstinate even than the soul, than the
tomb, than the enchantment of magicians. It has its caves and
its attics, it has its obscure abodes, its luminous beaches.
My head, for example, my head: what a strange cavern that
opens onto the external world with two windows. Two openings
– I am sure of it, because I see them in the mirror, and also
because I can close one or the other separately. And yet,
there is really only one opening – since what I see facing
me is only one continuous landscape, without partition or gap.
What happens inside of this head? Well, things come to lodge
themselves inside it. They enter – and I am certain that things
enter my head when I look, because the sun, when it is too

strong and blinds me, rips through to the back of my brain.
And yet, these things that enter my head remain on the outside,
since I see them in front of me, and in order to reach them
I must come forward in turn. Incomprehensible body, penetrable
and opaque body, open and closed body, utopian body. Absolutely
visible body, in one sense. I know very well what it is to
be looked over by someone else from head to toe. I know what
it is to be spied from behind, watched over the shoulder,
caught off guard when I least expect it. I know what it is
to be naked. And yet this same body, which is so visible
is also withdrawn, captured by a kind of invisibility from
which I can never really detach it. This skull, the back of
my skull, I can feel it, right there, with my fingers. But
see it? Never. This back, which I can feel leaning against
the pressure of the mattress, against the couch when I am
lying down, and which I might catch but only by the ruse of
the mirror. And what is the shoulder, whose movements and
positions I know with precision, but that I will never be
able to see without dreadfully contorting myself? The body
– phantom that only appears in the mirage of the mirror, and
then only in fragmentary fashion – do I really need genies
and fairies, and death and the soul, in order to be, at the
same time, both visible and invisible? Besides, this body is
light; it is transparent; it is imponderable. Nothing is less
thing than my body: it runs, it acts, it lives, it desires.
It lets itself be traversed, with no resistance, by all my
intentions. Sure. But until the day when I hurt, when a pit is
hollowed out in my belly, when my chest and throat choke up,
block up, fill up with coughs. Until the day that a toothache
crazes in the back of my mouth. And then, I cease to be
light, imponderable, et cetera. I become thing… fantastic and
ruminated architecture. No really, there is no need for magic,
for enchantment. There's no need for a soul, nor a death for
me to be both transparent and opaque, visible and invisible,
life and thing. For me to be a utopia, it is enough that I be
a body. All those utopias by which I evaded my body – well they
had, quite simply, their model and their first application,
they had their place of origin, in my body itself. I really
was wrong, before, to say that utopias are turned against
the body and destined to erase it. They were born from the
body itself, and perhaps afterwards they turned against it.
In any case, one thing is certain: that the human body is the
principal actor in all utopias. After all, isn't one of the
oldest utopias about which men have told themselves stories
the dream of an immense and inordinate body that could devour
space and master the world? This is the old utopia of giants
that one finds at the heart of so many legends in Europe,
in Africa, in Oceania, in Asia – this old legend that for so

long fed the Western imagination, from Prometheus to Gulliver.
The body is also a great utopian actor when it comes to
masks, makeup, and tattoos. To wear a mask, to put on makeup,
to tattoo oneself, is not exactly (as one might imagine)
to acquire another body, only a bit more beautiful, better
decorated, more easily recognizable. To tattoo oneself, to put
on makeup or a mask, is probably something else: It is to place
the body in communication with secret powers and invisible
forces. The mask, the tattooed sign, the face-paint – they
lay upon the body an entire language, an entirely enigmatic
language, an entire language that is ciphered, secret, sacred,
which calls upon this body the violence of the God, the silent
power of the Sacred, or the liveliness of Desire. The mask, the
tattoo, the make-up: They place the body into an another space.
They usher it into a place that does not take place in the
world directly. They make of this body a fragment of imaginary
space, which will communicate with the universe of divinities,
or with the universe of the other, where one will be taken
by the gods, or taken by the person one has just seduced. In
any case the mask, the tattoo, the make-up, are operations by
which the body is torn away from its proper space and projected
into an other space. Listen, for example, to this old Japanese
tale, and to the way a tattoo artist makes the body of the
young woman he desires pass into a universe that is not ours:

"The morning sun glittered on the river, setting the eight-
mat studio ablaze with light. Rays reflected from the water
sketched rippling golden waves on the paper sliding screens
and on the face of the girl, who was fast asleep. Seikichi had
closed the doors and taken up his tattooing instruments, but
for a while he only sat there entranced, savoring to the full
her uncanny beauty. He thought that he would never tire of
contemplating her serene mask-like face. Just as the ancient
Egyptians had embellished their magnificent land with pyramids
and sphinxes, he was about to embellish the pure skin of this
girl. Presently he raised the brush which was gripped between
the thumb and last two fingers of his left hand, applied
its top to the girl's back, and, with the needle which he
held in his right hand, began pricking out a design." (1)

And if one considers that clothing, sacred or profane,
religious or civil, allows the individual to enter into the
enclosed space of the monk, or into the invisible network of
society, then one sees that everything that touches the body –
drawing, colors, diadems, tiaras, clothes, uniforms, all that
– lets the utopias sealed in the body blossom into sensible and
colorful form. And perhaps, then, one should descend beneath
the clothes – one should perhaps reach the flesh itself, and

then one would see that in some cases even the body itself turns its own utopian power against itself, allowing all the space of the religious and the sacred, all the space of the other world, all the space of the counter world, to enter into the space that is reserved for it. So the body, then, in its materiality, in its flesh, would be like the product of its own phantasm. After all, isn't the body of the dancer precisely a body dilated along an entire space that is both exterior and interior to it? And the drugged, also? And the possessed? The possessed, whose bodies become hell; the stigmatized, whose bodies become suffering, redemption and salvation: a bloody paradise. Really, it was silly of me, before, to believe that the body was never elsewhere, that it was an irremediable here, and that it opposed itself to any utopia. My body, in fact, is always elsewhere. It is tied to all the elsewheres of the world. And to tell the truth, it is elsewhere than in the world; because it is around it that things are arranged. It is in relation to it - and in relation to it as if in relation to a sovereign - that there is a below, an above, a right, a left, a forward and a backward, a near and a far. The body is the zero point in the world. There, where paths and spaces come to meet, the body is nowhere. It is at the heart of the world, this small utopian kernel from which I dream, I speak, I proceed, I imagine, I perceive things in their space, and I negate them also by the indefinite power of the utopia I imagine. My body is like the City of the Sun. It has no place, but it is from it that all possible places, real and utopian, emerge and radiate. After all, children take a long time to know that they have a body. For months, for more than a year, they only have a dispersed body of limbs, cavities, orifices. And all of this only gets organized, all of this gets literally embodied only in the image of the mirror. Stranger still is the way Homer's Greeks had no word to designate the unity of the body. As paradoxical as it may be, on the walls defended by Hector and his companions, facing Troy, there was no body. There were raised arms, there were brave chests, there were nimble legs, there were helmets shimmering atop heads – there was no body. The Greek word for "body" only appears in Homer to designate a corpse. It is this corpse, consequently, it is the corpse and it is the mirror that teach us - or at least that taught the Greeks then, and that teach the children now – that we have a body, that this body has a form, that this form has an outline, that in this outline there is a thickness, a weight. In short, that the body occupies a place. It is the mirror and it is the corpse that assign a space to the profoundly and originally utopian experience of the body. It is the mirror and it is the corpse that silence, and appease, and shut into a closure (for us now sealed) this great utopian

rage that dilapidates and volatilizes our bodies at every
instant. It is thanks to them, thanks to the mirror and to the
corpse, that our body is not pure and simple utopia. And yet,
if one considers that the image of the mirror resides for us
in an inaccessible space, and that we will never be able to be
where our corpse will be; if one thinks that the mirror and
the corpse are themselves in an invincible elsewhere, then one
discovers that only utopias can close in on themselves, and
hide, for an instant, the profound and sovereign utopia of
our body. Maybe it should also be said that to make love is to
feel one's body close in on oneself. It is finally to exist
outside of any utopia, with all of one's density, between the
hands of the other. Under the other's fingers running over you,
all the invisible parts of your body begin to exist. Against
the lips of the other, yours become sensitive. In front of his
half-closed eyes, your face acquires a certitude. There is a
gaze, finally, to see your closed eyelids. Love also, like
the mirror and like the death - it appeases the utopia of your
body, it hushes it, it calms it, it encloses it as if in a box,
it shuts and seals it. This is why love is so closely related
to the illusion of the mirror and the menace of death. And if,
despite the two perilous figures that surround it, we love so
much to make love, it is because, in love, the body is here.

(1) This unidentified passage is excerpted from Junichiro Tanizaki's
The Tattooer, a short story published in 1910.

Michel Foucault, *Le corps utopique*, translated by Lucia Allais in
consultation with Caroline A. Jones and Arnold Davidson from Michel
Foucault, *Utopies et Hétérotopies*, a CD release of two 1966 radio
broadcasts published in 2004 by the Institut National d'Audiovisuel, Paris.

SELF-DETACHMENT

FROM THE SERIES MIRRORS AND MASKS, 2013.
SCULPTURES, WOODEN MASK, MIRROR, STEEL, VIEW AT KW - INSTITUTE FOR CONTEMPORARY ART -
BERLIN, 2013.

Dear Olivier,

In my work, the issue of repair is first broached concretely and only then does it become more metaphorical, even metaphysical. At the beginning, I showed significant interest in great paradoxes of the modern 20th century, of which World War I is one of the symptoms. That conflict brought the 19th century (and the classical war skills of the time) to a close while also introducing the 20th century to the power of a weaponry power that would kill, destroy and leave its mark on humanity forever. At about the same time, and according to those paradoxes, millions of objects taken from colonized traditional cultures constituted ethnological collections in Western countries, but still according to a Euro-modern vision of the world. During the Great War, the millions of injured people called "les gueules cassées" did not only undergo physical but also psychological pain.

You and I once talked about pain and you explained that this sensation is a creation of the brain, in short, that it does not exist... What would you say about physical and psychological pain caused by such trauma? Does the brain have a certain hierarchy for the pain it creates?

Looking forward to hearing from you.

Talk to you real soon,

Kader

—

Dear Kader,

It is a pleasure to talk with you again. Pain could be described as a sense, just like taste, hearing, touch, smell and sight, or even balance and movement. All these sensory systems imply "sensors" (responsive cells reactive to specific physicochemical stimuli) connected to particular brain centers that manifest sensations (mainly objective) and perceptions (mainly subjective). Contrary to other senses that tell you about your relation to the world, pain will tell you about yourself and your own physical integrity (most research in neurophysiology focuses on physical pain). However, the notion of pain as a sense of both the person's physical and psychological integrity could be widened. Indeed, the loss of identity or even the difficulty to build one causes suffering. You mentioned with the "gueules cassées" of World War I. These soldiers went through one significant trauma with consequences (physical, psychological and cognitive) that ended up disturbing the individual's sense of continuity and identity. Brain-damaged patients I see at the hospital as part of my neuropsychologist training must go through serious "mourning" caused by a disruption in their being that has shaken their memory and identity.

Mourning is often described as a state of depression, yet you could just as well talk about actual pain echoing the concept of the person's sense of physical integrity. As a matter of fact, when you talk about depression, you think about "ill-being", and there you can see the notion of suffering and pain is real. This "ill-being" lets you see every disorder related to a person's identity. There are many examples: a traumatizing experience (post-traumatic stress following a serious accident, rape, having to face an "inhuman" situation...), the intense "fragmentation" stages of schizophrenia, a teenager trying to figure out who he is, a mixed-race person whose cultural roots grant him a rich but complex identity, a migrant who has to let go of part of himself in order to integrate some new

socio-cultural environment, anyone who loses someone dear... These are all painful experiences. If, with physical pain, it is easy for scientists to spot the sensors of physical integrity distributed in our entire body and organs and that are sensitive to particular aggressions (heat, stretching, pressure, acidity...) and cause relatively well located painful sensations, then what about the sensors of our psychological identity? In the same way, brain centers for physical pain have been defined, however, does psychological pain lie in the same areas? We know about pain neurochemistry with endorphins and their receptors, and when morphine enables to ease physical pain, does it also ease psychological suffering?

I recall an image, actually a photograph of a man lying on his stomach. He was looking up and his gaze seemed lost in the horizon. It was a black and white picture. The man, lying on his stomach, head up, with his hallucinated blank stare, was a World War I survivor. His trauma was due to keeping watch right above a trench. The picture was taken in the hospital where he was being treated. The caption stated that he spent the rest of his days in that position. At first sight, you do not think of a physical injury, because you cannot see a wound, yet the blank stare and his bright wide eyes tells all about his suffering. I hope you will be satisfied with my answer, and of course I remain available for any other questions.

Your friend,

Olivier

—

Dear Olivier,

Thank you for such an enriching answer. My study on the concept repair, of traditional extra-Western cultures to modern Western cultures, just keeps bringing to light the infinite presence of the mysterious "re" process.

At first, I showed interest in the contrasting analogies between broken and fixed objects within their initial context, and repairs in physical injuries relating to European wars, especially World War I and the extraordinary four year development that embodied a dazzling breakthrough from "brutality to subtlety" in terms of modern maxillofacial surgery...

For a few years now, this study has taken a more "psychological" turn. In fact, it became clear that the essential aspect in any traditional and modern repair is inherent to two conditions: the apprehension of its reality and its virtuality. In order to read and understand each repair, you have to take the visible and invisible reality of each thing into consideration.

Repair stems from a real situation and context; by inference, it marks the repaired thing's materiality...yet, what makes modern and traditional cultures different surely is the misunderstanding on the immateriality of things. In *The Order of Things*, Michel Foucault makes a clear description of how, from the Middle Ages to the classical age, and finally up to modern thinking, the conception of all thing falls under a genealogy that has been structured along the eras, it falls under constant links established between things; from cultural to natural ones. He sums it up with words clearly using a comparison mode: analogio, simulatio, emulatio. "I know this plant is a plant because it sprouts from earth just like any other and grows branches out to the sky." "Every plant sprouts from earth to the sky, yet not all plants are green." The progressive relation of things throughout their studied history is perfectly concrete. Extra-Western cultures follow an almost similar reading of the world. Still, it changes according to the seer's position in time and space. "I know the dog before my eyes that just crossed the village is a dog when I see it, but I know nothing about its shape when it is out of sight." It might be a ghost willing to cross the village unnoticed by daylight so it adopted the shape of an animal. In Pygmy culture, there are children's games where you have to draw well-known geometric shapes, circles for example, with the help of others while sitting on the ground…These immaterial objects bring joy and fear based on games that are not physically real.

This permanent link to what modern thinking calls the irrational now seems to be the most inconceivable thing to think about. There are so many pictures of trances, yet the West is still dubious towards the reality of what is often said to be mere staging imposed by the camera (see Jean Rouch's *Les Maîtres Fous – The Mad Masters*).

Europe is now completely excluded from intentional physical traumatisms created in most ethnic groups since the origins of mankind. Such practices are now disappearing in extra-Western cultures, too. I'm thinking about scarifications and body transformation, from lengthened craniums to penile sub-incision done by Aboriginals and some groups from Papua New Guinea. Having made it through circumcision without anesthetics and operated by an imam with his old rusty razor, I still have a lot of trouble with descriptions of certain rituals linked to mutilation. Sub-incision and excision are the two things that cause violent physical reactions in me. Nevertheless, I keep wondering: is the pain caused by intentional mutilation more traumatic than one that is not, like war injuries for example? In the immaterality of cult and ritual, is there not some form of control upon fear, some social group desire to sublimate it, since the person most directly concerned goes through utter suffering at the moment?

All the best,
Kader

—

Dear Kader,
I find myself in the impossibility to carry on our conversation even though it pains me to do so. Actually, my mother suffers from a neurodegenerative disease. She struggles against the progressive numbing of her cognitive abilities, yet her condition is progressing like some ill-fated wind blowing away her burning urge to stay with us.

The disease echoes your work and our talk on repair. The repair and cure concepts are indeed more subtle than they seem to be at first. "In order to read and understand each repair, you have to take the visible and invisible reality of each thing into consideration" you said. In order to understand healing, you have to go through the same elements. Each fracture causes a visible and invisible disruption with past coherence ("the being's immateriality" as you would say). Therefore, one can wonder whether repairing or healing lets you return to the original state. I get your fascination for progress in reconstructive surgery during the war. Perhaps there was an urgent need to mend mutilated bodies as a way to end the nightmare and come back to the "original" state; reconstructive surgery's amazing progress accompanied a kind of denial about the world collapsing in violence and pain. The progressive and irreversible character of neurodegenerative diseases forbids any hope of returning to what used to be. Actually, such is true with every disease, which you learn from you learn from immunology. Recovering from a cold is finding a balance that takes past experience into consideration. The "repaired" body is not the same anymore since it has been strengthened with a system of antibodies that was not there before. The healed body, just like the repaired object, is a new construction that has recieved a new personality, a new intimacy. Yet it is not always easy, not to say impossible, to build (oneself) a new personality. The construction, as you highlight, is a matter of genealogy, but some disruptions make it hard, even chaotic, to restore intimacy. Still, you are probably right: the permanent link to irrationality is the most unconceivable thing there is to modern man, as it is to me. Perhaps there is some subtle link to the "whole" (the irrational, that which escapes understanding, almighty nature, the divine…) which allows mankind to keep real integrity beyond disruptions, beyond disease. Nevertheless, I think the condition for a possible harmonious reconstruction goes not through the individual, but through the group. It is the group's gaze that makes all singular existence possible, or at least that can make it easier or harder. Nowadays, it is quite complicated to attribute identity to an old person whose cognitive faculties seem to have disappeared and therefore, it is quite complex for an old person to build an identity within such a social environment and for their singularity to be acknowledged.

I do not know if you will be able to use this e-mail in your book. I'm still sending it, as I've mainly talked about my current worries, for which I am sorry (I did not answer the issue of ritual mutilation, an enthralling and legitimate subject for your work on repair).

Yours truly,
Olivier.

Translated from French by Joël Mallet

Olivier Galaverna, PhD in neurosciences and scientific director of Art dans la cité, met Kader Attia in 2009 during his artistic residency in the Rouffach hospital complex, a psychiatric complex inaugurated in 1909 to treat patients from Haut-Rhin, where Attia first installed Untitled (Al Aqsa).

UNTITLED (AL AQSA), 2009.
INSTALLATION, CYMBALS, STEEL STICKS, VIEW AT PSYCHIATRIC HOSPITAL OF ROUFFACH - ROUFFACH, 2009.

UNTITLED (AL AQSA), 2009.
INSTALLATION, CYMBALS, STEEL STICKS, VIEW AT TUILERIES GARDENS, PARIS,
PROJECT OF GALERIE CHRISTIAN NAGEL - PARIS, 2009.

HOLY LAND, 2006.
INSTALLATION, MIRROR, VIEW AT THE 1ST BIENNALE OF ART, ARCHITECTURE, AND LANDSCAPE
OF THE CANARY ISLANDS - FUERTEVENTURA, 2006.

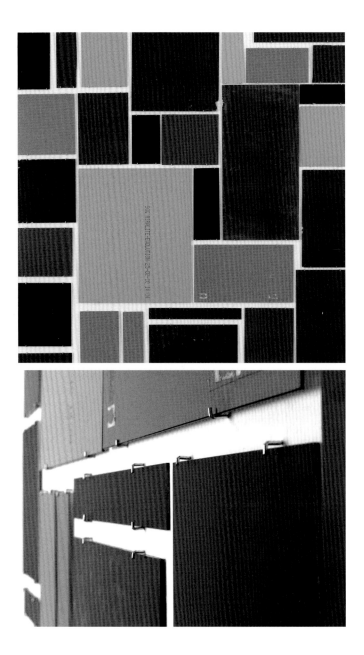

UNTITLED (MIRRORS), 2009.
WALL SCULPTURE, MIRRORS, VIEW AT GALLERIA CONTINUA - SAN GIMIGNANO, 2012.

CHILDHOOD #1, 2005.
INSTALLATION, SLIDE, MIRRORS, TILES, RAZOR BLADES, BROKEN GLASS,
BLACK LEATHER DOG NECKLACES, DOLL, HAIR, VIEW AT MARCEL DUCHAMP PRIZE - PARIS, 2005.

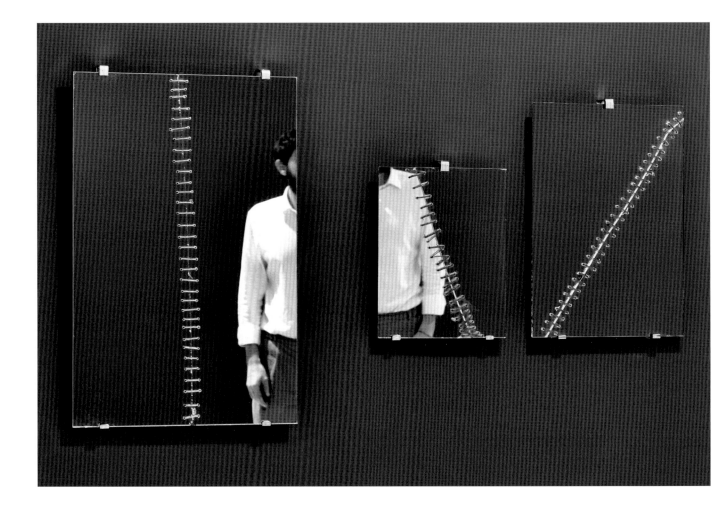

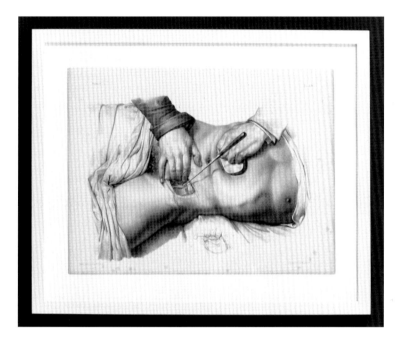

FROM THE SERIES REPAIR ANALYSIS, 2013.
REPAIRED MIRRORS AND 19TH CENTURY LITHOGRAPHS, MIRROR, COPPER WIRE, DETAIL,
VIEW AT CCC STROZZINA, PALAZZO STROZZI – FLORENCE, 2013.

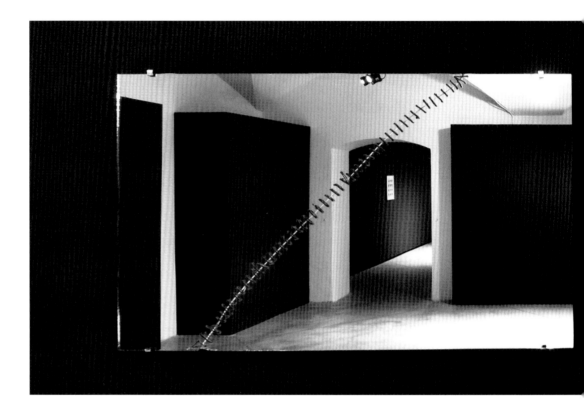

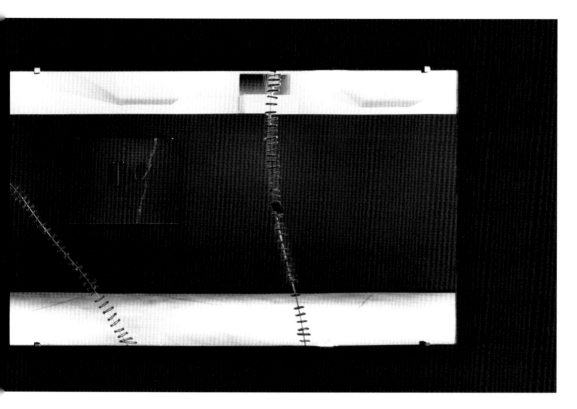

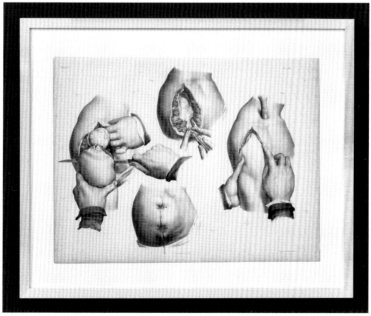

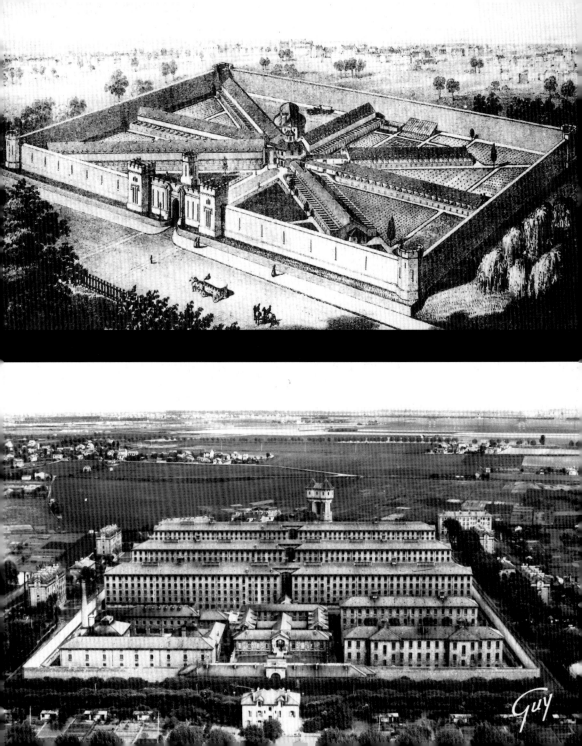

427. CANNES — Île Sainte-Marguerite
Prison du Masque de Fer

ÉTABLISSEMENTS PÉNITENTIAIRES DE FRESNES
Bâtiments des divisions du grand Quartier — La Chapelle-École

ATHENES — Prison de Socrate
ATHENS. — Socrate's Prison.

Women's Prison, Auburn State Prison, Auburn, N. Y.

Traditionally, power was what was seen, what was shown, and what was manifested… Disciplinary power, on the other hand, is exercised through its invisibility; at the same time it imposes on those whom it subjects a principle of compulsory visibility. In discipline, it is the subjects who have to be seen. Their visibility assures the hold of the power that is exercised over them. It is this fact of being constantly seen, of being able always to be seen, that maintains the disciplined individual in his subjection. And the examination is the technique by which power, instead of emitting the signs of its potency, instead of imposing its mark on its subjects, holds them in a mechanism of objectification. In this space of domination, disciplinary power manifests its potency essentially by arranging objects. The examination is, as it were, the ceremony of this objectification.

Michel Foucault, *Discipline and Punish: The Birth of the Prison*, 1975.

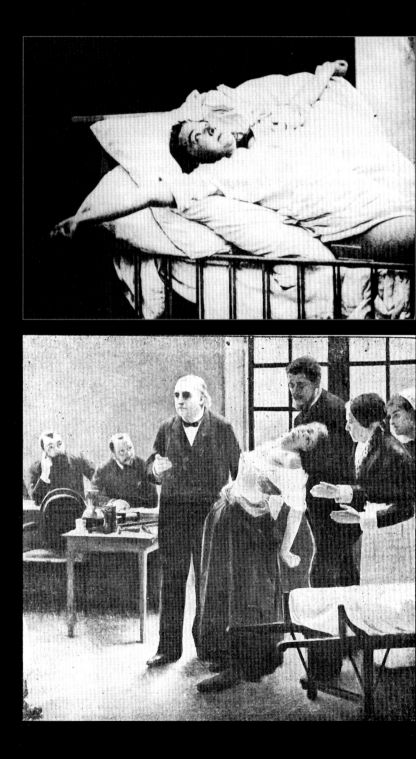

Left: Jérôme Bosch's painting *Ship of Fools*, around 1500.
Top: Late 19th century photograph showing hysteric people.

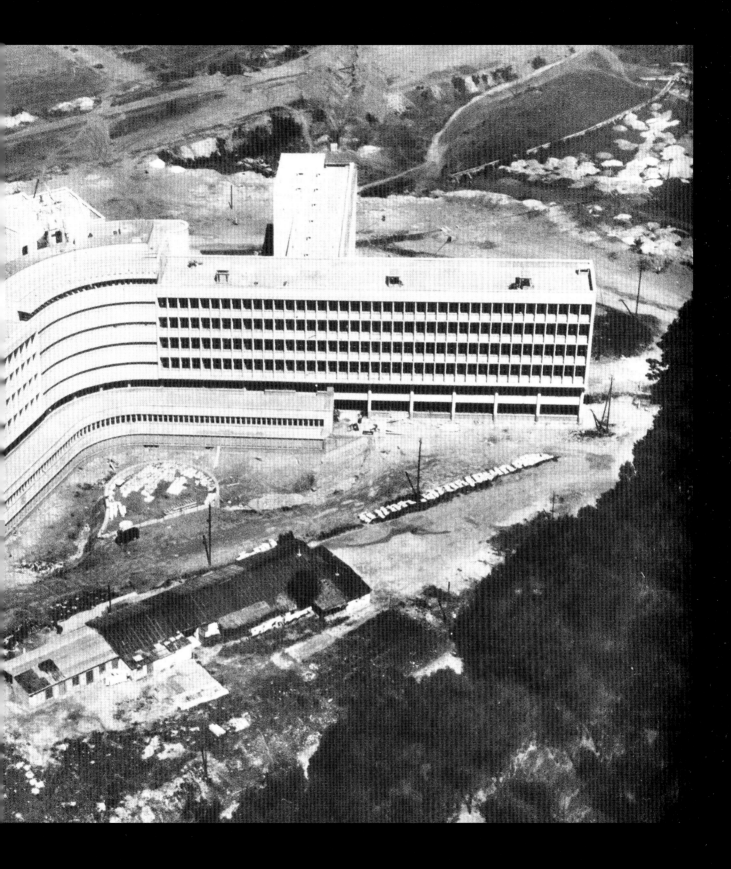

Modern hospital architecture in Algeria.

But the war goes on; and for years to come we will have to bind up the many, sometimes ineffaceable wounds that the colonialist onslaught has inflicted on our people. That imperialism which today is fighting against a true liberation of mankind leaves in its wake, here and there, tinctures of decay which we must search and mercilessly expel from our land and our spirits. We shall deal here with the problem of mental disorder which arise from the war of national liberation which the Algerian people are carrying on. We cannot be held responsible that in this war, psychiatric phenomena entailing disorders affecting behavior and thought have taken on importance, where those who carry out the "pacification" are concerned, or that these same disorders are notable among the "pacified" population. The truth is that colonialism in its essence was already taking on the aspect of a fertile purveyor for psychiatric hospitals. Since 1954, in various scientific works, we have drawn the attention of both French and international psychiatrists to the difficulties that arise when seeking to "cure" a native properly, that is to say, when seeking to make him thoroughly a part of a social background of the colonial type. Because it is a systematic negation of the other person and a furious determination to deny the other person all attributes of humanity, colonialism forces the people it dominates to constantly ask themselves the question: "in reality, who am I?" The defensive attitudes created by this violent bringing together of the colonized man and the colonial system form themselves into a structure which then reveals the colonized personality. This sensitivity is easily understood if we simply study and are alive to the number and depth of the injuries inflicted upon a native during a single day spent amidst the colonial regime. It must in any case be remembered that a colonized people is not simply a dominated people. Under the German occupation, the French remained men; under the French occupation, the Germans remained men. In Algeria there is not simply the domination, but a by-the-book decision not to occupy anything more than the sum total of the land. The Algerians, the veiled women, the palm trees and the camels make up the landscape, the natural background to the human presence of the French. Hostile nature, obstinate and fundamentally rebellious, is in fact represented in the colonies by the bush, by mosquitoes, natives, and fever. And colonization is a success when all this indocile nature has finally been tamed. Railways across the bush, the draining of swamps and a native population which is politically and economically non-existent are in fact one and the same thing. In the period of colonization when there is no contestation by armed resistance, when the sum total of harmful, nervous stimuli overstep a certain threshold, the defensive attitude of the natives gives way and they then find themselves crowding the mental hospitals. Thus, during this calm period of successful colonization, there is a regular and important mental pathology which is the direct product of oppression.

Frantz Fanon, *The Wretched of the Earth*, 1965.
Translated from French by Constance Farrington.

CONTRE NATURE

FLYING RATS, 2005.
INSTALLATION, CAGE, LIFE-SIZE SCULPTURES OF CHILDREN IN SEED, CLOTHING, WIGS, BAGS,
AND 250 LIVING PIGEONS, VIEW AT THE 8TH LYON BIENNALE - LYON, 2005.

KADER ATTIA: I have been working for several years now on what I called reappropriation, and I have come to the conclusion that reappropriation is repair. It is a huge problematic also linked to the issue of repetition, transmission or education. Through different works, I could explore this notion, from ephemeral to "eternal" proposals, from the organic to the mechanical, from Nature to Culture. The installation *Flying Rats*, which represents a life-sized group of 53 kids made of bird seeds, dressed in human second hand clothes and being eaten by 153 living pigeons, is one of them. More recently and in a more minimal way, *Mimetism as Resistance* consists of a five minute film running in a continuous loop on a small plasma screen (30 inches) in a 400m² space showing a lyre-bird mimicking complex sounds made by other birds, such as the kookaburra; but more surprisingly, it also reproduces industrial machines like chainsaws cutting the trees in its surrounding environment. These perfectly mimicked sounds seem to be a reappropriation of Nature's superiority. I would be very interested to know what you think about this.

I'm indeed really interested in your approach as an ornithologist, who always sees further than the horizon of the laboratory. The first time we met, you showed me films about experiments with birds dancing at the same time, doing the same movements, creating a sort of camouflage...

NICKY CLAYTON: These are blue manakins living in South America, especially in Brazil, Paraguay, and importantly, Argentina. They are tiny little birds, not more than 40 or 50 grams. Here are two birds dancing together, one is the leader, the other the follower; I call it "avian tango." I'm specifically referring to Argentine tango. One of the theories about the evolution of Argentine tango is that it started in the 1800s with African slaves and other immigrants, and they were mainly single men, so tango was initially danced by male couples, the inexperienced follower learning the moves from the more experienced leader. *The compadritos* then took the dance to the *Corrales Viejos* district of Buenos Aires, where they could dance with women in brothels and other low-life establishments where dancing could take place. In the case of the birds, it's also two males dancing together: the alpha male and its apprentice. During nine months, they spend about 90% of their daylight hours doing this to woo the ladies. The female birds mate with the best dancers, and they are almost always the male leaders. It takes the blue manakins eight years to learn this dance. They do not start practicing until they are two, they do not start on a proper dancing perch until they're four, and it is not until they are eight that they stand a chance of becoming a leader and actually being a principal male. I thought it was a wonderful example because it has all the parallels we wanted to bring out in Mark Baldwin's choreographic work *Comedy of Change*, with this whole notion of time (past/future), and the idea of individual variation, which we called same/different – of how two individuals could be effectively the same (the same species, and in this case the same sex), and yet so different (they are individuals after all, not mere clones). In this movie clip I'm showing you, one of them is brilliant at dancing, the other one is a youngster and still has a lot to learn. It also illustrates the camouflage, a theme Mark and I called conceal and reveal. On the one hand, when they are dancing there is this amazing swirl of blue, and you can barely tell where the birds are because everything is happening so fast, creating this beautiful hypnotic display of exquisite movements in which it is hard to see who is who. And then, when the birds stop dancing in the middle of this clea-

ring they are so visible and be seen so easily. However, their camouflage is richer than this, for when they go back into the undergrowth of the jungle, under the dark leaves, leaves, they can barely be seen at all despite their showy blue colours, and look almost black and hidden. I love this idea that you can be brightly colored in one light, so obvious and easy to detect, and in other circumstances you cannot because of where you have chosen to hide, or because you have made such a flamboyant display that you have become almost invisible for a whole different reason, namely that you have confused the perceptions of the onlooker. We humans are always searching for new ways of seeing, to see the unseen. Nature finds such clever ways to achieve just that.

K. A.: We met thanks to Mark Baldwin, the choreographer on the *Comedy of Change* project, which is actually a project involving you, Mark, the composer Julian Anderson, musicians, light designers, dancers and me, around an idea that was a kind of tribute to Charles Darwin's theories. I remember the different conversations we had about how to pass from a totally scientist/theorist project to an artistic one. What could you tell me about the issue of camouflage in terms of the repair, rectification, or correction of something that has to be "reoriented"?

N. C.: It was one of the three themes we picked for *Comedy of Change. Camouflage,* which Mark and I interpreted as conceal/reveal, same/different, was inspired by Charles Darwin's theory of natural selection, for which the currency is individual variation; and thinking about the fact that change always occurs over time, which led us to the notion of past/future. Three apparent paradoxes that are all interrelated. There's a sense in which you can think of camouflage as communicating with the environment – knowing when to conceal and when to reveal, and the costs and benefits of that. So, biologically, if you are a bird doing a fancy display or a giant octopus, on the one hand you want to display and woo and impress the ladies with showy moves. But, at another level, that comes at a cost because local predators might notice it as well, and once you are on their radar, you could easily be their lunch or dinner. It is about perspective taking, the ability to understand that there are two sides to every coin: everything can be both "a thing" and a "no thing". You can think of camouflage as this trade-off between knowing when to conceal and when to reveal, with all the nuances of how one might engage in camouflage. One way is by sheer confusion, for example when the birds are performing their hypnotic dancing display, or a murmuration of starlings where it is very difficult to see one individual starling – you just see this swirl of black across the sky, or the octopus and squid with their ink-jets who paint the world black and meticulously disappear. Another way to conceal is when the animal in question changes its manners, movements, colors, patterns and shapes to mimic the background and blend in that way, which is probably the way that most people think of camouflage. They probably would not think of the ink-jet as camouflage, more the starling murmurations and zebra stripes, yet all these are forms of concealment because the observer becomes distracted and, in that very moment, misses the very things they are trying to see. You can also think of these things as being changes that occur in space and time, and ask questions about what it is like to mentally travel in time to revisit a memory. Am I now back in the past, while being in the present, or am I actually in a future that resembles the past? For each time you revisit a memory you often end up changing it, altering it, maybe even in undetectable ways, but recreating it none the less. Which memory is the real one, all of them, none of them, or just the original one?

K. A.: Do you mean camouflage could be a disconnection from the now?

N. C.: Yes, I think it is, in a sense. Perhaps that is the yogi in me, which for me is origami for the body and meditation in motion. You have to transcend the present in order to truly be in the moment, and I think that means disconnecting with the here and now. You know, every time you make something new there is a sense in which you are bringing all the past to bear on it, so any re-creation, although it is new, is also not new because it is based on all this old stuff that is part of you, your past and your identity. They are all forms of making a mark, part of the whole idea that the way in which you make something says so much about who you are, how you think and how you explore the world. Every time you make something new, you are also thinking about the future because you are thinking about the finished product. And the finished product is repairing or re-creating an old thing, there is always a wonderful juxtaposition of whether it is the same as the old thing or different from it. Where does the old end, and the new begin? There is always an old bit to the new bit, whether you like it or not. It was the thing that it was, no matter how much you change it, or maybe it is trying to be a replica, but copies are never identical... There is always something that has changed in space and/or time, and in the mind of the creative maker.

K. A.: Is there a subjective camouflage rather than an objective one?

N. C.: Oh, well, that is a very interesting question. It would be wonderful to know what a giant squid or an octopus experiences when they make these changes, and I wonder what it is like when they are lateralized. Half of them is in one mode, and half of them is in another mode. Is that purely objective, or do they have subjective experiences too? As humans we certainly have subjective camouflage – I'm using the word camouflage in a very loose sense now. Role playing would be one example, as the ability to think about other minds and other times. You can think of that as a camouflage, or the way we choose to dress in order to reveal and conceal things of importance to us, for example.

K. A.: Years ago, I worked with transsexuals and transgender people. This is also interesting because there is no camouflage anymore: a transgender just repairs "Nature's failure." I remember a scene with a transsexual friend of mine who had a beautiful feminine body and a male organ, she was totally androgynous. She was depressed because she had to see a psychologist before the surgery to have the agreement. I can still see her, looking at herself in the mirror, almost crying and telling me, "There is a mistake somewhere, this has to be repaired..."

N. C.: The whole idea of masks is fascinating – I told you a bit about one of the projects that my tango partner, Clive Wilkens, and I are doing with the self, what lies beneath, and another one, the altered self – the storm within consciousness. One of the things we do in our lecture is a demonstration in which Clive puts on a latex mask. The distortion of the face is so powerful it gets to your very core. You feel really ill at ease even though you know that it's the same person underneath, and you feel this sense of relief when the mask is removed and normality resumed. Even though the body is there, and the eyes are still there, the fact that the rest of the face has changed so suddenly and so dramatically is really, really freaky. There are people for whom this is a reality, for example those who have been very badly mauled and have had plastic surgery on their face. This must have a profound impact on their identities... There is something about the face, it is so intimately connected with the self.

K. A.: As an artist, I'm fascinated by the idea that culture could be a repair of nature. I would like to hear what you have to say about something I experienced a few years ago: in the north of France, I had installed twenty-six mirrors (six feet eight inches high and three feet four inches wide) in a huge field. One day I received a phone call from the field owners who told me that for the past few weeks, a couple of crows came every evening to watch themselves in the mirrors, dancing with their reflections, and then attacked the mirror... at the beginning they were only two, but when they called me the whole colony was there... What do you think about this based on your own experiences?

N. C.: Scientists have often wondered whether other animals might have a sense of self. Obviously, the concept of self and identity, and the rich, myriad cognitive skills that it brings, is central to our own species, our society and our culture. How on earth might one go about testing whether an animal – that does not talk and cannot communicate with us in an obvious way through language – has a sense of self? You can speculate philosophically, you can use your intuition, and you can interact with the animal and test hypotheses based on how animals react and respond. But, of course, you never know whether they really have a self, or whether your self is so busy trying to connect with with their potential selves that it is just a reflection of your self that has come back on you – just like a mirror image. It was Gordon Gallup who developed the "Mark Test" or the "Rouge Test" (people have done it with little babies as well). What you do is you place a big red mark somewhere on the face that the beholder cannot possibly see and you look at how the subject responds to what it sees in the mirror. You tend to get two types of reactions: some animals look at the mirror image and they attack it, whereas a select few in "The Clever Club" use the mirror to inspect the image before them searching for things they would otherwise not be able to see. Many animals look at the mirror image of themselves and just attack it, and the idea there is that it might suggest that when they see their own reflection they do not realize that it has anything to do with them, it is just another individual. The idea is conveyed quite well in *Winnie the Pooh*, the Disney version to be precise. Tigger takes a look at himself in the mirror and says, "Oh my God! I thought I was the only one!" and scurries under the bed. Pooh in the background muses "Well, who's that then?" and then Tigger comes out from under the bed and starts attacking his mirror image. So, that is one way of responding to mirrors, and probably what the crows were almost certainly doing in the first instance because even those in "The Clever Club" need some experience of mirrors. But those in "The Clever Club" seem to be able to learn that the mirrored reflection isn't another individual. The question is, what exactly does it say about themselves? The highest level interpretation would be that they understand that the mirror reflection is them – the very same self, their mirrored reflection. A lower level interpretation is that they have a partial understanding so that they realize it is not another individual, but rather "it is like me." You can see this distinction between "it is me" and "it is like me" in the Disney film where Pooh Bear – being a greedy teddy bear who's a bit over-partial to honey – has split his sides. He is a stuffed teddy bear after all, and he uses the mirror to sew himself up. This suggests that he understands something about the image in the mirror corresponding to him, and that he can use the mirror to reveal a part of him that he cannot see. But it is the failures within successes that reveals so much more. Curiously, Pooh Bear thanks the mirror and says, "it is like me" as opposed to, "it is me" suggesting he only has a partial understanding of what a mirror reflection really means about the self. There are not many animals that pass the Mark Test, but guess what, members of the crow family do pass, along with chimpanzees, dolphins and elephants.

In truth we do not really know what it means to pass the Mark Test, but it does seem to be a sign of intelligence in the members of this select "Clever Club" who seem to be able to understand that this image of themselves tells them something about themselves.

K. A.: There is also this experience with crows you told me about: they understand that to throw stones in a bowl raises the water level... How do you define this? Is it intelligence?

N. C.: It is about the ability to come up with innovative ways of solving problems. It is about being able to think through problems and reason about them. There are a host of things that would fall into this category. We call the experience you are speaking about the Aesop's fable task. In the original fable, a thirsty crow puts the stones into a vessel of water in order to raise the water level so that he could drink. We have done a series of experiments on a variety of species of crows, including rooks and jays and New Caledonian crows... and also on children. It's such a simple task – it's basically a vessel of water and some stones, and we float a reward on the top so that the subject does not need to be thirsty. The idea is that to get the reward, which is out of beak reach or out of finger reach, you need to put stones in to raise the water level and get the food. Then you can start to change certain parameters, and in doing so try to figure out how the animals and children are solving the test, how they might be reasoning about it. For example, we've been able to show that the birds seem to understand that it only works with a liquid. If the reward is resting on a solid substrate, like sawdust or sand, then stones won't solve the problem. The birds only put stones into the tube if it contains a liquid. And if you give them new objects, some of which sink and some of which float, they also understand that it's only the sinkable ones that are going to work. That has been fascinating, because we have tested children, and children do not pass the test until they are eight years old. I have some footage that the BBC took for us which shows this poor little boy who is so frustrated because he has put all the floating objects, and of course it has blocked the

reward and jammed it at the top, and he looks at it like he is about to burst into tears.

K. A.: Does that reaction from the birds prove that any life system – birds in this case – is able to, as Charles Darwin would have said, adapt to the problematics of each environment to survive?

N. C.: We have tested New Caledonian crows, which are famous for making and using tools. We have also tested rooks and jays, which do not use tools in the wild. And in all cases, we found that they do not spontaneously use stones as tools. They seem to need to see a stone drop, but once they have seen it, and understand that you can use other objects, they immediately transfer to the notion that it only works with liquid and that they need things that are going to sink and not float. So it is quite interesting that there is this one very simple step; but without that, they do not do it at all. So it is a mixture of serendipity and forethought. You might see a problem and have no idea how to approach it, then one little glimpse sets a whole train of thought in motion. Without that trigger, none of the rest of the thought processes would happen, even though the processes might be far more complex than the tiny little trigger. The way in which minds work is fascinating. You have got to have the idea, and the moment you have a trigger you can go in interesting directions, but without the trigger it would never have happened. That is why perspective taking is so important – it is a way of allowing you to see things from different points of view, and with luck and a bit of creative foresight, to think outside the box.

K. A.: How do you understand that children under eight can not do the same things as birds?

N. C.: It suggests that children and crows might be approaching the problem in different ways. One can make a distinction between the product and the process. The product, or output, is about whether or not they pass the task. The process concerns how they solve the problem, the factors they consider, what they see and what goes unseen. We do not know for sure yet of course, but we suspect that crows and children might be using different ways of thinking, and that is why the young children fail some versions of the tasks that the crows can pass, including the sinking-floating variant. There are other versions of the tasks that only the children pass, however. In one variant of the task we presented the birds and children with two big wide tubes that you can put stones in to raise the water level, and a little tube in the middle that is too narrow to put the stone in. The conundrum is that the little narrow tube contains the prize: for the children it's a little sticker; and for the jays and crows it's a worm. Now the prize that's in the narrow tube in the middle is out of finger or beak reach, because the water level is too low. Unbeknown to the crows and the children, in fact one of the big wide tubes is attached to the little tube via a u-shaped tube that is hidden from view. So all the children and jays can see are three tubes: a thin one, and two thick ones. In truth there are only two tubes, a U-tube which is big at one end and narrow at the other, and another big tube placed equidistant to the narrow part of the U-tube. The question is, can the subjects learn to put the stones in a particular big tube without an explanation why, because when you put stones in that particular tube the water level in the narrow one rises and grants access to the prize. The birds were never able to learn to do this, and it isn't that they can't learn that one tube leads to the reward while the other doesn't – if they can see the observable causes for the effects they have no problem doing it, but in this case it is an unobservable cause because you cannot see that the tubes are connected. Now, little children could not pass this test either until they were seven or eight. None of the birds ever actually passed the test. The other interesting thing about it is when you ask the children how it works, they could not describe how – none of them said, "Oh, that is because this tube is connected to this one through a U-tube, or that the tubes are somehow connected". They simply explained it away as magic. I think the whole idea that we can be sufficiently imaginative to state "well, this is how it works", without really understanding exactly why, is a fascinating phenomenon. It is like magic, in a way – you see an effect ,and you know that it is different from reality because it is a physical impossibility – you know you are missing some critical information. Often we do not know how the effect works, and my tango partner Clive – who is also a professional magician – has led me to understand that magicians have multiple ways of creating the same effect. Although most people think they know how the effects work, they don't – unless they are magicians themselves. Magic is effective because our brains are selective. We miss so much and tend to make connections or associations between things to fill in the 'unseen' gaps, to anticipate what we know we failed to see.

K. A.: If I understand well these two examples, the first one shows that in placing the stones, the birds understand that the water rises with each stone, but until the age of eight, children are unable to observe, understand, and then come up with this solution. It somehow raises the question, or at least questions the meaning, of what intelligence is. On the other hand, in situations with an unobservable system the birds are unable to get it while the children do, showing that it is less about intelligence than imagination. The idea is to conceptualize another part of the story, a hidden reason from which we have visible results, and hidden causes from which we have the results.

N. C.: Absolutely, imagination is key. A crucial question is about how you might solve problems using different ways of thinking. We're back to the idea of same/different again. Both the children and the crows can pass the basic Aesop's fable task, and you might be tempted to assume they are doing so in similar ways, but various interventions with different versions of the task suggest they are not – they are solving the problem in different ways, using different thinking patterns. So I think the whole idea that this alien mind, wearing these beautiful black feathers and this big pale beak in the case of the rooks, or this big feathered crest in the case of the jays, might actually be solving the task in a fundamentally different way from the way we and young children do it is fascinating. It raises all kinds of interesting questions about what it means to think: the extent to which we think in a particular way because of language, or whether we think in a particular way because of something else to do with being human, of which language is merely a reflection of the particular patterning or thought processes. But is there any one, or two, or three, or very small and finite number of thinking patterns available

to any kind of mind – human, animal, alien, who knows? It is back to the question of thinking about patterns, with and without words, and how they are expressed through some form of energy, chemical or electrical, from ion channels to Hebbian synapses. I think of it as energy moving through space and time. A key principle, I believe, is to search for combinatorial patterns of failures embedded within successes. In tango we have a saying, "where mistakes become moves". Looking at mistakes in the system may be much more revealing about what it means to think and the kinds of thought processes available – this is what might help us see the unseen. Why is it that the crows fail the U-tube version of the task? Would they learn if they watched another individual solving it? And what of the children who failed the sinking-floating task, would they pass if they could see someone else solving it? How is it that the human brain does seems to be able to grapple with unobservable causes in a way that the crow's brain cannot? What is it about the animal mind that prevents it from being able to reason about unobservable causes? And what is it about our imaginations that allows us to do so? Are we the only living life form in the universe that can do this? If there are other life forms, what do those look like, and are their thought processes the same as ours or different, or neither and both ?

K. A.: If until the age of eight, children are unable to do what the birds are able to, would it be possible that this ability comes from education, culture, which would mean that the heaviness of this education makes them unable to understand what the bird does until the age of eight?

N. C.: I think one question that might be very interesting anthropologically would be to look at other cultures where making materials and interacting with the physical world has more salience, to investigate whether children from such cultures could pass these tests earlier or whether these are universal facets of the human mind. If one were to show that these were universals of the human mind, then that would suggest that the developmental trajectory for such problem solving skills has nothing to do with education. By contrast, if one were to show that there were these big cultural differences in when children develop such skills and pass such tests, then we could start to try to think about what it is about education that is constraining physical cognitive development. Is it coming from education, from parents, from social media and television, or combinations of those and other factors we have yet to discover? Perhaps we are so used to having various technological gadgets that we no longer really know how they work, we just know what buttons to press to get them to do what we need them to do. I have no idea how my iPhone works but I just turn it on and use it for the things I need. The same is true of my computer. We live in an age of specialization, no longer trained to be our own craftsmen. Children are accomplished at using all these computerized and other electrical devices, but they do not have the same practical opportunities to make, to create physically with their hands. There's so much pressure to understand the nuances of the social world, too. If you make a mistake and a physical problem occurs, it is not really going to be a big deal – if you break it, mummy will probably buy you a new one anyway and it is not that important. But if you were to get the social nuances wrong, you would probably be ridiculed by other children. So maybe there has been much more pressure to focus on getting a lot of the social stuff right. Perhaps it is a selective attention problem, a conflict between focusing on the social and the physical. Perhaps it is not a failure to understand per se but simply a few blind spots that are just not being seen. We are back to the notion of thinking about how to see the unseen and how that would help our powers of imagination. It is one thing to know that we can reason about unobservable causes; it is quite another to be able to figure out what those unobservables are and how they look. Experiments about planning ahead are interesting in that regard, both because they require imagination, and because you have to visualize a future outcome in some way. We know, for example, that jays can plan for the future at least at a rudimentary level. They can also think about other minds as well as other times. The ability to understand what another individual is thinking and what another individual wants is interesting because again you can not see what somebody else wants, you have to imagine it. I suspect there are probably forms of imagination that you can do through experience projection by putting yourself in their shoes, which is quite a different process from reasoning about an unobservable cause. In the case of experience projection, it is something that in principle can be seen, just not in the immediate moment. You could have seen it from another view point, which requires remembering that viewpoint, putting yourself back where you were when you experienced it, and reviewing what you can no longer see. However, it does not require you to see what has never been seen, which might be an interesting distinction.

K. A.: Our conversation brings us, again and again, to this idea that every system of life is ruled by a kind of rebirth instinct, of "re". You said that anything that is done leaves stress, leaves marks somewhere, and that there is no re-creation. I absolutely do believe in this and I think it is interesting to talk about this with you, because, I always saw this through philosophical and cultural issues. I would like to know if you remember the film we saw together in which, either feeling endangered or to protect itself, apparently feeling endangered, or to protect itself, a biological organism – I think it was a squid – used camouflage to change into something that looked like coral?

N. C.: It was a piece of coral I think. The giant squid and the octopus are interesting because of all invertebrates, they seem to show certain levels of intelligence that are unexpectedly complex. How on earth can an animal without a backbone and with a brain that is distributed throughout the body transform itself? These cephalopods are masters of camouflage. In the movie clip that I showed you, the squid had transformed itself to look like a piece of coral, in shape and size, in color, and in its texture and pattern. Then all of a sudden, as the camera came closer, half of the "coral" transformed again, staying the same colour but changing its shape and texture into a giant squid. In the next bit of the sequence, the camera came closer and out spurted the ink-jet, turning everything black so the animal was totally concealed. It shows the dynamics of change, the magic of movement, the way in which the animal can conceal and reveal; the way in which the animal, in repairing itself, reverts back to how it was. But is that true? It is how it was, and it is not how it was, all rolled into one because the environment has changed subtly in time and space. The organism is also not just the organism itself but the environment that it inhabits. The environment is dynamic in space and time, amongst other things, and so it may have reverted back to the original, but it is both the same as, and different from, that original individual in much the same way as our memories are transformed by time and our need to re-create them. When we go back to revisit a memory, we do not just replay it, we relive it and in doing so, we re-create it. I think that is a big part of what we are and how the world works, how the universe works. Our imaginations and creativity are a fundamental part of change. In speaking of repair, do you try to conceal change and make the repair in the image of the original, or do you try to mark the change and acknowledge that it is no longer the same? In making that acknowledgement, do you emphasize the sameness or the difference, or do you allow both points of view to shimmer and shine, even when they are imperceptible?

Nicky Clayton is a Professor of Comparative Cognition in the Department of Psychology at the University of Cambridge, a Fellow of Clare College and a Fellow of the Royal Society. Her expertise lies in the contemporary study of comparative cognition, integrating knowledge of both biology and psychology to introduce new ways of thinking about the evolution and development of intelligence in non-verbal animals and pre-verbal children. She is also Rambert Dance Company's first Scientist in Residence. She collaborates with Mark Baldwin, the Artistic Director, on new choreographic works inspired by science.

SNAILS, 2009.
LIGHTBOX, 146 X 181 X 17 CM.

MEASURE AND CONTROL, 2013.
SERIES OF 5 VINTAGE VITRINES CONTAINING STUFFED ANIMALS, AFRICAN MASKS,
CAMERA LENS, PHOTOGRAPHS, MICROSCOPE, TELESCOPE, BOOK, STEEL, WOOD,
VIEW AT KW, INSTITUTE FOR CONTEMPORARY ART - BERLIN, 2013.

MIMESIS AS RESISTANCE, 2013.
VIDEO INSTALLATION, 2 MIN 18 SEC,
VIEW AT KW, INSTITUTE FOR
CONTEMPORARY ART - BERLIN, 2013.

VIEW OF THE EXHIBITION CONTRE NATURE, BEIRUT ART CENTER – BEIRUT 2014.

NATURE'S AGENCY, 2014.
INSTALLATION, INKJET PRINTS, BOOK AND TEXT BY VLADIMIR NABOKOV,
VIEW AT THE BEIRUT ART CENTER - BEIRUT, 2014.

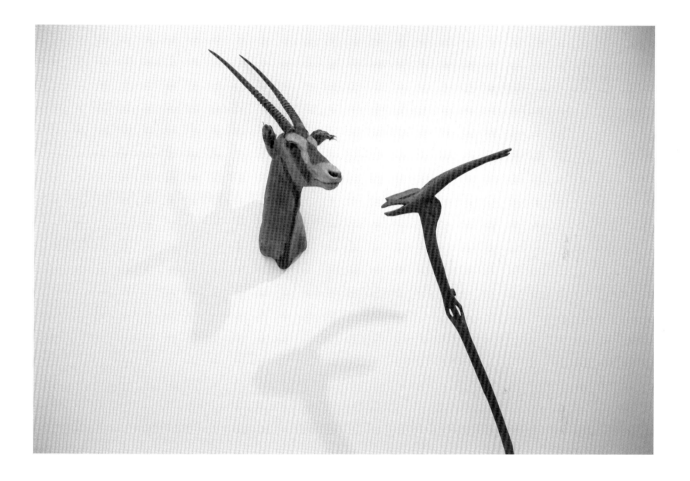

CULTURES ARE FOLLOWING THE SAME ANIMAL #1, 2014.
SERIES OF DIPTYCHS, STUFFED ANTELOPE HEAD AND WOODEN SCULPTURE OF AN ANTELOPE
FROM THE DOGON ETHNIC GROUP (MALI), VIEW AT THE BEIRUT ART CENTER - BEIRUT, 2014.

19th century etching, stuffer in his workshop in Africa.

9th century etching, scene of affection between animal and man

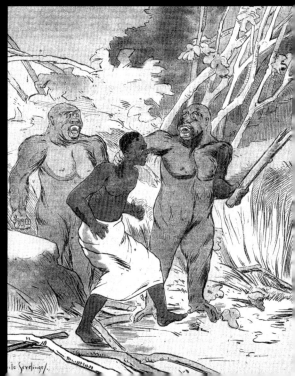

Ritter gegen Tod und Teufel

S. 106. Das Nilpferd wird an Land geschafft

Early photo framing, archive from the newspaper *The Baltimore Sun*

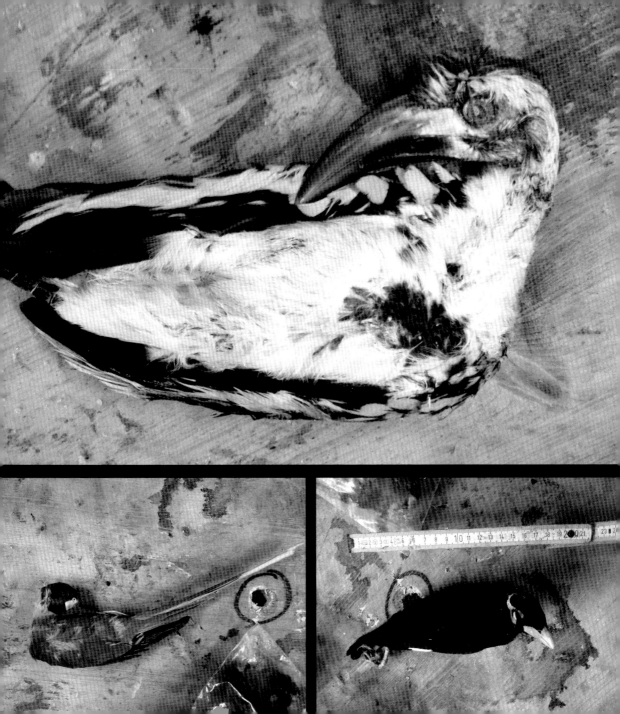

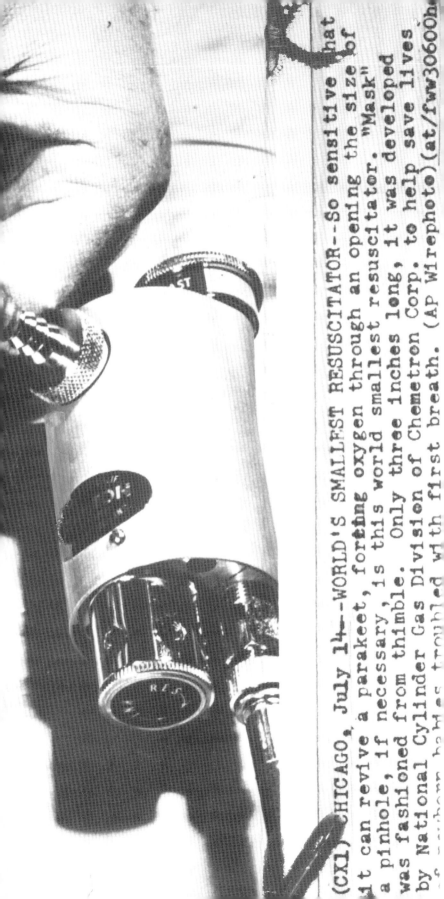

(CXL) CHICAGO, July 14—WORLD'S SMALLEST RESUSCITATOR—So sensitive that it can revive a parakeet, forcing oxygen through an opening the size of a pinhole, if necessary, is this world smallest resuscitator. "Mask" was fashioned from thimble. Only three inches long, it was developed by National Cylinder Gas Division of Chemetron Corp. to help save lives of newborn babies troubled with first breath. (AP Wirephoto)(at/fww30600h

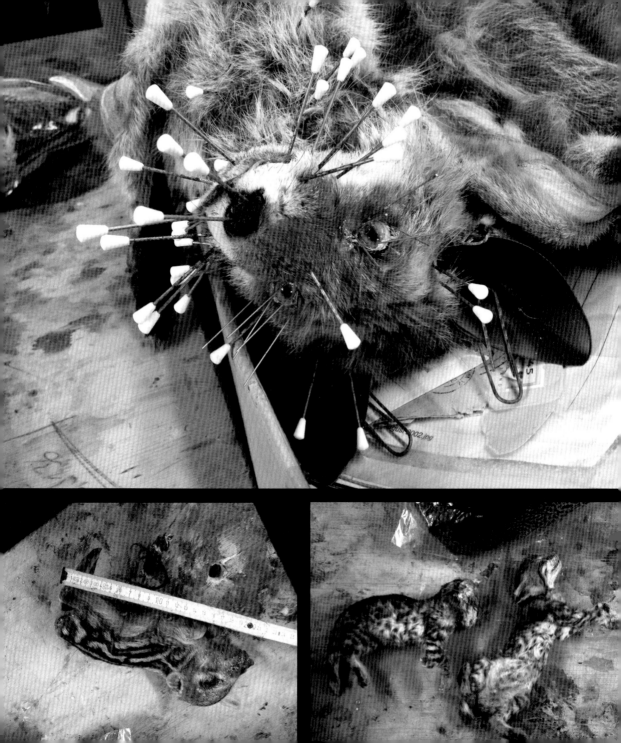

The mysteries of mimicry had a special attraction for
me. Its phenomena showed an artistic perfection usually
associated with man-wrought things. Consider the imitation
of oozing poison by bubblelike macules on a wing (complete
with pseudo-refraction) or by glossy yellow knobs on a
chrysalis ("don´t eat me - I have already been squashed,
sampled and rejected"). Consider the tricks of an acrobatic
caterpillar (of the Lobster Moth) which in infancy looks
like bird´s dung, but after molting develops scrabbly
hymenopteroid appendages and baroque characteristics,
allowing the extraordinary fellow to play two parts at
once (like the actor in Oriental shows who becomes a pair
of intertwisted wrestlers): that of a writhing larva and
that of a big ant seemingly harrowing it. When a certain
moth resembles a certain wasp in shape and color, it also
walks and moves its antennae in a waspish, unmothlike
manner. When a butterfly has to look like a leaf, not
only are all the details of a leaf beautifully rendered
but markings mimicking grub-bored holes are generously
thrown in. "Natural selection", in the Darwinian sense,
could not explain the miraculous coincidence of imitative
aspect and imitative behavior, nor could one appeal to
the theory of "the struggle for life" when a protective
device was carried to a point of mimetic subtlety,
exuberance, and luxury far in excess of a predator´s power
of appreciation. I discovered in nature the nonutilitarian
delights that I sought in art. Both were a form of magic,
both were a game of intricate enchantment and deception.

Vladimir Nabokov, *Speak, Memory: An Autobiography Revisited*, 1966.

RICHARD JEFFERIES

AFTER LONDON

THE GREAT FOREST

The old men say their fathers told them that soon after the
fields were left to themselves a change began to be visible.
It became green everywhere in the first spring, after London
ended, so that all the country looked alike. The meadows were
green, and so was the rising wheat which had been sown, but
which neither had nor would receive any further care. Such
arable fields as had not been sown, but where the last stubble
had been ploughed up, were overrun with couch-grass, and where
the short stubble had not been ploughed, the weeds hid it. So
that there was no place which was not more or less green; the
footpaths were the greenest of all, for such is the nature
of grass where it has once been trodden on, and by-and-by,
as the summer came on, the former roads were thinly covered
with the grass that had spread out from the margin. In the
autumn, as the meadows were not mown, the grass withered as
it stood, falling this way and that, as the wind had blown
it; the seeds dropped, and the bennets became a greyish-
white, or, where the docks and sorrel were thick, a brownish-
red. The wheat, after it had ripened, there being no one to
reap it, also remained standing, and was eaten by clouds of
sparrows, rooks, and pigeons, which flocked to it and were
undisturbed, feasting at their pleasure. As the winter came
on, the crops were beaten down by the storms, soaked with
rain, and trodden upon by herds of animals. Next summer the
prostrate straw of the preceding year was concealed by the
young green wheat and barley that sprang up from the grain
sown by dropping from the ears, and by quantities of docks,
thistles, oxeye daisies, and similar plants. This matted mass
grew up through the bleached straw. Charlock, too, hid the
rotting roots in the fields under a blaze of yellow flower.
The young spring meadow-grass could scarcely push its way up
through the long dead grass and bennets of the year previous,
but docks and thistles, sorrel, wild carrots, and nettles,
found no such difficulty. Footpaths were concealed by the
second year, but roads could be traced, though as green as the
sward, and were still the best for walking, because the tangled
wheat and weeds, and, in the meadows, the long grass, caught
the feet of those who tried to pass through. Year by year the
original crops of wheat, barley, oats, and beans asserted their
presence by shooting up, but in gradually diminished force,
as nettles and coarser plants, such as the wild parsnips,
spread out into the fields from the ditches and choked them.
Aquatic grasses from the furrows and water-carriers extended
in the meadows, and, with the rushes, helped to destroy or
take the place of the former sweet herbage. Meanwhile, the
brambles, which grew very fast, had pushed forward their
prickly runners farther and farther from the hedges till

they had now reached ten or fifteen yards. The briars had
followed, and the hedges had widened to three or four times
their first breadth, the fields being equally contracted.
Starting from all sides at once, these brambles and briars
in the course of about twenty years met in the centre of
the largest fields. Hawthorn bushes sprang up among them,
and, protected by the briars and thorns from grazing animals,
the suckers of elm-trees rose and flourished. Sapling ashes,
oaks, sycamores, and horse-chestnuts, lifted their heads.
Of old time the cattle would have eaten off the seed leaves
with the grass so soon as they were out of the ground, but
now most of the acorns that were dropped by birds, and the
keys that were wafted by the wind, twirling as they floated,
took root and grew into trees. By this time the brambles and
briars had choked up and blocked the former roads, which were
as impassable as the fields. No fields, indeed, remained,
for where the ground was dry, the thorns, briars, brambles,
and saplings already mentioned filled the space, and these
thickets and the young trees had converted most part of the
country into an immense forest. Where the ground was naturally
moist, and the drains had become choked with willow roots,
which, when confined in tubes, grow into a mass like the
brush of a fox, sedges and flags and rushes covered it. Thorn
bushes were there, too, but not so tall; they were hung with
lichen. Besides the flags and reeds, vast quantities of the
tallest cow-parsnips or "gicks" rose five or six feet high,
and the willow herb with its stout stem, almost as woody as
a shrub, filled every approach. By the thirtieth year there
was not one single open place, the hills only excepted,
where a man could walk, unless he followed the tracks of wild
creatures or cut himself a path. The ditches, of course, had
long since become full of leaves and dead branches, so that
the water which should have run off down them stagnated,
and presently spread out into the hollow places and by the
corner of what had once been fields, forming marshes where
the horsetails, flags, and sedges hid the water. As no care
was taken with the brooks, the hatches upon them gradually
rotted, and the force of the winter rains carried away
the weak timbers, flooding the lower grounds, which became
swamps of larger size. The dams, too, were drilled by water-
rats, and the streams percolating through, slowly increased the
size of these tunnels till the structure burst, and the current
swept on and added to the floods below. Mill-dams stood longer,
but, as the ponds silted up, the current flowed round and even
through the mill-houses, which, going by degrees to ruin, were
in some cases undermined till they fell. Everywhere the lower
lands adjacent to the streams had become marshes, some of
them extending for miles in a winding line, and occasionally

spreading out to a mile in breadth. This was particularly
the case where brooks and streams of some volume joined the
rivers, which were also blocked and obstructed in their turn,
and the two, overflowing, covered the country around; for the
rivers brought down trees and branches, timbers floated from
the shore, and all kinds of similar materials, which grounded
in the shallows or caught against snags, and formed huge piles
where there had been weirs. Sometimes, after great rains,
these piles swept away the timbers of the weir, driven by
the irresistible power of the water, and then in its course
the flood, carrying the balks before it like battering rams,
cracked and split the bridges of solid stone which the ancients
had built. These and the iron bridges likewise were overthrown,
and presently quite disappeared, for the very foundations were
covered with the sand and gravel silted up. Thus, too, the
sites of many villages and towns that anciently existed along
the rivers, or on the lower lands adjoining, were concealed by
the water and the mud it brought with it. The sedges and reeds
that arose completed the work and left nothing visible, so that
the mighty buildings of olden days were by these means utterly
buried. And, as has been proved by those who have dug for
treasures, in our time the very foundations are deep beneath
the earth, and not to be got at for the water that oozes into
the shafts that they have tried to sink through the sand and
mud banks. From an elevation, therefore, there was nothing
visible but endless forest and marsh. On the level ground
and plains the view was limited to a short distance, because
of the thickets and the saplings which had now become young
trees. The downs only were still partially open, yet it was
not convenient to walk upon them except in the tracks of
animals, because of the long grass which, being no more
regularly grazed upon by sheep, as was once the case, grew
thick and tangled. Furze, too, and heath covered the slopes,
and in places vast quantities of fern. There had always
been copses of fir and beech and nut-tree covers, and these
increased and spread, while bramble, briar, and hawthorn
extended around them. By degrees the trees of the vale seemed
as it were to invade and march up the hills, and, as we see
in our time, in many places the downs are hidden altogether
with a stunted kind of forest. But all the above happened
in the time of the first generation. Besides these things
a great physical change took place; but before I speak of
that, it will be best to relate what effects were produced
upon animals and men. In the first years after the fields
were left to themselves, the fallen and over-ripe corn crops
became the resort of innumerable mice. They swarmed to an
incredible degree, not only devouring the grain upon the straw
that had never been cut, but clearing out every single ear in

the wheat-ricks that were standing about the country. Nothing remained in these ricks but straw, pierced with tunnels and runs, the home and breeding-place of mice, which thence poured forth into the fields. Such grain as had been left in barns and granaries, in mills, and in warehouses of the deserted towns, disappeared in the same manner. When men tried to raise crops in small gardens and enclosures for their sustenance, these legions of mice rushed in and destroyed the produce of their labour. Nothing could keep them out, and if a score were killed, a hundred more supplied their place. These mice were preyed upon by kestrel hawks, owls, and weasels; but at first they made little or no appreciable difference. In a few years, however, the weasels, having such a superabundance of food, trebled in numbers, and in the same way the hawks, owls, and foxes increased. There was then some relief, but even now at intervals districts are invaded, and the granaries and the standing corn suffer from these depredations. This does not happen every year, but only at intervals, for it is noticed that mice abound very much more in some seasons than others. The extraordinary multiplication of these creatures was the means of providing food for the cats that had been abandoned in the towns, and came forth into the country in droves. Feeding on the mice, they became, in a very short time, quite wild, and their descendants now roam the forest. In our houses we still have several varieties of the domestic cat, such as the tortoise-shell, which is the most prized, but when the above-mentioned cats became wild, after a while the several varieties disappeared, and left but one wild kind. Those which are now so often seen in the forest, and which do so much mischief about houses and enclosures, are almost all greyish, some being striped, and they are also much longer in the body than the tame. A few are jet black; their skins are then preferred by hunters. Though the forest cat retires from the sight of man as much as possible, yet it is extremely fierce in defense of its young, and instances have been known where travellers in the woods have been attacked upon unwittingly approaching their dens. Dropping from the boughs of a tree upon the shoulders, the creature flies at the face, inflicting deep scratches and bites, exceedingly painful, and sometimes dangerous, from the tendency to fester. But such cases are rare, and the reason the forest cat is so detested is because it preys upon fowls and poultry, mounting with ease the trees or places where they roost. Almost worse than the mice were the rats, which came out of the old cities in such vast numbers that the people who survived and saw them are related to have fled in fear. This terror, however, did not last so long as the evil of the mice, for the rats, probably not finding sufficient food when together, scattered abroad, and were destroyed singly by the cats and dogs, who slew them by thousands, far more than they could afterwards eat, so that the carcases were left to decay. It is said that, overcome with hunger, these armies of rats in some cases fell upon each other, and fed on their own kindred. They are still numerous, but do not appear to do the same amount of damage as is occasionally caused by the mice, when the latter invade the cultivated lands. The dogs, of course, like the cats, were forced by starvation into the fields, where they perished in incredible numbers. Of many species of dogs which are stated to have been plentiful among the ancients, we have now nothing but the name. The poodle is extinct, the Maltese terrier, the Pomeranian, the Italian greyhound, and, it is believed, great numbers of crosses and mongrels have utterly disappeared. There was none to feed them, and they could not find food for themselves, nor could they stand the rigour of the winter when exposed to the frost in the open air. Some kinds, more hardy and fitted by nature for the chase, became wild, and their descendants are now found in the woods. Of these, there are three sorts which keep apart from each other, and are thought not to interbreed. The most numerous are the black. The black wood-dog is short and stoutly made, with shaggy hair, sometimes marked with white patches. There can be no doubt that it is the descendant of the ancient sheep-dog, for it is known that the sheep-dog was of that character, and it is said that those who used to keep sheep soon found their dogs abandon the fold, and join the wild troops that fell upon the sheep. The black wood-dogs hunt in packs of ten or more (as many as forty have been counted), and are the pest of the farmer, for, unless his flocks are protected at night within stockades or enclosures, they are certain to be attacked. Not satisfied with killing enough to satisfy hunger, these dogs tear and mangle for sheer delight of blood, and will destroy twenty times as many as they can eat, leaving the miserably torn carcases on the field. Nor are the sheep always safe by day if the wood-dogs happen to be hungry. The shepherd is, therefore, usually accompanied by two or three mastiffs, of whose great size and strength the others stand in awe. At night, and when in large packs, starving in the snow, not even the mastiffs can check them. No wood-dog, of any kind, has ever been known to attack man, and the hunter in the forest hears their bark in every direction without fear. It is, nevertheless, best to retire out of their way when charging sheep in packs, for they then seem seized with a blind fury, and some who have endeavoured to fight them have been thrown down and seriously mauled. But this has been in the blindness of their rush; no instance has ever been known of their purposely attacking man. These black wood-dogs will also chase and finally pull down cattle, if they can get within the enclosures, and even horses have fallen victims to their untiring thirst for blood. Not even the wild cattle can always escape, despite their strength, and they have been known to run down stags, though not their usual quarry. The next kind of wild wood-dog is the yellow, a smaller animal, with smooth hair inclining to a yellow colour, which lives principally upon game, chasing all, from the hare to the stag. It is as swift, or nearly as swift, as the greyhound, and possesses greater endurance. In coursing the hare, it not uncommonly happens that these dogs start from the brake and take the hare, when nearly exhausted, from the hunter's hounds. They will in the same way follow a stag, which has been almost run down by the hunters, and bring him to bay, though in this case they lose their booty, dispersing through fear of man, when the hunters come up in a body. But such is their love of the chase, that they are known to assemble from their lairs at the distant sound of the horn, and, as the hunters ride through the woods, they often see the yellow dogs flitting along side by side with them through bush and fern. These animals sometimes hunt singly, sometimes in couples, and as the season advances, and winter approaches, in packs of eight or twelve. They never attack sheep or cattle, and avoid man, except when they perceive he is engaged in the chase. There is little doubt that they are the descendants of the dogs which the ancients called lurchers, crossed, perhaps, with the greyhound, and possibly other breeds. When the various species of dogs were thrown on their own resources, those only withstood the exposure and hardships which were naturally hardy, and possessed natural aptitude for the chase. The third species of wood-dog is the white. They are low on the legs, of a dingy white colour, and much smaller than the other two. They neither attack cattle nor game, though fond of hunting rabbits. This dog is, in fact, a scavenger, living upon the carcases of dead sheep and animals, which are found picked clean in the night. For this purpose it haunts the neighbourhood of habitations, and prowls in the evening over heaps of refuse, scampering away at the least alarm, for it is extremely timid. It is perfectly harmless, for even the poultry do not dread it, and it will not face a tame cat, if by chance the two meet. It is rarely met with far from habitations, though it will accompany an army on the march. It may be said to remain in one district. The black and yellow dogs, on the contrary, roam about the forest without apparent home. One day the hunter sees signs of their presence, and perhaps may, for a month afterwards, not so much as hear a bark. This uncertainty in the case of the black dog is the bane of the shepherds; for, not seeing or hearing anything

of the enemy for months altogether, in spite of former
experience their vigilance relaxes, and suddenly, while they
sleep, their flocks are scattered. We still have, among
tame dogs, the mastiff, terrier, spaniel, deerhound, and
greyhound, all of which are as faithful to man as ever.

WILD ANIMALS

When the ancients departed, great numbers of their cattle
perished. It was not so much the want of food as the inability
to endure exposure that caused their death; a few winters are
related to have so reduced them that they died by hundreds,
many mangled by dogs. The hardiest that remained became
perfectly wild, and the wood cattle are now more difficult
to approach than deer. There are two kinds, the white and
the black. The white (sometimes dun) are believed to be the
survivors of the domestic roan-and-white, for the cattle in
our enclosures at the present day are of that colour. The black
are smaller, and are doubtless little changed from their state
in the olden times, except that they are wild. These latter
are timid, unless accompanied by a calf, and are rarely known
to turn upon their pursuers. But the white are fierce at all
times; they will not, indeed, attack man, but will scarcely
run from him, and it is not always safe to cross their haunts.
The bulls are savage beyond measure at certain seasons of the
year. If they see men at a distance, they retire; if they come
unexpectedly face to face, they attack. This characteristic
enables those who travel through districts known to be haunted
by white cattle to provide against an encounter, for, by
occasionally blowing a horn, the herd that may be in the
vicinity is dispersed. There are not often more than twenty
in a herd. The hides of the dun are highly prized, both for
their intrinsic value, and as proofs of skill and courage, so
much so that you shall hardly buy a skin for all the money
you may offer; and the horns are likewise trophies. The white
or dun bull is the monarch of our forests. Four kinds of wild
pigs are found. The most numerous, or at least the most often
seen, as it lies about our enclosures, is the common thorn-
hog. It is the largest of the wild pigs, long-bodied and flat-
sided, in colour much the hue of the mud in which it wallows.
To the agriculturist it is the greatest pest, destroying or
damaging all kinds of crops, and routing up the gardens. It
is with difficulty kept out by palisading, for if there be a
weak place in the wooden framework, the strong snout of the
animal is sure to undermine and work a passage through. As
there are always so many of these pigs round about inhabited
places and cultivated fields, constant care is required,
for they instantly discover an opening. From their habit of

haunting the thickets and bush which come up to the verge of
the enclosures, they have obtained the name of thorn-hogs.
Some reach an immense size, and they are very prolific, so
that it is impossible to destroy them. The boars are fierce
at a particular season, but never attack unless provoked to do
so. But when driven to bay they are the most dangerous of the
boars, on account of their vast size and weight. They are of a
sluggish disposition, and will not rise from their lairs unless
forced to do so. The next kind is the white hog, which has
much the same habits as the former, except that it is usually
found in moist places, near lakes and rivers, and is often
called the marsh-pig. The third kind is perfectly black, much
smaller in size, and very active, affording by far the best
sport, and also the best food when killed. As they are found
on the hills where the ground is somewhat more open, horses can
follow freely, and the chase becomes exciting. By some it is
called the hill-hog, from the locality it frequents. The small
tusks of the black boar are used for many ornamental purposes.
These three species are considered to be the descendants of
the various domestic pigs of the ancients, but the fourth, or
grey, is thought to be the true wild boar. It is seldom seen,
but is most common in the south-western forests, where, from
the quantity of fern, it is called the fern-pig. This kind is
believed to represent the true wild boar, which was extinct,
or merged in the domestic hog among the ancients, except in
that neighbourhood where the strain remained. With wild times,
the wild habits have returned, and the grey boar is at once
the most difficult of access, and the most ready to encounter
either dogs or men. Although the first, or thorn-hog, does
the most damage to the agriculturist because of its numbers,
and its habit of haunting the neighbourhood of enclosures,
the others are equally injurious if they chance to enter the
cultivated fields. The three principal kinds of wild sheep are
the horned, the thyme, and the meadow. The thyme sheep are
the smallest, and haunt the highest hills in the south, where,
feeding on the sweet herbage of the ridges, their flesh is
said to acquire a flavour of wild thyme. They move in small
flocks of not more than thirty, and are the most difficult to
approach, being far more wary than deer, so continuously are
they hunted by the wood-dogs. The horned are larger, and move
in greater numbers; as many as two hundred are sometimes seen
together. They are found on the lower slopes and plains, and
in the woods. The meadow sheep have long shaggy wool, which
is made into various articles of clothing, but they are not
numerous. They haunt river sides, and the shores of lakes and
ponds. None of these are easily got at, on account of the wood-
dogs; but the rams of the horned kind are reputed to sometimes
turn upon the pursuing pack, and butt them to death. In the

extremity of their terror whole flocks of wild sheep have been
driven over precipices and into quagmires and torrents. Besides
these, there are several other species whose haunt is local. On
the islands, especially, different kinds are found. The wood-
dogs will occasionally, in calm weather, swim out to an island
and kill every sheep upon it. From the horses that were in use
among the ancients the two wild species now found are known to
have descended, a fact confirmed by their evident resemblance
to the horses we still retain. The largest wild horse is almost
black, or inclined to a dark colour, somewhat less in size than
our present waggon horses, but of the same heavy make. It is,
however, much swifter, on account of having enjoyed liberty
for so long. It is called the bush-horse, being generally
distributed among thickets and meadow-like lands adjoining
water. The other species is called the hill-pony, from its
habitat, the hills, and is rather less in size than our riding-
horse. This latter is short and thick-set, so much so as not
to be easily ridden by short persons without high stirrups.
Neither of these wild horses are numerous, but neither are
they uncommon. They keep entirely separate from each other.
As many as thirty mares are sometimes seen together, but
there are districts where the traveller will not observe one
for weeks. Tradition says that in the olden times there were
horses of a slender build whose speed outstripped the wind,
but of the breed of these famous racers not one is left.
Whether they were too delicate to withstand exposure, or
whether the wild dogs hunted them down is uncertain, but they
are quite gone. Did but one exist, how eagerly it would be
sought out, for in these days it would be worth its weight
in gold, unless, indeed, as some affirm, such speed only
endured for a mile or two. It is not necessary, having written
thus far of the animals, that anything be said of the birds
of the woods, which every one knows were not always wild,
and which can, indeed, be compared with such poultry as are
kept in our enclosures. Such are the bush-hens, the wood-
turkeys, the galenæ, the peacocks, the white duck and the
white goose, all of which, though now wild as the hawk, are
well known to have been once tame. There were deer, red and
fallow, in numerous parks and chases of very old time, and
these, having got loose, and having such immense tracts to
roam over unmolested, went on increasing till now they are
beyond computation, and I have myself seen a thousand head
together. Within these forty years, as I learn, the roe-deer,
too, have come down from the extreme north, so that there are
now three sorts in the woods. Before them the pine-marten
came from the same direction, and, though they are not yet
common, it is believed they are increasing. For the first few
years after the change took place there seemed a danger lest

the foreign wild beasts that had been confined as curiosities in menageries should multiply and remain in the woods. But this did not happen. Some few lions, tigers, bears, and other animals did indeed escape, together with many less furious creatures, and it is related that they roamed about the fields for a long time. They were seldom met with, having such an extent of country to wander over, and after a while entirely disappeared. If any progeny were born, the winter frosts must have destroyed it, and the same fate awaited the monstrous serpents which had been collected for exhibition. Only one such animal now exists which is known to owe its origin to those which escaped from the dens of the ancients. It is the beaver, whose dams are now occasionally found upon the streams by those who traverse the woods. Some of the aquatic birds, too, which frequent the lakes, are thought to have been originally derived from those which were formerly kept as curiosities. In the castle yard at Longtover may still be seen the bones of an elephant which was found dying in the woods near that spot.

Richard Jefferies, *After London* (1885), Part I – The Relapse into Barbarism, chapters 1 and 2, 1885.

COURTESY PHOTOS CREDITS

p.12-14: Kasbah, 2008, courtesy the artist, private collection and Galerie Krinzinger, photo credit: Aurélien Mole

p.15: Kasbah, 2008, courtesy the artist, private collection and Galerie Krinzinger, photo credit: François Fernandez

p.16-17: Kasbah, 2008, courtesy the artist, private collection and Galerie Krinzinger, photo credit: Kader Attia

p.18-19: Kasbah, 2008, courtesy the artist, private collection and Galerie Krinzinger, photo credit: Ferran Martin

p.20-1: Kasbah, 2008, courtesy the artist, private collection and Galerie Krinzinger, photo credit: David Timperley

p.36-9: From the series Following the Modern Genealogy, 2012, courtesy the artist, private collection and Galerie Krinzinger

p.41: Dé-construire Ré-inventer, 2012, courtesy the artist, private collection and Galleria Continua

p.42-3: Satellite Dishes, 2009, courtesy the artist, private collection and Galerie Krinzinger

p.44-5: From the series The Arch of Tazoult, 2012, courtesy the artist, Musée d´Art Moderne de la Ville de Paris, and Galleria Continua

p.46: Narcisse, 2012, courtesy the artist and Galleria Continua, photo credit: Michele Alberto Sereni

p.47: Halam Tawaaf, 2008, courtesy the artist, private collection, Lehmann Maupin Gallery, Galerie Krinzinger, Galerie Nagel Draxler, and Galleria Continua, photo credit: Kader Attia

p.48-9: Untitled (Concrete Blocks), 2008, courtesy the artist, Collection Tate Modern – London, Galerie Nagel Draxler and Galleria Continua, photo credit: Kader Attia

p.50: Untitled (Concrete Pillars), 2007, courtesy the artist and Galerie Nagel Draxler, photo credit: Ed Reeve

p.51: Untitled (Concrete Blocks), 2008, courtesy the artist, Collection Tate Modern – London, Galerie Nagel Draxler and Galleria Continua, photo credit: Jean-Philippe Humbert

p.52-3: Hallal, 2004, courtesy the artist, photo credit: all rights reserved

p.54-5: The Sweatshop, 2004, courtesy the artist, photo credit: Kader Attia

p.56: Colonne sans fin, 2008, courtesy the artist and Fond National d'Art Contemporain, photo credit: Jean-Philippe Humbert

p.57: Recovery as Resistance, 2011, courtesy of the artist and Galleria Continua, photo credit: Alicia Luxem

p.58-9: Correspondance, 2003, courtesy the artist and Cité Nationale de l'Histoire de l'Immigration – Paris

p.62-3: © FLC/ADAGP, 2014

p.90-1: Ghost, 2007, courtesy the artist, Collection Centre Georges Pompidou – Paris, private collection, and Galerie Nagel Draxler, photo credit: Kader Attia

p.92: Ghost, 2007, courtesy the artist, Collection Centre Georges Pompidou – Paris, private collection, and Galerie Nagel Draxler, photo credit: Ludger Paffrath

p.93-5: Ghost, 2007, courtesy the artist, Collection Centre Georges Pompidou – Paris, private collection, and Galerie Nagel Draxler, photo credit: Jean-Pierre Duplan

p.106: Le Vide / Le Plein (Emptiness / Fullness), 2008, courtesy the artist and Galerie Nagel Draxler, photo credit: Kader Attia

p.107: The more we know the smaller we are, 2012, courtesy the artist, Izolyatsia Collection – Donesk, and Galleria Continua, photo credit: Alicia Luxem

p.108: Untitled (Plastic Bags), 2008, courtesy the artist, photo credit: Aurélien Mole

p.424: Untitled (Mirrors), 2009, courtesy the artist, private collection, Galerie Nagel Draxler and Galleria Continua, photo credit: Michele Alberto Sereni

p.425: Childhood #1, 2005, courtesy the artist and Collection Jumex – Mexico DF, photo credit: Laurent Lecat

p.426-9: From the series Repair Analysis, 2013, courtesy the artist, private collection, and Galerie Krinzinger, photo credit: Martino Margheri

p.440-7: Flying Rats, 2005, courtesy the artist and private collection, photo credit: Kader Attia

p.455: The Myth of Order I, courtesy the artist and Galerie Krinzinger, photo credit: Kader Attia

p.456-7: Snails, 2009, courtesy the artist, private collection, and Galerie Krinzinger, photo credit: Kader Attia

p.458-465: Measure and Control, 2013, courtesy the artist, Galerie Nagel Draxler and Galleria Continua, photo credit: Simon Vogel

p.466-7: Mimesis as Resistance, 2013, courtesy the artist, Galerie Nagel Draxler, Galleria Continua, and Galerie Krinzinger, photo credit: Uwe Walter

p.468-9: View of the exhibition Contre Nature at the Beirut Art Center – Beirut, 2014, photo credit: Kader Attia

p.470: Nature's Agency, 2014, courtesy the artist, Galerie Nagel Draxler, Galleria Continua, Galerie Krinzinger, Lehmann Maupin Gallery, photo credit: Kader Attia

p.471: Cultures are following the same animal #1, 2014, courtesy the artist, Galerie Nagel Draxler, Galleria Continua, Galerie Krinzinger, Lehmann Maupin Gallery, photo credit: Kader Attia

KADER ATTIA

Born 1970 in Dugny (Seine Saint-Denis)
Lives and works in Berlin and Algiers

SOLO SHOWS

2015
Musée Cantonal des Beaux-Arts de Lausanne, Lausanne | Switzerland
Galerie Nagel Draxler, Berlin | Germany
Galerie Krinzinger, Vienna | Austria

2014
NATURE, ANOTHER CULTURE REPAIRED, Middelheim Museum, Antwerpen | Belgium
CONTRE NATURE, Beirut Art Center, Beirut | Lebanon
BEGINNING OF THE WORLD, Galleria Continua, Beijing | China
SHOW YOUR INJURIES, Lehmann Maupin Gallery, New York | USA

2013
CONTINUUM OF THE REPAIR : THE LIGHT OF JACOB'S LADDER, Whitechapel Gallery, London | UK
LES TERRASSES, Public Commission, outdoor work, La Digue du Large, Marseille | France
REPAIR. 5 ACTS, KW Institute for Contemporary Art, Berlin | Germany

2012
CONSTRUIRE, DÉCONSTRUIRE, RECONSTRUIRE : LE CORPS UTOPIQUE, Musée d'Art Moderne de la Ville de Paris, Paris | France
COLLAGES, Galerie Christian Nagel, Berlin | Germany
ESSENTIAL, Galleria Continua, San Gimignano | Italy

2011
GHOST, Galerie Christian Nagel, Antwerp | Belgium

2010
HOLY LAND, Galleria Continua, San Gimignano | Italy

2009
PO(L)ETICAL, Galerie Krinzinger, Vienna | Austria
AS A FOLD, HORIZON IS NOT A SPACE, Galerie Christian Nagel, Berlin | Germany
KASBAH, Centre de Création Contemporaine de Tours, Tours | France
SIGNS OF REAPPROPRIATION, SCAD, Savannah | USA

2008
SIGNS OF REAPPROPRIATION, SCAD, Atlanta | USA
BLACK & WHITE : SIGNS OF TIMES, Centro de Arte Contemporaneo Huarte, Huarte | Spain
KADER ATTIA - NEW WORKS, Henry Art Gallery, Faye G. Allen Center for the Visual Arts, University of Washington, Seattle | USA

2007
MOMENTUM 9, ICA, Boston | USA
SQUARE DREAMS, BALTIC Center for Contemporary Art, Newcastle | UK
DO WHAT YOU WANT BUT DON'T TELL ANYBODY, Christian Nagel gallery, Berlin | Germany

2006
TSUNAMI, Magasin, CNAC, Grenoble | France
KADER ATTIA, Musée d'Art Contemporain de Lyon, Lyon | France
SWEET SWEAT, Andréhn-Schiptjenko Gallery, Stockholm | Sweden

2004
HALLAL, Kamel Mennour Gallery, Paris | France

2002
ALTER EGO, Kamel Mennour Gallery, Paris | France

2001
PHOTOSTORIES, Martine et Thibault de la Châtre, Paris | France

2000
LA PISTE D'ATTERRISSAGE, l'Atelier, Centre National de la Photographie, Paris | France

1997
INSTANTS URBAINS, Galerie L'œil du huit, Paris | France

1996
HUMANISTES AU CONGO, Centre culturel Français de Brazzaville, Brazzaville | Congo

GROUP SHOWS

2014

Kochi-Muziris Biennale, Kochi | India
WHEN NOWHERE BECOMES HERE, Poznan
Biennale, Poznan | Poland
THE THEORY OF COLOUR, Museo
Universitario Arte Contemporáneo-UNAM,
Mexico DF | Mexico
THE RELUCTANT NARRATOR, Museu Coleçào
Berardo, Lisbon | Portugal
HERE, ELSEWHERE, New Museum,
New York | USA
DAK'ART 2014, 11ème Biennale de l'Art
Africain Contemporain, Dakar | Senegal
WHERE ARE WE NOW ?, 5th Marrakech
Biennial, Marrakech | Morocco
THE CRIME WAS ALMOST PERFECT, Witte
de With, Center for Contemporary Art,
Rotterdam | The Netherlands
INVISIBLE VIOLENCE, Artium, Basque
Museum-Centre of Contemporary Art,
Vitoria | Spain, and Museum of
Contemporary Art, Belgrade | Serbia
PROJECT HLYSNAN: THE NOTION
AND POLITICS OF LISTENING,
Casino Luxembourg – Forum d'Art
Contemporain, Luxembourg | Luxembourg
ART HISTORIES, MdM Salzburg,
Salzburg | Austria
DOUBLE JEU, FRAC Centre – Orléans,
Orléans | France
DIVINE COMEDY, MMK Museum für Moderne
Kunst, Frankfurt | Germany

2013

AFTER YEAR ZERO, Haus der Kulturen
der Welt, Berlin | Germany
SALON DER ANGST, Kunsthalle Wien,
Vienna | Autsria
43 SALÓN (INTER) NACIONAL DE
ARTISTAS, Medellin | Colombia
UNSTABLE TERRITORY, Centre for
Contemporary Culture Strozzina,
Palazzo Strozzi, Florence | Italy
MUSEUM OFF MUSEUM, Bielefelder
Kunstverein, Bielefeld | Germany
ALTÉRITÉ, JE EST UN AUTRE, Espace
Culturel Louis Vuitton, Paris | France
ART UNLIMITED, ArtBasel 44, Basel |
Switzerland
LE PONT, Musée d'Art Contemporain de
Marseille, Marseille | France
TERMS AND CONDITIONS, The Singapore
Art Museum, Singapore | China

THE WORLD TURNED INSIDE OUT, Witte de
With, Center for Contemporary Art,
Rotterdam | The Netherlands
EVERY DAY MATTERS, Faurschou
Foundation, Copenhagen | Denmark
LE CAPC A 40 ANS, CAPC, Bordeaux | France
MODERNITY? PERSPECTIVES FROM FRANCE AND
TURKEY, Istanbul Modern, Istanbul | Turkey
ICI, AILLEURS, La Friche La Belle de
Mai, Marseille | France

2012

dOCUMENTA (13), Fridericianum Museum,
Kassel | Germany
PERFORMING HISTORIES(1), MoMA,
New York | USA
10 ANS DU PROJET POUR L'ART CONTEMPORAIN,
Centre Pompidou, Paris | France
MIRAGES D'ORIENT, GRENADES ET FIGUES
DE BARBARIE, CHASSÉ-CROISÉ EN
MÉDITERRANÉE, Collection Lambert,
Avignon | France
THE FAR AND THE NEAR: ST IVES AND
INTERNATIONAL ART, Tate St Ives, St
Ives | UK
DIE STADT, DIE ES NICHT GIBT, Ludwig
Forum für Internationale Kunst,
Aachen | Germany
LIVERPOOL BIENNIAL 2012, TATE
LIVERPOOL COLLECTION EXHIBITION :
THRESHOLDS, Liverpool | UK
CARTOGRAPHIES OF HOPE: CHANGE NARRATIVES,
DOX – Centre for Contemporary Art,
Prague | Czech Republic
NEWTOPIA: THE STATE OF HUMAN RIGHTS,
exhibition for the City of Mechelen,
Mechelen | Belgium
THE RITUALS OF CHAOS,The Bronx
Museum, New York | USA
GLISSEMENT DE TERRAIN: IMPERTIENCE-
RESISTANCE-SURVIVANCE, Ianchelevici
Museum, La Louvière | Belgium
WHERE IS THE TIME?, Foundation
Izolyatsia, Donetsk | Ukraine
RAÜME DER ERINNERUNG, Kunsthalle
Düsseldorf, Düsseldorf | Germany
SKYSCRAPER: ART AND ARCHITECTURE
AGAINST GRAVITY, Museum of
Contemporary Art Chicago, Chicago | USA
THE BEST OF TIMES, THE WORST OF TIMES,
1st Kiev International Biennale of
Contemporary Art, Kiev | Ukraine
CHKOUN AHNA, Carthage National Museum,
Carthage | Tunisia

IN OTHER WORDS, NGBK, Berlin | Germany
VIVEMENT DEMAIN, Mac/Val, Vitry-sur-Seine | France
HAJJ, Journey to the heart of Islam, the British Museum, London | UK
BEIJING ONLINE INLIVE - 10 HANDS 100 FINGERS, Galleria Continua, Beijing | China

2011
COLLECTOR, Collection of the Fond National d'Art Contemporain, Le Tri Postal, Lille | France
DRIFT - AN EXPLORATION OF URBAN AND SUBURBAN LANDSCAPES, Sharjah Art Foundation, Sharjah | UAE
SPHERES 2011, 7 ÉNERGIES AUTOUR D'UNE NOUVELLE EXPÉRIENCE D'EXPOSITION, Galleria Continua, Le Moulin | France
4TH MOSCOW BIENNALE, Moscow | Russia
WUNDER. KUNST, RELIGION UND WISSENSCHAFT VOM 4. JAHRHUNDERT BIS ZUR GEGENWART, Deichtorhallen Hamburg, Hamburg | Germany
THE GLOBAL CONTEMPORARY. ART WORLD AFTER 1989, ZKM, Karlsruhe | Germany
DUBLIN CONTEMPORARY, Biennale of Dublin, Dublin | Ireland
CONTESTED TERRAINS, Tate Modern, London | UK
EVERGREEN, Crédit Agricole de Montrouge, Montrouge | France
PARIS - DELHI - BOMBAY, Centre Georges Pompidou, Paris | France
ENTRE-TEMPS, Minsheng Art Museum Shanghai, Shanghai | China
PAX, Fondation Francès, Senlis | France
FRENCH WINDOW, Mori Museum, Tokyo | Japan
STRIKE OPPOSE, Barjeel Art Foundation, Sharjah | UAE
LIVING ROOM EXOTICA, Kunsthaus Glarus, Glarus | Switzerland
DE LEUR TEMPS (3), FRAC d'Alsace - Sélestat, Grenoble | France
PROJECT EUROPA: IMAGINING THE (IM) POSSIBLE, The Miriam and Ira D. Wallach Art Gallery, Columbia University, New York | USA

2010
TOLD | UNTOLD | RETOLD, Arab Museum of Modern Art, Doha | Qatar
SUD2010, Douala | Cameroon
SPHERES 2010, 7 ÉNERGIES AUTOUR D'UNE NOUVELLE EXPÉRIENCE D'EXPOSITION, Galleria Continua, Le Moulin | France

LA ROUTE DE LA SOIE, Le Tri Postal, Lille | France
PICHA, THE IMAGE ENCOUNTERS OF LUBUMBASHI, Lubumbashi | DRC
UTOPIA AND MONUMENT II. ON VIRTUOSITY AND THE PUBLIC SPHERE, Exhibition for the public space, Steirischer Herbst, Graz | Austria
CENTENARY OF MUSEO NACIONAL DE BELLAS ARTES, Santiago de Chile | Chile
THE FUTURE OF TRADITION - THE TRADITION OF FUTURE, Haus der Kunst, Munich | Germany
MAKE YOURSELF AT HOME, Kunsthal Charlottenborg, Charlottenborg | Denmark
LIVING IN EVOLUTION, Busan Biennale, Busan | South Korea
CENTENARY OF MUSEO NACIONAL DE BELLAS ARTES, Santiago de Chile | Chile
STREET & STUDIO - FROM BASQUIAT TO SÉRIPOP, Kunsthalle Wien, Wien | Austria
GEO-GRAPHICS, A MAP OF ART PRACTICES IN AFRICA, PAST AND PRESENT, Palais des Beaux Arts, Brussels | Belgium
THE FLOWER OF MAY, Kunsthalle Gwangju and City Museum, Gwangju | South Korea
UNERWARTET. VON DER ISLAMISCHEN KUNST ZUR ZEITGENÖSSISCHEN KUNST, Kunstmuseum Bochum, Bochum | Germany
ART UNLIMITED, Art Basel 41, Basel | Switzerland
THE BEAUTY OF DISTANCE: SONGS OF SURVIVAL IN A PRECARIOUS AGE, BIENNALE OF SYDNEY, Sydney | Australia
DREAMLANDS, Beaubourg - Centre Georges Pompidou, Paris | France
PROJECT EUROPA: IMAGINING THE (IM) POSSIBLE, The Samuel p. Harn Museum of Art - University of Florida, Gainesville | USA

2009
MEHR ALS EIN T-SHIRT, Bielefelder Kunstverein, Bielefeld | Germany
DISORIENTATION II, Sharjah Art Foundation, Abu Dhabi | UAE
LOS DE ARRIBA Y LOS DE ABAJO, Sala de Arte Público Siqueiros, Mexico DF | Mexico
FIAC, Musée national d'art moderne et contemporain, Algiers | Algeria
FRONTIÈRES, 8th African Biennale of Photography, Bamako | Mali
SPHERES, Le Moulin, Paris | France
DISPOSITIVOS ÓPTICOS, Centro Andaluz de Arte Contemporáneo, Seville | Spain

CARGO, Autocenter, Berlin | Germany
PULSIONI PERFORMATIVE NELL'ARTE
CONTEMPORANEA, Torrione Passari,
Molfetta | Italy
ENTRE-TEMPS, Espaço Cultural Oi
Futuro, Rio de Janeiro | Brazil
LOUIS VUITTON: A PASSION FOR
CREATION, Hong Kong Museum of Art,
Hong Kong | SAR
TIME OUT OF JOINT : RECALL AND
EVOCATION IN RECENT ART, The Kitchen,
New York | USA
PRAXIS, ART IN TIMES OF UNCERTAINTY,
Thessaloniki Biennale,
Thessaloniki | Greece
COLLECTION 10, IAC - Institut d´art
contemporain - Frac Rhône-Alpes,
Villeurbanne | France
LA FORCE DE L'ART 02, Paris
Triennial, Galeries nationales du
Grand Palais, Paris | France
FIAC 2009, Tuileries Gardens,
Paris | France
ENTRE-TEMPS, MIS - Museu da Imagem E
Do Som, Sao Paulo SP | Brazil
INTEGRATION AND RESISTANCE IN THE
GLOBAL ERA, 10th Havana Biennale,
Havana | Cuba
GAGARIN THE ARTISTS IN THEIR OWN WORDS -
THE FIRST DECADE, SMAK, Gent | Belgium
NATION STATE, Goodman Gallery Cape,
Cape Town | South Africa
LOOKING INSIDE-OUT, Kunstnernes,
Oslo | Norway
UNVEILED: NEW ART FROM THE MIDDLE
EAST, Saatchi Gallery, London | UK

2008
THE OTHER, 11th Cairo Biennale,
Cairo | Egypt
CROSSINGS TRAVERSÉES, Darb 1718
Contemporary Art and Culture Center,
Cairo | Egypt
TRAVESIA, Centro Atlántico de Arte
Moderno, las Palmas de Gran Canaria,
Canary Islands | Spain
RÉFLÉCHIR LE MONDE, La Centrale
Electrique, Brussels | Belgium
IN THE DESERT OF MODERNITY, Haus der
Kulturen der Welt, Berlin | Germany
DEFENSE, Skeppsholmen, Stockholm | Sweden
PONTEVEDRA BIENNALE, Pontevedra | Spain
REPRESENTATIONS OF THE ARTIST AS AN
INTELLECTUAL, D21 Kunstraum, Leipzig |
Germany

TRAVERSÉE, Art Paris, Paris | France
ELEFANTE NEGRO, Diego Rivera Museum,
Mexico DF | Mexico

2007
SUITE FRANÇAISE, Krinzinger Projekte,
Vienna | Austria
THE BIG EASY, ACC Galerie Weimar,
Weimar | Germany
THE BIG EASY: RELOCATING THE MYTH OF
THE "WEST", Stiftung Federkiel -
Halle 14, Leipzig | Germany
LES RENCONTRES INTERNATIONALES PARIS |
BERLIN | MADRID, Galerie nationale du
Jeu de Paume, Paris | France
DE LEUR TEMPS (2), Musée de Grenoble,
Grenoble | France
FRIEZE ART FAIR, Sculpture Park,
London | UK
EQUATORIAL RHYTHMS, Stenersen Museum,
Oslo | Norway
THEATER OF CRUELTY, White Box,
New York | USA
SIGNES D'EXISTENCE, MAC Museo de Arte
Contemporáneo. Universidad de Chile,
Santiago | Chile
NEW ECONOMY, Artists Space,
New York | USA
DIALOGUES MÉDITERRANÉENS, St Tropez |
France
ACCÉLÉRATION, Centre d'Art Neuchâtel,
Neuchâtel | Switzerland
L´EMPRISE DU LIEU #4, Domaine Pommery,
Reims | France

2006
1ST ART, LANDSCAPE & ARCHITECTURE
BIENNIAL, Canary Islands | Spain
BLACK PARIS. KUNST UND GESCHICHTE
EINER SCHWARZEN DIASPORA, Iwalewa-
Haus, Bayreuth | Germany
NUIT BLANCHE, Paris | France
INFINITIES, ART UNLIMITED, Art Basel
37, Basel | Switzerland
NOTRE HISTOIRE : UNE SCÈNE ARTISTIQUE
FRANÇAISE ÉMERGENTE, Palais de Tokyo,
Paris | France

2005
MEETING POINT, Stenersen Museum,
Oslo | Norway
IN BETWEEN TIMES, Tramway, Glasgow | UK
REGARDS DES PHOTOGRAPHES ARABES
CONTEMPORAINS, Institut du Monde Arabe,
Paris | France

EXPÉRIENCE DE LA DURÉE, 8th Lyon
Biennale, Lyon | France
LIVING FOR THE CITY, J. Shainman
Gallery, New York | USA
THE LOOP, ART UNLIMITED, Art Basel 36,
Basel | Switzerland
SINGULIERS, Guangdong Museum of Art,
Canton | China

2004
THE SWEATSHOP, ART POSITION, Art Basel
Miami, Miami | USA
NEAR EAST PROJECT, Schirn Kunsthalle,
Frankfurt | Germany
CONTINENTAL BREAKFAST, Belgrade | Serbia
SHAKE, OK Centrum für Gegenwartskunst,
Linz | Austria
SHAKE, Villa Arson, Nice | France

2003
CORRESPONDANCE, STATEMENT AREA, Art
Basel 34, Basel | Switzerland
FAULT LINES, CONTEMPORARY AFRICAN ART
AND SHIFTING LANDSCAPES, 50th Venice
Biennale, Venice | Italy
VOYAGES D'ARTISTES, Foundation Electra,
Paris | France
OUVERTURES ALGÉRIENNES : CRÉATIONS
VIVANTES, La Criée, Rennes | France

2002
LES VERTUS SONT DES TITRES, LES
SOUFFRANCES SONT DES DROITS, FRAC
Poitou-Charentes, Angoulême | France

2001
L'ALCHIMIE DE LA RENCONTRE, FRAC
Champagne-Ardenne, Reims | France
THE STATE OF THINGS, PART.1, Kunst-
Werke, KW Institute for Contemporary
Art, Berlin | Germany

**SYMPOSIUMS |
LECTURES | OTHERS**

2014
KADER ATTIA - SPECIAL EVENT,
Whitechapel, London | UK
KADER ATTIA IN CONVERSATION WITH
MAGNUS AF PETERSENS, Whitechapel,
London | UK
KADER ATTIA IN CONVERSATION WITH KOYO
KOUOH, MMK Museum for Modern Art,
Frankfurt | Germany
KADER ATTIA - ARTIST TALK, NICC,
Brussels | Belgium
COLLECTING GEOGRAPHIES, Stedelijk
Museum, Amsterdam | The Netherlands

2013
SUSPENDED SPACES - DISCOVER | UNCOVER
MODERNISM, Paris | France
Whitechapel, London | UK
DOCUMENT, FICTION ET DROIT, Wiels,
Brussels | Belgium
AFTER YEAR ZERO, Haus der Kulturen
der Welt, Berlin | Germany
INVENTIONS ET RÉINVENTIONS DES ARTS
PRIMITIFS, Musée du Quai Branly,
Paris | France
THE CULTURE OF FEAR: AN INVENTION
OF EVIL, Witte de With, Rotterdam |
The Netherlands
HOMEWORKS, Ashkal Awan,
Beirut | Lebanon
CURATORIAL | Knowledge seminar,
Goldsmiths, London | UK

2012
MATTERS OF COLLABORATIONS,
Collaboratoire 3, Dakar | Senegal
MODERN MONDAY, MoMA, New York | USA
Musée d'Art Moderne de la Ville de
Paris | France

2011
INTERFACE, Université La Sorbonne,
Paris 1 | France
A BRAS LE CORPS, UNITÉS D'HISTOIRE
DE L'ART ET DES ÉTUDES GENRE DE
L'UNIVERSITÉ DE GENÈVE (UNIGE), Haute
école d'art et de design genevoise
(HEAD), Genève | Suisse
SUSPENDED SPACES, Beirut Art Center,
Beirut | Lebanon
INTERFACE, Université La Sorbonne,
Paris 1, Paris | France
UN TEMPS DE L'ART, Université
Rennes 2, Ecole supérieure européenne
d'art de Bretagne, Rennes | France
FESTIVAL DE L'HISTOIRE DE L'ART,
Fontainebleau | France
KUNST AFRIKAS, Freie Universität
Berlin, Berlin | Germany

2010
THE SERPENTINE MAP MARATHON,
Serpentine Gallery, London | UK
WARSAW UNDER CONSTRUCTION II, Muzeum
Sztuki Nowoczesnej w Warszawie,
Warsaw | Poland
THE BRITISH MUSEUM, IN COLLABORATION
WITH THE TATE : KADER ATTIA : VOID'S
GEOMETRIES, London | UK

THE FALMOUTH CONVENTION, University College Falmouth, Falmouth | UK
AFTER POST-COLONIALISM: TRANSNATIONALISM OR ESSENTIALISM?, panel discussion, Tate Modern, London | UK
SITAC VIII, International Symposium on Contemporary Art Theory, Mexico DF | Mexico
CLINICAS SYMPOSIUM, Mexico DF | Mexico

2009
EASTWARDS = WESTWARDS, Jan van Eyck Academie, Maastricht | The Netherlands
Artistic design of the ballet "Comedy of Change" by Rambert Dance Company, UK

RESIDENCY PROGRAMS

2014
ARTPACE, San Antonio | USA

2010
THE BANFF CENTRE, Banff | Canada

2008
IASPIS, Stockholm | Sweden

GRANTS FELLOWSHIPS PRIZES

2014
Kunstpreis Berlin Jubiläumsstiftung 1848|1948, Akademie der Künste, Berlin | Germany

2010
Paul D. Fleck Fellowship, Banff | Canada
Smithsonian Institution Artist Research Fellowship Program, Washington DC | USA
Abraaj Capital Prize, Dubai | UAE

2008
Cairo Biennale, Prize of the Biennale, Cairo | Egypt

2005
Nominee for the Marcel Duchamp Prize, Paris | France

1997
The Leica Special Prize | "Une Algérie d'Enfance", Paris | France

PUBLIC AND PRIVATE COLLECTIONS

MoMA, New York | USA
Margulies Collection, Miami | USA
Tate Modern, London | UK
Boston ICA, Boston | USA

Barjeel Art Foundation | UAE
Sharjah Art Foundation | UAE
MAHTAF | Qatar
Jumex Collection, Mexico DF | Mexico
Musée d'Art Moderne de la Ville de Paris | France
Collection Centre Georges Pompidou, Paris | France
Musée d'Art Contemporain de Lyon, Lyon | France
Mac/Val, Vitry-sur-Seine | France
Société Générale, Paris | France
Géotec Collection | France
Fondation Francès | France
Fond National d'Art Contemporain | France
Fond Régional d'Art Contemporain Centre - Orléans | France
Fond Régional d'Art Contemporain Poitou-Charente | France
Fond Régional d'Art Contemporain des Pays de la Loire | France
Fond Régional d'Art Contemporain Lorraine | France
IAC Villeurbaine | France
MMK Frankfurt | Germany
UniCredit Art Collection | Austria
Vanmoerkerke Collection | Belgium
La Collection Uhoda | Belgium
Sammlung zeitgenössischer Kunst der Bundesrepublik Deutschland | Germany
Deutsche Bank Collection | Germany
Fondation Louis Vuitton pour la Création, Paris | France
Irene Panagopoulos Collection, Athens | Greece

ACKNOWLEGMENTS

Kader Attia would like to thank:

Léa Gauthier, Léa Chevrier, Jean-Michel Diaz, Kobena Mercer, Achille Mbembe, Marion Von Osten, Jacinto Lageira, Ana Teixeira Pinto, Richard Klein, Serge Gruzinski, Amanda Crawley Jackson, Benard Mole, Françoise Vergès, Hélène Hazéra, Olivier Galaverna, Nicky Clayton, Monique Jeudy-Ballini, Brigitte Derlon and Yves Michaud.

Galerie Nagel Draxler, Galleria Continua, Galerie Krinzinger, Lehmann Maupin Gallery, le Centre National des Arts Plastiques - Paris, France, Gérard Alaux and Fondation nationale des arts graphiques et plastiques - Paris, France, Hortensia Völckers and the Kulturstiftung des Bundes (German Federal Cultural Foundation), Carolyn Christov-Bakargiev, Koyo Kouoh, Kitty Scott, Manthia Diawara, Souleymane Bachir Diagne, Sabine Breitwieser, Hélène des Rieux, Kamara Sassi, Gabriela Acha, Elisa Ganivet, Capitaine Tabbagh and Musée du Service de Santé des Armées - Paris, France, Martin Monestier, Yves Le Fur and Musée du Quai Branly - Paris, France, Christine Kreamer and National Museum of African Art, Smithsonian Institution - Washington DC, USA, Anne-Marie Bouttiaux and Royal Museum for Central Africa - Tervuren, Belgium, Museum der Kulturen - Basel, Switzerland, Staatliches Museum für Völkerkunde - München, Germany, Institut für Geschichte und Ethik der Medizin, Ruprecht-Karls-Universität Heidelberg, Germany, Clémentine Deliss and Weltkulturen Museum Frankfurt - Frankfurt, Germany, Musée d'Ethnographie de Neuchâtel - Neuchâtel, Switzerland, Deutsches Hygiene Museum Dresden - Dresden, Germany, Charité Museum Berlin - Berlin, Germany, Historisches Museum Frankfurt - Frankfurt am Main, Germany, National Veterans Art Museum - Chicago, USA, Fondation Le Corbusier - Paris, Akademie der Künste, Berlin, Walter Benjamin Archiv, Nathalie Hazan-Brunet, Aurélien Mole, Taiyana Pimentel and the team of Sala de Arte Público Siqueiros - Mexico DF, Mexico, David Elliott, Régis Durand, Gabriela Rangel, Elizabeth Brown and the team of Henry Art Gallery - Seattle, USA, Doual'Art, Nicolas Baume, Sandra Dagher, Lamia Joreige and the team of the Beirut Art Center - Beirut, Lebanon, Magnus af Petersens and the team of Whitechapel Gallery - London, UK, Ellen Blumenstein and the team of KunstWerke - Institute for Contemporary Art - Berlin, Germany, Laurie Ann Farrell and the team of SCAD - Atlanta, USA, Tami Katz-Freimann, Alain Julien Laferrière and the team of CCC de Tours - Tours, France, Thierry Raspail and the team of Musée d'Art Contemporain de Lyon - Lyon, France, Abdelkader Damani and the team of Dak'Art - Dakar, Senegal, Alexia Fabre and the team of Mac/Val - Vitry-sur-Seine, France, Gilles Fuchs, Boris Hirmas, Philippe Van Cauteren, Kim West, Emilie Butler, Yola Noujaim, Caroline David and the team of Lille 3000 - Lille, France, Dr Susanne Gaensheimer and the team of MMK - Frankfurt, Germany, the team of Bozar - Bruxelles, Belgium, Alain Le Comte, Philippe Regnier, Christine Tohme, Anselm Franke, Philippe Dagen.

BLACKJACK ÉDITIONS

Editor: Léa Gauthier
Art direction: Jean Michel Diaz
Graphic design: Léa Chevrier,
Costanza Della Cananea (cover)
Proofreading: Maya Dalinsky,
Tess Edmonson, Joël Mallet
Translations: Vanessa Ackerman, Maya
Dalinsky, Lisa Damon, Hoda Fourcade
Zeid, Joël Mallet

Printed in 2014 by Cassochrome
(Belgium)

Distribution:
Les Presses du Réel
www.lespressesdureel.com

International:
Idea Books
www.ideabooks.nl

Blackjack éditions
103 rue du Cherche Midi 75006 Paris
(France)

www.blackjackeditions.com
editions.blackjack@gmail.com

Book published with the support of:

Galerie Nagel Draxler (formerly
Galerie Christian Nagel) - Berlin
Galerie Krinzinger - Vienna
GALLERIA CONTINUA, San Gimignano /
Beijing / Les Moulins
Lehmann Maupin Gallery - New York

Book also published with the support
of the Centre National des Arts
Plastiques ꞏ, ministry of culture
and communication (support programs
for publishing costs), France.
Ouvrage édité avec le soutien
du Centre National des Arts
Plastiques, ministère de la culture
et de la communication (aide
à l'édition), France.